TOWARD A
NEW BEHAVIORISM

The Case Against
Perceptual Reductionism

SCIENTIFIC PSYCHOLOGY SERIES

Monographs

William R. Uttal • Toward a New Behaviorism: The Case Against Perceptual Reductionism

Gordon M. Redding and Benjamin Wallace • Adaptive Spatial Alignment

John C. Baird • Sensation and Judgment: Complimentarity Theory of Psychophysics

John A. Swets • Signal Detection Theory and ROC Analysis in Psychology and Diagnostics: Collected Papers

William R. Uttal • The Swimmer: An Integrated Computational Model of a Perceptual–Motor System

Stephen W. Link • The Wave Theory of Difference and Similarity

Edited Volumes

F. Gregory Ashby • Multidimensional Models of Perception and Cognition

Hans-George Geissler, Stephen W. Link, and James T. Townsend • Cognition, Information Processing, and Psychophysics: Basic Issues

TOWARD A
NEW BEHAVIORISM

The Case Against
Perceptual Reductionism

WILLIAM R. UTTAL
Arizona State University

 LAWRENCE ERLBAUM ASSOCIATES, PUBLISHERS
1998 **Mahwah, New Jersey**   **London**

Lawrence Erlbaum Associates, Inc., Publishers
10 Industrial Avenue
Mahwah, New Jersey 07430

Library of Congress Cataloging-in-Publication Data

Uttal, William R.
Toward a new behaviorism : the case against perceptual
reductionism / William R. Uttal.
p.   cm.
Includes bibliographical references and indexes.
ISBN 0-8058-2738-2 (alk. paper).
1. Visual perception. 2. Behaviorism (Psychology). I. Title.
BF241.U865 1998
152.1–dc21   97-19624
                                                            CIP

Books published by Lawrence Erlbaum Associates are printed on acid-free paper,
and their bindings are chosen for strength and durability.

Printed in the United States of America
10 9 8 7 6 5 4 3 2 1

BOOKS BY WILLIAM R. UTTAL

- *Real Time Computers: Techniques and Applications in the Psychological Sciences*
- *Generative Computer Assisted Instruction* (With Miriam Rogers, Ramelle Hieronymus, and Timothy Pasich)
- *Sensory Coding: Selected Readings* (Editor)
- *The Psychobiology of Sensory Coding*
- *Cellular Neurophysiology and Integration: An Interpretive Introduction*
- *An Autocorrelation Theory of Form Detection*
- *The Psychobiology of Mind*
- *A Taxonomy of Visual Processes*
- *Visual Form Detection in 3-Dimensional Space*
- *Foundations of Psychobiology* (With Daniel N. Robinson)
- *The Detection of Nonplanar Surfaces in Visual Space*
- *The Perception of Dotted Forms*
- *On Seeing Forms*
- *The Swimmer: An Integrated Computational Model of a Perceptual–Motor System* (With Gary Bradshaw, Sriram Dayanand, Robb Lovell, Thomas Shepherd, Ramakrishna Kakarala, Kurt Skifsted, and Greg Tupper)
- *Toward a New Behaviorism: The Case Against Perceptual Reductionism*
- *A Vision System* (With Ramakrishna Kakarala, Sriram Dayanand, Thomas Shepherd, Jaggi Kalki, Charles Lunskis, and Ning Liu)
- *A Psychophysical Behaviorism*

CONTENTS

PREFACE

The purpose of this book is to examine the scientific basis of reductionist approaches to understanding visual perception. It is my belief that, for a variety of reasons, contemporary perceptual and cognitive science has gone off onto what can only be described as a wild-goose chase. In this book I consider some specific and general examples of this misdirection and suggest an alternative future course for our science.

For most of the last forty years I have been a student of human visual perception. I was drawn out of a graduate program in physics to the excitement of what was then called physiological psychology by the teaching of Professor Donald R. Meyer of Ohio State University. My interests were focused on the more specific area of vision by the late Professor Philburn Ratoosh. For most of my career I have taught, experimented, theorized, and written about visual sensation and perception. My technique of the moment might have been psychophysical or neurophysiological experimentation, computational modeling, or even synoptic review. In each case, my goal has always been to answer for myself one of the most persistent questions of science: How do we see? Even a brief excursion into somatosensory research was aimed at determining some general principles of sensory and perceptual research in the hope that my vision of vision could be sharpened.

My early enchantment with sensory psychophysiology (or as the field later came to be called, sensory neuroscience) was based on the possibility of explaining perceptual processes by reference to the underlying neurophysiological mechanisms. From my first days as a physiological psychologist, it seemed to me that we were on the threshold of a solution to not only the visual problem, but also the age-old question of how the nervous system accounts more generally for our mental experiences. Indeed, the quest did seem to be proceeding wonderfully well as we attempted to show and then succeeded in showing some relationships between perceptual responses and neural activity in peripheral mechanisms.

The last half century has seen an unprecedented explosion in our knowledge of the function and structure of neurons. The pioneering neurophysiological work of Sherrington (1940), Granit (1955), Eccles (1953), Hartline (1938), and Loewenstein (1961); the remarkable discoveries of biochemists such as Wald (1945) concerning the biochemistry of the retinal receptors; and the enormous contributions of other more recent neurophysiologists such as Hubel and Wiesel (1959) and Lettvin, Maturana, McCulloch, and Pitts (1959), among many others, promised to link perceptual psychology and neurophysiology in a way that could not have been imagined even as recently as the middle of the twentieth century. The invention of the microelectrode by Ling and Gerard (1949) and the pioneering anatomical studies of Polyak (1941, 1957) all added to our understanding of the nature of the sensory nervous system and to the hope that a truly neuroreductive perceptual science was at hand.

To a certain degree, that hope was fulfilled. The explanation of some phenomena, at least with regard to transformations produced by the early or peripheral portions of the sensory pathways, was to a very satisfying degree accomplished in the second half of the twentieth century. We came to understand something about the language of the peripheral nerves and thus how information was transmitted along the afferent visual pathways. Many perceptual phenomena were shown to reflect, in a more or less direct way, the effects of neuronal transformations in the most peripheral portions of the sensory systems. Dark adaptation, the Mach band, the blind spot, color sensitivity, and a number of other phenomena were shown to have fundamental causative factors located in the peripheral nervous system.

However tantalizing and exciting these accomplishments were, I have now come to believe that these early successes were misleading in subtle and significant ways. They have affected our conceptualization of the continuing problem of how our perception is related to higher level neural mechanisms in profound ways. We have learned a great deal about the transmission codes—the nature of the signals that carried information about the stimulus up to those still unknown parts of the brain where that information was transformed into mental experiences. We have also learned a great deal about the organization of the anatomy of the visual brain. We have even learned a lot about where some functions may be localized in the brain.

What we have not learned is how these signals actually become the equivalents of those perceptual responses in those central structures. Somewhere along the line, we have forgotten that transmission processes are not the same as the psychoneural equivalents of the mental experiences. By *psychoneural equivalents*, I am referring to the actions of those parts of the brain that are the same as the mental experiences. Certainly, the sensory message could be modified and transformed by the peripheral coding processes and interactions, including those occurring in the brainstem and early cerebral areas. Nevertheless, there is no logical reason that these regions should be presumed, a priori, to be the locus of the central psychoneural equivalents, the identification of which is the heart of the brain–perceptual experience problem.

It is now clear that our perceptions of the world around us are driven by a cascade of forces that include far more than just the physical properties of the stimulus, their interactions with the sensitivities of the receptors, or the interconnections of simple neural nets. Our perceptions are also influenced, and perhaps even dominated, by other factors that are far more complex and much less amenable to neurophysiological examination than are the events taking place in peripheral portions of the sensory system. Decades of research on the psychophysics of perception have taught us that the higher levels of nervous activity—processes just hinted at by such terms as *schema, memory, relationships*, and *meaningfulness*—also can determine the perceptual outcome. In spite of this high influence, which can be summed up by the term *cognitive penetration* (of both conscious and unconscious kinds), there has been a pervasive tendency in the vision sciences to peripheralize explanations of various visual processes. Explanations of complex visual illusions, which many of us now feel must depend more on interpretations of the symbolic meaning of a stimulus pattern than on the raw physics and geometry of the stimulus, are still being sought at relatively low levels of the cerebral cortex—erroneously, I believe.

The very fact that we know a lot about information coding and transformation in the peripheral nervous system has impelled us toward neuroreductionist arguments and explanations in those terms and at that level. The impulse to peripheralize our neural models is still very strong, sometimes leading to wildly incorrect ideas about the locus of one or another psychoneural equivalent.

Some years ago I set out to educate myself about the many levels of visual science by writing a series of synoptic reviews. This project has so far resulted in the publication of four books entitled *The Psychobiology of Sensory Coding* (1973), *The Psychobiology of Mind* (1978a), *A Taxonomy of Visual Processes* (1981a), and penultimately, *On Seeing Forms* (1988). The present work, *Toward a New Behaviorism: The Case Against Perceptual Reductionism*, is intended as an interpretive and conceptual summary and integration of those earlier books and as a current statement of what happened to my thinking about the basic nature of perception as I worked my way through these successively more complex levels of visual science.

It is very clear to me that something quite profound did happen to my personal scientific philosophy as I tried to answer, to my own satisfaction, questions such as: What are the goals of this science? What empirical data do we have? What theories guide our thinking? and What general principles seem to be emerging? What happened was that I began to lose my confidence (and perhaps my scientific innocence) that the goals and hopes of a reductionist perceptual science could be obtained. Somewhere in the third volume (*A Taxonomy*), it became clear to me that, beyond some of the simpler stimulus, receptor, and network influences in the periphery, many, if not most, theories of sensation and perception were overly simplistic. This was true if they were based on either a neural or a cognitive (mental architecture) approach. Some theories were cloaked in esoteric mathematical reasoning; some were merely verbal; some were just numerical analogs and metaphors based on curve fitting by functions that seemed to have the same number of degrees of freedom as a first approximation to the observed phenomenon; some were judgments that some neurophysiological data "were not inconsistent" with some perceptual data. Regardless of the theoretical method, it became increasingly clear to me that many of these approaches to solving the problem either obscured or ignored some fundamental logical, and very relevant, issues.

This evolution in my thoughts has brought me to a stage that I could never have imagined when I set out on this quest. I am not sure how many of my colleagues would agree with some of my conclusions and views, but I am sure that all would consider the problems just mentioned to be of considerable importance to the serious student of visual perception. In this book I elaborate on the reasons that have convinced me that:

- First, all mathematical and computational models of perceptual phenomena are absolutely neutral with regard to the underlying neural mechanisms.

- Second, many theoretical bridges built between neural and psychophysical data are extreme stretches of the imagination, often based on narrowly defined microuniverses of experimentation and/or superficial analogies, if not spurious ones. Substantial speculative theories are sometimes based on fragmentary or disputed neurophysiological data.

- Third, many attempts at cognitive reductionism (i.e., the search for the underlying mental architecture) are not justifiable given certain intrinsic constraints based on matters of both principle and practice. Many of the assumptions required to carry out this task are insupportable.

- Fourth, if perceptual psychology is to survive, and not be inappropriately absorbed into the neural or computational sciences in the next millennium, it will have to return to its behaviorist, positivist roots.

- Fifth, my goal in this book has to be limited to suggesting revisions in the assumptions and ways in which we interpret some theories and data. I am not aiming at a major sea change in the direction of our empirical research activities, only a reconsideration of the underlying assumptions built into our perceptual science.

These five assertions, both individually and collectively, are, of course, contrary to much of the reductionist *zeitgeist* of contemporary perceptual science. One does not have to go far in perusing the literature to appreciate that these personal convictions on my part are probably held by a very small minority of my colleagues. As I set out on this fifth volume, it is with an awareness of that fact.

I am, nevertheless, convinced that a reconstruction of the conceptual foundations of perceptual science is necessary if it is to continue to flourish. Sooner or later, an unfulfilled promise of a chimerical reductionist science will come back to haunt us. Therefore, if it is not too ostentatious, I would like to suggest that, given the inevitable judgment of scientific history, the great hope of perceptual psychology is its conversion (or, rather, reconversion) back into the operational, positivist, behaviorist traditions of the past. Our subject matter is observable behavior and the phenomenology it reflects. As we shall see, there are formidable barriers to doing anything more in terms of attempts to understand the internal architecture of the mind or the incalculably complex and cognitively relevant neural nets of the brain. To ignore these barriers must ultimately be disastrous for our science as well as for the deepest goal of all—a legitimate and valid understanding of how our perceptual system works.

I should note that the evolution of my thoughts was no sudden brainstorm. For many years I picked at some of the details. In articles that I wrote years ago, I find the roots of this book and can discern the trend from the young, eager, optimistic, and very reductionist physiological psychologist I was then to a somewhat older and definitely iconoclastic critic. Nevertheless, I still consider myself a bright-eyed, if not bushy-tailed, student and champion of perceptual science.

Should any one ever wish to track this evolution of my thinking, they might be interested in looking at some of these following harbingers of my current point of view.

1. Do compound evoked potentials reflect psychological codes (Uttal, 1965)?
2. Evoked brain potentials: Signs or codes (Uttal, 1967)?.
3. Emerging principles of sensory coding (Uttal, 1969).
4. The psychobiological silly season, or what happens when neurophysiological data become psychological theories (Uttal, 1971a).

5. Codes, sensations, and the mind–body problem (Uttal, 1978b).

6. On the limits of sensory neuroreductionism (Uttal, 1981b).

7. Neuroreduction dogma: A heretical counterview (Uttal, 1982).

There are also two papers that form the basis for chapters 2 and 5, respectively, in this book.

8. On some two way barriers between theories and mechanisms (Uttal, 1990).

9. Toward a new behaviorism (Uttal, 1993).

Clearly, many of the views that have matured enough to be presented in this book have been in the works for some time. This is neither a late-in-life nor a sudden conversion.

I would like to deal with one potential criticism in advance. Some will suggest that I am arguing for a return to the past when I champion a new version of an operational and behavioral perceptual science. It could be objected that I am ignoring the truly wonderful accomplishments of this science in the last four or five decades. Such a criticism misses the point. I am arguing for a reconsideration of the *meaning* of what we are doing. I cannot imagine any kind of experiment that I would argue should not have been done (within the limits of our very contemporary ethical standards, of course). Many of our formal theories, furthermore, are absolutely elegant and sometimes even effective in predicting the future outcome of some system's function. I could hardly argue that mathematics is not a powerful tool or that a computer has not opened to us new ways to guarantee rigor in our theories. What I ask is that we consider a bit more critically what a mathematical model is, what it does, what it means, and what it can be. Neural comparisons with psychophysical data have been powerful heuristics in helping both fields achieve their maturity. However, I also ask that we be a little more critical when we attempt to build a bridge that is dangerously frail as we attempt to cross from one field to the other.

Likewise, despite an enormous amount of ingenious theorizing, I argue that it is not really feasible, given the assumptions that must be invoked, to use psychological studies to determine the organization of internal thought processes. In short, let us bring our current approach to perceptual science out of a world of weak correlations, buckling conceptual bridges, fantastic extrapolations, unreplicated findings, and flawed assumptions. We must transform it from nothing more than an expression of our hopes and dreams into a reasonable, rational, and critical maturity. Only by achieving a level of true, if limited, understanding can we avoid the historical tendency to change our fundamental interpretations of our science every couple of decades or so. Somewhere in the midst all of this data exists a psychobiological reality. Most other sciences have built a pyramid of ever more inclusive understanding on their conceptual and empirical primitives. We need to do the same thing so that we do not perpetuate the theoretical instability of the past century.

The instability of perceptual science has not led to a continuous evolutionary improvement in our understanding. Perceptual psychology has returned again and again to older ideas. Indeed, as I pointed out in *The Taxonomy* (Uttal, 1981a), there has been a continuing tendency for psychological theory to swing back and forth between two extremes—one holistic and synthetic and one elementalist and analytic—throughout its history. Figure P.1 is taken from that book and is my interpretation of the historical swings of that multidimensional theoretical pendulum. Theories of the moment swing back and forth between a more holist point of view and a more elementalist point of view, even as they alternate between rationalist and empiricist foundations. All of the perspectives on the left side of this figure are essentially synthetic in the sense that they purport to deal with the molar attributes of the mind, whereas those on the right side are designed to tear thoughts and percepts into their constituent pieces. Of course there

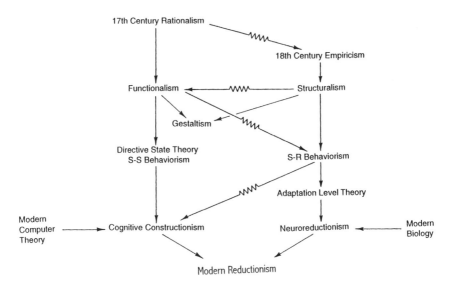

FIG. P.1. History of psychological theories and the intellectual sequence that led to the modern reductionist approach. Straight arrows indicate positive trends from one theory to another. Broken arrows indicate developments that were essentially reactions to the perceived failures of the other type of theory. The important idea here is that psychological theories have oscillated from more holist to more elementalist ideas throughout the history of this science. From Uttal (1981a). Adapted with permission from Lawrence Erlbaum Associates.

are other stress points—for example, the disputes between those who argued for introspection and those who declined to use this tool. But I see the main contending forces as those championing holism and rationalism against elementalism and empiricism, respectively. Clearly, elementalism reached its peak in recent years under the influence of the enormous successes in both modern computer theory and modern biology. This new form of elementalism has also fostered an essentially empiricist perspective in recent years.

This holistic–elementalist dichotomy is also the focus of much of the stress in contemporary theory. As I summarize in chapter 5 of this book, I believe that it is necessary that we return to a perceptual science that is mathematically descriptive, nonreductionist, holist, rationalist, and mentalist. (These badly overused and poorly defined technical terms are defined later.) If one puts this all together, one comes up with a new way to look at an old friend, nothing other than a new version of an operational and nonreductionist behaviorism.

This book is, by intent and definition, a polemic. In it, I draw together my thoughts, as they have evolved in the last four decades, into a counterargument to the elementalist, empiricist, reductionist *zeitgeist*. I must also acknowledge at the outset that I am not attempting to develop an even-handed and balanced review of the literature or by any means to make it complete. There is enough breadth in the empirical literature to allow one to support virtually any point of view, particularly in the context of the topics I consider here. My citations of the work of others is, therefore, selective. Occasionally, I "view with alarm and point with concern" at a specific study, but only as it represents a class of similar work. I am particularly drawing on what I believe are some of the most important ideas of workers from the last half century, sometimes at the expense of ignoring something more recent but less relevant. We tend to forget that all of our work is based on that of our predecessors and that many ideas and formulations have a much longer history than the last issue of our favorite journal. Impact and relevancy are more important than recency as I work my way through these chapters.

I am also drawing on some of my earlier writings in critical places where I find that what I said before captured, after some editing, the point I now want to make. Chapters 3 and 5, in particular, are heavily reworked versions of essays that I had published previously. Placing them in the context of the other new chapters made them more relevant for me, and I hope they also make the entire story I have to tell coherent.

I also have to acknowledge that many of the ideas that I present and argue for cannot be proven in a strong scientific sense. Many of the arguments I make are those of judgment, point of view, and conviction. Some of my readers may dislike this limitation, but little more can be said for the conclusiveness of many of the current neuroreductionist and cognitive reductionist theories that I discuss. Indeed, much of what we call perceptual theory today is based on very weak logical foundations of proof. But that is not unusual. All sciences, including perceptual psychology, are forced to examine only vague symbols and traces of the actual reality in which they are interested. Astronomers can no more directly examine a star than a psychologist can directly measure a percept. The problem for perceptual scientists is that the possible interferences between themselves and their objects of interest—thoughts and percepts—are far greater than those obscuring the astronomer's view. Cognitive penetration is far more difficult to measure, analyze, and comprehend than is the absorption spectrum of interstellar dust.

Finally in this preface, I do want to make one additional disclaimer, one that is repeated throughout the book simply because I know that this will inevitably be one of the criticisms that will be lodged against some of the unpopular ideas about limits and barriers in this book. If I may paraphrase the words of our not-too-lamented past president: "I am not a dualist." The criticism of reductionism that I present here is in no way intended to suggest that I am not a practicing, deeply committed, materialist monist. I am absolutely convinced of what I call the basic principle of psychobiology. That is: *The mind and all of its accoutrements are nothing more nor nothing less than the processes of the material brain.* To reject this fundamental principle is to take the subject matter about which I am writing out of the realm of science itself, and that would be wrong on many counts. Perception is a matter for scientific investigation. However profoundly its progress may be limited by certain constraints and barriers, perceptual science is absolutely and finally placed in the domain of experimentation and theory that characterizes all other kinds of science. The debate is only over what kind of a science it will ultimately be.

A book like this is much easier to write than were its predecessors. My convictions are more firmly set, I am not trying to exhaustively review all relevant literature, and I know very well what my message is at this stage of the game. I have no illusions about how this critique of contemporary science is likely to be accepted. I expect that, should this book be of any interest to any of my colleagues, it will be considered extremely controversial, if not easily rejectable. It is, without question, an attempted refutation of some of the primary assumptions of contemporary theory. My hope is that I am not too far off base according to some other criterion than contemporary popularity. Of course, I also hope that history will support my position. If not, so be it. This book sums up my convictions concerning some of the most important questions of human nature. It is a statement of a point of view that has provided a framework for my personal answers to some of the most important questions of human history. Right or wrong, in detail or in general, I am convinced that this personal synthetic act is not performed often enough. That in itself may be one of the main reasons some of the misconceptions that I criticize here have emerged.

ACKNOWLEDGMENTS

In the past there have been many people who have supported and nourished the intellectual environment that I have enjoyed. In each of my books, I have tried to thank those who were most helpful to me during the time each was prepared. The last five years have been in a new environment for me, one that was made possible by Professor Charles Backus, who was dean of the of the College of Engineering and Applied Sciences at Arizona State University, and by Professor Philip Wolfe, who was chair of the Department of Industrial and Management Systems Engineering when I moved over here. I will be grateful for a very long time to them for their confidence simply because this has been a wonderful place for a psychologist to work, study, teach, and write. A critical stage of editing and writing was done while I was a visiting professor in the Department of Electrical and Electronics Engineering at the University of Auckland in New Zealand. This trip was arranged by my friend and colleague Dr. Ramakrishna Kakarala. Ram and his competent wife–colleague, Dr. Lara Ruffolo, went far beyond ordinary hospitality to make my trip both professionally productive and personally enjoyable. Lara went even further and applied her excellent literary skills to editing this book at a critical point in my work. Final copyediting was done by Sondra Guideman of LEA.

Several of my colleagues have read and commented on the more technical aspects of various chapters. In each case I have profited from their attention even when they did not agree with everything I wrote. I am especially grateful to Dr. Satoru Susuki, during the course of his postdoctoral visit to the Perception Laboratory at Arizona State University. My long discussions with Satoru added immeasurably to my understanding of the difficult topics that I have chosen to write about. My colleague Peter Killeen has been a wise guide and mentor through the complexities of behaviorist thinking. I would also like to acknowledge the important influence on my thinking exerted by Robert Pachella of the University of Michigan. His prescient article of 1974 should have had a much greater influence than it did at the time. Hopefully it will be appreciated for its pioneering ideas in the future.

There have also been many others who have stimulated some thought, *en passant* so to speak, with a written or spoken communication. I know that I have not remembered or mentioned all of them, but their influence has left its marks throughout this book. Of course, in the final analysis, only I bear the responsibility for the successes and blunders of both expression and of conceptualization.

As ever, whatever I have done is mainly due to the companionship and love of over forty years from my dearest Mit-chan. Thank you, sweetheart.

1

INTRODUCTION:
THE WAY THINGS ARE

PERCEPTUAL SCIENCE YESTERDAY AND TODAY

Our understanding of how we see has gone through an extraordinary period of growth and development in the last half century. It shares with many of the other sciences the fact that this has been a time unequaled in human history for progress toward a deep understanding of both our world and ourselves. The study of vision, however, in all of its many forms, has undergone a paradigmatic revolution that is quite different from those experienced by many of the physical and behavioral sciences. The enormous change for vision science is characterized by the fact that it was transmuted from what was purely a phenomenological and even philosophically speculative endeavor to one based on the natural sciences. Physics, chemistry, geology, and most other forms of the natural sciences had already made that transition centuries earlier. Most of the other forms of nonexperimental psychology have yet to cross that threshold.

Along with this transition of vision science from a pre-science to a full-blown science came a diversification of its methods and theories. The availability of such devices as the intracellular microelectrode, high-gain, high-impedance electronic signal amplifiers, the digital computer, the functional magnetic resonance imaging (fMRI) and positron emission tomography (PET) scanners, and other ingenious devices has changed not only what perceptual scientists do, but also what they think. As recently as a half century ago we were only able to ask people "what did you see" and record their verbal or simple motor responses, whereas we now are able to look at the activity of both single neurons and large chunks of the visual pathway at virtually all of its levels. We can simulate and model visual processes with mathematical formulas, statistical analyses, computer programs, and even, in some cases, programs that mimic networks of neurons. We are now able to measure the phenomenon of vision psychophysically with a new precision and breadth of inquiry using tools such as cathode ray tube (CRT) displays and computationally modified stimulus images. All of this progress and development would have been unimaginable only a few years ago.

Methods and techniques that were unknown a half century ago are now commonplace. For example, our awareness of the chemistry of light absorption by the cones has been one of the great intellectual accomplishments of our times. The biochemistry of the retinal receptors provided insight into the color vision process, which was originally measured in terms of color mixing responses gathered in psychophysical experiments. Some of the questions that were impenetrable to those methods were answered with the development of electrodes small enough to enter single retinal receptors. We even are beginning to know something about the genetic codes that guide the development of the retinal photochemicals.

In the reverse direction, a belated (Fourier published his theorem in 1822) application of Fourier analysis techniques to image manipulation has provided us a powerful means of controlling the details of pictures presented as stimuli. Previously there had not been any satisfactory and convenient way to manipulate a picture in a controlled manner so that its properties could be used as controlled variables in psychophysical experiments.

This powerful Fourier theorem has even become the basis of a entirely new theory of how the visual system is anatomically and physiologically organized—what we might call the "Fourier" theory of vision. The key idea in this model is that the visual system is composed of a set of real (in a physiological and anatomical sense) spatial frequency-sensitive components in much the same way that the Fourier theory suggested that any pattern could be broken up into a hypothetical set of orthogonal sinusoidal functions (De Valois & De Valois, 1988). Even though I argue against the use of this particular approach as a physiological theory later in this book, this application of this complex mathematical theorem to vision has to be considered to be one of the supreme intellectual accomplishments of this science. For example, measures of visual form acuity such as the contrast sensitivity function (CSF)—a spatial frequency-based idea—provide a novel and precise way of studying form perception. Hitherto, this topic has always been made difficult by the lack of a satisfactory way of quantifying form—the critical independent variable in many important experiments.

The impact of all of this progress has not only been to enormously expand the database but also, in a much more fundamental and important way, to alter our perceptions of perception. Our theories have gone through an evolutionary, if not revolutionary, process in the past few decades. Computer theories, including the well-known connectionist or neural net ideas have been extremely influential not only in stimulating new ideas but also in practical applications. Computational modeling has become a major activity of vision scientists. The comparisons of neurophysiological data with psychophysical data in an effort to build bridges between the two domains has become a ubiquitous part of contemporary perceptual science. Neural net models, as well as neurophysiological findings, are frequently invoked to explain perceptual phenomena. Computational models are commonly developed to simulate or mimic visual processes.

The excitement of the progress that has been made in psychophysics, neurophysiology, modeling, and theory sometimes obscures the fact that there is still a tenuous basis for much of what passes for theory in contemporary vision science. Many of our theories of how we see are based on known neurophysiological relationships, but most of these data come from the less complicated, peripheral portions of the visual pathway. Although we know a lot about the action of single neurons at all levels of the visual pathway, we know virtually nothing about that which is the essence of the relationship between perception and neurons—the complex web of interactions between these neural components at high levels. I argue in this book that the complexity of that web is so great that it is impossible in both a practical sense and in principle (due to the limits on analyzability imposed by thermodynamics, numerousness, and chaos) to unravel it. That is, the simple facts of the huge numbers of involved neurons and computational complexity will forever prohibit us from understanding how central neural processes become perceptual experience.

Furthermore, we now appreciate that many perceptual phenomena are "cognitively penetrated." That is, many visual responses seem not to be determined solely by the raw physical aspects of the stimulus or simple peripheral neural interactions, but also by the symbolic significance or inferred meaning, or even the spatial or temporal relations of the stimulus or the situation. My use of the term *cognitive penetration* includes both conscious and unconscious processes. The key idea is that the determination of the perceptual response depends on factors beyond those of the raw physical attributes of the stimulus or even the simple low level transformations by simple neural processes. What a stimulus means or what it implies can sometimes determine the perceptual outcome more effectively than the wavelength of the light or the geometry of its retinal projection.

Another very important controversy revolves around the question: What is more important, the nature of the parts of the stimulus figure or the arrangement of the parts? In many instances, the visual experience is determined not by the detailed properties of the individual parts of a stimulus, but by the spatial or temporal relations of one part of the stimulus scene to others. To me this implies the prepotent influence of the highest, most complex levels of the cerebral cortex in determining our perceptions. All too often, however, contemporary psychobiologists "peripheralize" their explanatory models by placing the critical locus of the perceptual experience in the earliest or lowest levels of the visual pathway.

I cannot overstate my conviction as we progress through this book that, at the present time, we have no idea what the logical rules and laws are that govern the transmutation of neural activity into perceptions. Indeed, we do not even know where in the brain that this mysterious and wonderful process takes place, if it is localized at all. I believe this lacuna in our knowledge to be the main driving force, if not the exclusive reason, for the predominance of theories stressing the peripheral location of the salient mechanisms. I believe this emphasis to be mainly incorrect. Many of my colleagues agree with this emphasis, as is clearly indicated by the abundance of top-down theories of cognition. Many others, however, seek peripheral explanations of perception at low levels that seem to many of us to be irrelevant to the essence of the process.

In *A Taxonomy of Visual Processes* (Uttal, 1981a), I spelled out in detail what I thought was a plausible broad-brush approach to a multi-influence or -level theory of visual perception. I argued that we could categorize the factors that affect the visual perception of a stimulus into six levels of influence. They were:

- Level 0—The preneural physics of the outside world
- Level 1—Receptor properties
- Level 2—Neuronal interactions
- Level 3—Perceptual organization
- Level 4—Relational factors
- Level 5—Cognitive and attentive manipulation

My contention is that each of the five levels of processing leaves its traces in the perceptual experience. Certainly the physics of the stimulus has a significant impact on what we see. If it did not, we could not survive. Poor quality of our adaptive responses to visual stimuli would challenge not only our personal existence, but that of our species. The important thing to keep in mind is that, in addition to the raw attributes of the stimulus, there are also many other modifying influences between the stimulus and our percepts. The nature of the retinal receptors determines what we will see, as do the interactions that occur between neurons in the retina and throughout the visual nervous system. In the periphery, we have been able to make progress in understanding some of these influences. In the higher or more central portions of the visual nervous system, as I just noted and as I firmly believe, the complexities of the interactions are now, and probably forever, beyond us. The problem is that to understand these neural processes and interactions, we have to look at them in microscopic detail—and all at once. Unfortunately, a research strategy to do that is simply not available or foreseeable. Therefore, some students of vision tend to look at the collective, ensemble, cumulative behavior produced by the involved neurons. Such a molar strategy has come to be called *psychology*. There is nothing pejorative in this word. This macroscopic approach is exactly what physicists use with such complex ensembles as the dynamics of a tank of gas, a situation in which they are, likewise, confronted with an uncountable large number of component molecules. Others interested in the same problems prefer to study the individual neuronal components, one or a few at a time. This microscopic strategy is called *neurophysiology* and it is analogous to particle physics. Both approaches have much to offer in helping us to understand how we see. However, problems of both a practical and theoretical nature emerge when attempts are made to build conceptual bridges between the two domains.

To appreciate why, let's consider my taxonomy of visual processes in a little more detail. The first five levels (0–4 as described in *A Taxonomy of Visual Processes*, Uttal 1981a) were postulated to be essentially preattentive and automatic; the sixth level (5 as described in *On Seeing Forms*, Uttal, 1988) reflected a set of visual processes that seemed to require some kind of effortful activity on the part of the observer. To me, however, there is an even more important dividing line than the one between the attentive and the preattentive categories. That is the discontinuity that exists between level 2 (neural interactions) and level 3 (perceptual organization). Notwithstanding my complete adherence to the most basic and fundamental premise of this entire science—that all mental experiences are the equivalent of some neural process—it was here that I felt that we had to shift conceptual gears and go from microscopically organized reductive explanations to macroscopic descriptive ones. It was here that the sheer numerousness of the involved neurons and the complexity of the involved neural networks swamped any hope of a neuronal reductionism that was comprehensible at any level beyond the most peripheral.

The line of demarcation that I have suggested between the potentially microscopically reductive (level 2 and below) and the macroscopically descriptive (level 3 and above) is probably far lower than many of my colleagues would accept. For example, attempts to find simple neural network explanations for many of the visual illusions that I described in the *Taxonomy* book are a flourishing part of contemporary visual science. Exacerbating this disagreement is the fact that there is a very strong tendency to peripheralize the critical locus of the location of some of these phenomena. Such illusions as the waterfall illusion, the McCullough effect, the Muller–Lyer illusion, the neon color spreading effects, and the Kaniza triangle have all become grist for neuroreductionist arguments. The alternative, a molar, descriptive approach based on "perceptual organization," does not satisfy current tastes because it does not depend on the technological apparatus of computers and microelectrodes that is so popular these days. Nevertheless, it is this primarily phenomenological, operational, and positivistic approach (so well summed up in the distinguished article by Pomerantz & Kubovy, 1986) to which I have been drawn back in the course of the last few decades of considering these issues. This book spells out some of the reasons that argue for this kind of nonreductive, molar, and—if I dare use the word in today's cognitive climate—behaviorist approach to much of visual perception.

Before I proceed further into this discussion, I also want to make two very important personal points of view clear. First, as I have said in the preface and as I repeat in later chapters, I am not some kind of a closet metaphysical dualist asserting that mind and brain are examples of two different kinds of reality. I am a fully committed materialist monist and am completely convinced that the neural network of our brain is the necessary and sufficient apparatus for the creation of sentience, consciousness, awareness, mind, or whatever else one wishes to call it. This ontological monism is, however, tempered by an epistemological conservatism. I believe, and will try to convince my readers as we move through the chapters of this book, that there are substantial blocks, barriers, and obstacles to our ability to actually build the bridges from the microscopic to the macroscopic. In this regard, I find that I am in essential agreement with other antireductionist materialists such as Boyd (1980) and other philosophers of this same persuasion. Boyd argues strongly for a materialist theory of mental processes, but distinguishes between the mind as an expression of physical reality and the possibility that it can be reduced to the terms of its constituent components. He asserts that the operational or functional properties (mind?) that emerge from that physical structure (brain?) are usually immune to analysis. In Boyd's words:

> Materialists, quite rightly, have been careful to insist that each mental state is identical to, not merely correlated with some physical state. . . . I shall show that the version of materialist psychology best supported by available evidence entails that mental and psychological states are not definable in physical terms. (p. 86)

Boyd, thereby, distinguishes between the "doctrine that mental phenomena are physical phenomena" and that there necessarily exist "true mind-body identity statements linking rigid designators." His argument is primarily an attack on some earlier antimaterialist philosophies. But, his conclusion is the same as the point being made here—although mind is of brain, developing the links between the two domains may be both practically and theoretically impossible.

The intractability of brain–mind reductionism, in my view, arises because of the very nature of its material origins—the complexity of the critical functional interactions. In this regard, Boyd obviously shares with me a deep commitment to a material monism. We also agree, however, on somewhat different grounds, that in terms of an achievable epistemology (the issue of what we can know) we both are actually functioning as epistemological dualists!

In other words, there are two worlds of observation, even if there is only one of underlying reality. They are separated not by any mystical barrier, but simply by the computational load that would confront any theory attempting to build a bridge between the two. The barrier is, from one point of view, just a simple practical matter, but one that speaks loudly to the nature of current psychobiological theory. What this practical matter is saying is that the theoretical bridge between the mental and the physical is not just difficult to build, but it is impossible. The impracticality, however, merges into a matter of principle, which also adds to the intractability of the problem.

Second, although I am critical here and throughout this book of many of the reductive techniques and approaches, I value very highly the contributions from the individual sciences. Computational modelers have created wonders in programming algorithms that imitate the performance of human cognitive abilities (e.g., Grossberg & Mingolla, 1993a, 1993b). Neurophysiologists have discovered some of the details of the working of neurons and very simple neural nets that have enlightened and informed us about one of the most, if not the most, important systems of the organic world (e.g., Hartline, 1938; Hubel & Wiesel, 1968). Psychophysics, the primary tool of what may be called *applied epistemology* (a synonym for *perceptual science*), has contributed enormously to our understanding of the functional rules of visual perception (e.g., Campbell & Robson, 1968). Each of these sciences can and should stand on its own feet. The distinguished contributions of practitioners of each of these sciences offer much to understanding ourselves and the world we live in. I hope it is clear that I am not suggesting a cessation or even a reduction in the effort directed at each of these sciences. What I am proposing is a reevaluation of the meaning of the relationships among them and, perhaps, a somewhat calmer and more realistic evaluation of where reductionist approaches are plausible and where they strain credulity.

By intent, this book is an iconoclastic review, from the perspective of one perceptual scientist, of the meaning and justification of reductive techniques in modeling, psychophysics, and cognitive psychology, respectively. Iconoclasts, I appreciate, do not have a good reputation. In the ninth century they rushed about destroying great works of art and making a fuss at a time when more accepting folk were willing to accept contemporary traditions.

There is even a tinge of fanaticism in the appellation "iconoclast." One might exclaim—What presumptuousness! What gall! What *chutzpah*! What right does any individual have to take on the *zeitgeist*—the consensual community of agreement on basic scientific principles and assumptions? Frankly, I have no good answer to this question beyond that of a lifetime of study of the foundations of this science, a deep personal conviction that all is not well, and, fortunately, the support of an increasing number of colleagues. The arguments presented here will hardly be definitive or compelling; many are indirect and logical rather than empirical, or matters of taste rather than rigorous proof. Yet, I have to agree that, no matter how farfetched, the ability to cite a seemingly related experimental finding is always more compelling than a mathematical proof or a logical argument.

Nevertheless, I argue that scientists, both individually and collectively, are also capable of illusory misperceptions concerning the organization of their science and the meaning of their findings. History is glutted with examples of firmly held theories that were ultimately shown to be incorrect. One does not have to go as far back as the days of phlogiston, the ether, or stable continents to prove this point. Paleoanthropology, a science that shares some formal similarities with psychology (both are working with fragmentary data far removed from the real targets of their research), has been in the throes of argument and counterargument for the last decade concerning the interpretation of their very sparse evidence for the evolutionary history of our species. (See, e.g., Johanson and Shreeve, 1989, for a report on the disputational state of that science.)

Nor does one have to travel that far afield from biopsychology or psychiatry to appreciate that erroneous perspectives can emerge, just as one does not have to look that far back in time. Consider the book *Great and Desperate Cures: The Rise and Decline of Psychosurgery and Other Radical Treatments for Mental Illness* by the biopsychologist Elliot Valenstein (1986). Valenstein makes it clear how the mind–brain community, as a whole, can go off on wild tangents that are ultimately proven to be fallacious. For 20 years, a draconian reductive theory—a putative, but unsubstantiated, relationship of the frontal lobes to mental health—provided the rationale and foundation for a now totally discredited and, retrospectively, appallingly drastic surgical intervention. The number of people who were mutilated and tranquilized by lobotomies of one sort or another is shockingly described in Valenstein's important book.

Even more relevant to this discussion than the disastrous consequences of mistaken theories in psychosurgery, however, is that Valenstein emphasizes how easy it is for an entire scientific community to be fundamentally wrong with regard to its basic theories and concepts. It should not go unnoticed that it was in the field of the relation between the mind and the brain that the possibility for error was so drastically realized.

Valenstein's book is fascinating for another reason. It explores the non-scientific reasons that motivated the lobotomy pseudotheories. Sadly, these included such issues as economic debates between neurologists and psychiatrists concerning who would "serve" certain kinds of patients and, therefore, collect the fees. As remote as perceptual science is from the concerns of most of the public, it is also subject to the same kind of economic force that all too often drives other kinds of human behavior.

The topics that I consider in this book don't have the practical immediacy or visibility that these widely applied surgical techniques had at their heyday; the matters that I discuss here are far more arcane and esoteric and, in the main, less visible to the public at large. Thus unconstrained, and for other reasons to be introduced later, there has been far too little consideration of the significance and meaning of some of these theoretical approaches. Although many of these ideas may be mainly of interest at the present time to specialists, they do concern some of the most fundamental premises underlying understandings we have of our own nature. My goal in this book is to clarify at least partially contemporary thinking concerning the logical and conceptual underpinning of some widely accepted theoretical concepts and premises in perception science.

THE ISSUE—REDUCTIONISM

The main target of the iconoclastic thesis of this book is "reductionism" in a very particular domain—mind–brain relationships. I am considering our science's efforts to explain perceptual (and other mental functions) in the terms of either internal cognitive mechanisms, formal models, or the neural structures from which the brain, the organ of the mind, is constructed. There is no question that some kinds of reductionism have been enormously successful in some sciences. Our understanding of the nature of the physical world is truly impressive and is based on a progressive reduction in our models from various kinds of matter to molecules to atoms to the indivisible gravitons, photons, and leptons and the divisible (into quarks) hadrons. Clearly this kind of physical reductionism is one of the major achievements of modern science and has influenced our lives in both positive and negative ways that we have yet to appreciate or completely understand. Similarly, our understanding of the biology of reproduction, growth, and evolution, based on the structure of the large molecule called DNA (deoxyribonucleic acid), has not only been an intellectual accomplishment of the first water but also promises cures for some of the most feared of human afflictions.

In spite of these successes, there are differences between physical and genetic reductionism, on the one hand, and perceptual reductionism on the other. These differences should raise flags of caution as we extrapolate these past successes into future expectations. One of the major differences is all too often ignored. Physical and genetic reductionism are not of the same level of complexity as perceptual reductionism. Although reductive, the codes for the basic particles of physics are very simple—only a few particles are combined in only a few ways; there are only 6 quarks (12 if you count the antiquarks) and they can only be combined 3 at a time. Furthermore, electrons are all identical and are absolutely identified by a few "quantum numbers," whereas it is likely that no two neurons are the same. Finally, where one electron operates on another in a simple manner (electrostatic repulsion), the interactions between neurons are much more complex. Two neural centers do not interact by simple, single valence-type forces, but rather by complex multivariate coded messages.

Even within the relatively simple world of physics, the problems may be of such enormous complexity that they are, for all practical purposes, unsolvable. In recent years, for example, there has been considerable interest in the physical sciences in a new universal explanation of all of the forces of matter called *string theory*. String theory consists of families of equations that for all practical purposes are unsolvable if applied to the full complexity of our universe. Nevertheless, the approach is considered to be extremely valuable just because it is the only currently plausible unified theory that gathers together all of the particles and all of the forces of the physical world under the umbrella of a single mathematical description.

This esoteric mathematical approach to understanding physical nature is conceptually related to the question of reductionism in perceptual science in an important way. String theory, like perceptual science, invokes issues and problems that can be expressed and yet remain insoluble. It is curious that this limitation is acceptable in the physical sciences but difficult to accept by the brain sciences even though the problems encountered in the physical sciences are fundamentally much simpler.

In this same vein, the genetic code consists of only a few basic units (the four bases cytosine, guanine, thymine, and adenine) that can be combined to encode all organisms. Nevertheless, this important field of science also confronts its own barriers of complexity and intricacy. Decoding the structure of the human genome is underway, but at enormous cost and effort in spite of the logical simplicity of the linear code on the DNA molecule.

It is not just the fact that physics and DNA require the combination of only a few basic terms and that there may be many more kinds of synapses or neurons that suggests that decoding the brain will be a much more difficult task. Even more important, in comparing the difficulty of the codes instantiated in neural nets and those in the genetic codes, is the fact that although the genetic problem is essentially one dimensional, neural codes are almost certainly three-dimensional. The explosion of complexity (and the associated computational requirements for successful analysis) when one goes from a one- to a three-dimensional code should not be underestimated and can in some cases lead to what are totally intractable, although perfectly formulizable, problems.

It also is important to make a point here that is expanded considerably in the next chapter. Mathematical models are themselves neutral with regard to the underlying mechanics. String theory, for all its elegance and power, contains superfluous mathematical constructs, just as did its predecessor quantum mechanics. Current versions of string theory invoke 10-dimensional worlds even though one may wish to describe only the 4-dimensional one (x, y, z, and t) in which we live. To link the mathematical theory to the physical world requires other assumptions, premises, and linking hypotheses about which the mathematics says nothing. Yet that linkage is the essential aspect of the reductionist approach; it is not the mathematical model per se, no matter how comprehensive and successful it may be in *describing* the universe under investigation at its own level of discourse.

However easy it is to coin and use the word *reductionism*, clearly it has multiple meanings and is, along with a lot of the more sophisticated ideas in science, difficult to define precisely. One of the most interesting attempts at clarifying the multiple definitions of this term has been presented by the philosopher of psychology Daniel N. Robinson (1995). Robinson classified reductionism (in general) into four types:

Nominalistic Reductionism. A nominalist reductionist provides formal, abstract descriptions that list the components of which a thing is made, for example, "This chair has four legs." This kind of reductionism is purely a matter of naming. Examples of "theoretical" approaches in psychology in which nominalistic reductionism has been presented as theory are ubiquitous. Freudian psychoanalysis, with its id, ego, and superego, is a typical nominalistic reductionism.

Phenomenalistic Reductionism. Phenomenalistic reductionism links psychological responses and vocabulary, for example, "The taste of sugar is what is called sweet." Psychology has also frequently defined some of its constructs in terms of the inferred internal mental processes or mechanisms. Consider for example, what we mean by *motivation, affection, fear*, and other terms that describe private feelings.

Nomological Reductionism. To a nomological reductionist, reductionism is nothing more than a statement of a scientific law. Examples are, "The threshold for light under optimal conditions is only five to ten quanta" or "IQs decrease with the number of children in the family." In other words, this kind of reductionism is equivalent to the assertion of a replicable relationship between observations of a pair of variables.

Ontological Reductionism. Now we come to what Robinson and I both believe is the kind of reductionism that I am talking about in this book, for example, "Face recognition is the same thing as the response of a neuron (or a group of neurons) at some place in the nervous system and can be *explained* in terms of the neuronal response." This is the kind of reductionism in which descriptions of reality at one level are linked to descriptions at another, usually more microscopic, level. This kind of reductionism is the more demanding kind of reductionism. It requires a more or less complete definition of the way in which the microscopic parts of a system interact to produce molar behavior rather than just the naming of the parts. It is more than description; in fact, an ontological reduction is a metaphysical statement of the nature of things. Hartline's explanation of the Mach band in terms of the interactions of the neural signals in the ommatidia of the horseshoe crab's eye is an example of an ontological model. So, too, are the cognitive reductionist theories that attempt, for example, to separate reaction times into several component subprocesses.

It is this fourth definition—ontological reductionism—that I consider and criticize in the discussions that follow. Psychophysical–neurophysiological bridge building of the kind we call *neuroreductionism* is clearly an ontological enterprise. So, too, are the efforts to reduce behavioral observations to cognitive processes presumed to be going on as a result of the action of complex neural nets. Model building, as I shall demonstrate, is intrinsically nonontologically reductive (math is neutral), but is often presented as this kind of reductionism. The other three forms of reductionism to which Robinson refers are epistemological tools with which it is difficult to take offense, but they are not metaphysical entities in which the nature of reality is considered. Model building, neuroreductionism, and cognitive reductionism, the three topics to be considered in detail in later chapters in this book, are ontological issues that deal with the fundamental nature of reality. In other words, they are reductive enterprises. As such, they are very serious enterprises. However serious, it must not be overlooked that they are extremely vulnerable to logical, empirical, and conceptual difficulties.

At the risk of diminishing my reader's confidence in my expressed plan to be a dispassionate critic, I cannot avoid inserting this penetrating quotation from Robinson's (1995) provocative prose:

> Let me say only that reductive strategies of the materialistic stripe have *always* been either declared or undeclared wars on psychology, for such strategies have as their principle objective the elimination of all psychological entities from the domain of the actually existing. This is why it is so ironic, if not pathetic, to witness contemporary psychology lusting after them. (p. 6)

I don't agree with Robinson that there is necessarily any overt intent behind these "wars," but I do agree that scientific psychology is in jeopardy from the increasing trend toward computational and neuroreductionism in recent years as well as from its own ill-advised cognitive reductionism. If this were the natural course of events, well justified by new scientific discoveries and developments, I would be entirely comfortable with this development. However, along with a few others, I am convinced that there is a legitimate, and perhaps primary, role for a molar psychology studying the behavior of the entire creature, even in this world of increased (and increasing) emphasis on the microscopic components of the system. The reasons for this belief are spelled out in detail in the remainder of this book.

WHY REDUCTIONISM IS SEDUCTIVE

Why is reductionism so attractive to perceptual scientists? There are several answers to this question that I would now like to discuss. They include:

- Mind is, beyond doubt, a product of the brain.
- Humans have what appears to be an innate desire to explain that which is ponderable.
- Neuroreductionism has been successful, at least at some levels of the nervous system.
- There is neural "evidence" for almost any theory, no matter how far-fetched.
- There are many economic, social, and prestige pressures on perceptual science to simulate other natural sciences.

Mind Is Neural

One of the obvious reasons that neuroreductionism as an epistemological strategy is so attractive is that mind is, by its most fundamental nature and beyond any doubt, truly reductive in basic ontological principle. That is, there is no question that our mental processes are generated by our neural mechanisms. It is also true that the components of our neural mechanisms are discrete and that the critical transactions occur among vast numbers of the constituent neurons that make up the brain. It is this flow of information between and among the many involved cells that is the only possible mechanism that can be plausibly invoked to explain all of our mental life including our perceptual experiences. To go beyond this basic fact of the psychobiological sciences is to enter into a world of mysticism, theology, and fantasy that is far beyond any logical or scientific examination.

The key word, however, in the previous paragraph is *vast*. Although it is an axiomatic principle that mind emerges from brain, the number of involved neurons must be so great to instantiate even the simplest thought that, in practice, it is probably impossible to unravel. Therefore, an argument can be made on this basis that it is impossible to understand the neural network. Much more is made of this point in later chapters.

The Nature of the Human Mind

Another important compelling force that pushes us toward reductionism is, to put it baldly, that we perceptual scientists are as human as anyone else. This statement is obviously a superficial truism if considered out of the context of this discussion. Nevertheless, I believe it also holds a major truth about the intellectual enterprise that we are now considering. One of humankind's most important characteristics is that we are always searching for answers—we are a very curious animal. Human history is filled with systems of thought, some based on scientific evidence and others based on fragile wishes, that have been created to answer some of the very difficult conundrums that are continuously encountered by humans.

- What is life?
- Why do we die?
- What happens then?
- What is consciousness?
- What are the rules that should govern human interactions?
- What is our responsibility to our fellow human?
- What is beautiful and what is ugly?
- What is good and what is evil?
- What is the nature of the physical world of which we are a part?
- What are we?
- Where did we come from?
- Where are we going? That is, what is the purpose of our existence, if any?

These questions keep crowding into our lives and demanding answers—regardless of whether they are answerable. Our innate drive for answers and the awareness of at least some humans of at least some of these questions compels us to construct answers—any answers. There is no doubt that our lives are filled with questions of the utmost complexity. However, there is far less consideration of the ultimate answerability of the questions—itself a question that is ignored in the optimistic and uncritical hope that, as Sherlock Holmes put it, "all will be revealed in due time."

Driven by the basic human urge of curiosity, we create answers, sometimes simply for the sake of having an answer. Some of these answers are based on nothing more than a search for order in what otherwise would be an intellectual chaos. Intellectual structures, schema, philosophies, religions, and other guiding principles are sometimes built simply to organize the disorganized, the latter being a state that many scientists, in particular, find offensive. Some, like prejudices and stereotypes, are no more than efforts to simplify the complex in order to avoid the mental effort of dealing separately with the entire array of entities that is involved in any complex system, be it social or neural. Some answers are complex conceptual systems based on fundamental premises that themselves are far from being confirmable. Yet, once accepted, these premises can often lead through an impeccable logical progression to conclusions that are totally fallacious.

One has only to observe the plethora of false cults and quack cures to quickly become convinced of how compelling the human need for answers can be. We humans seem to exhibit an innate drive that abhors intellectual vacuums just as nature despises physical ones.

The problem is accentuated in science. The entire scientific enterprise is charged with the task of providing answers to specific questions. In this domain of human activity, we have institutionalized our basic human curiosity. We have added to this institution the responsibility to find answers to questions of enormous practical importance in health, commerce, and national defense. In light of these demands, it is not popular to even consider saying "I don't know" or, even worse, "It can't be known."

The situation pyramids on itself. Developments in one science are often seen as potential solutions to the problems of other sciences. Sometimes they are; sometimes they are but illusions of understanding. Throughout history, our psychobiological science has sought to answer questions about the nature of mental processes by providing solutions that were often based on the most recently available technology. Primitive reductionisms invoked mechanical, hydraulic, and even pneumatic technologies as answers to the question of the nature of mind. More modern ones have invoked electrical circuits, computers, and abstract ideas of organizational structures and processes. Most recently, I will argue, advances in cellular neurophysiology have become technological models of mental processes.

Doubts arise as we pass through this historical sequence, however. It may be that the properties of the neuron that make it important in producing mind are not the same as the ones that we can most easily measure. We know much about the membrane, receptor sites, and the general chemistry and physiology of these wonderful cells. It may just be, however, that the significant properties of the mind may be its informational attributes (e.g., the ways the neurons are interconnected) rather than its metabolic ones (e.g., what chemicals are used as transmitters or why electrotonic—i.e., passive—signals diminish with distance along a membrane).

There is another issue that is important as we consider this issue—the tractability of the questions that we are asking. The very human behavior of searching for answers and explanations is founded on the notion that answers are possible to even the most complex questions. As we see later, there is at least once science in which this is an open question—perceptual science.

Furthermore, the promise made by science, the social contract from which it derives its support from the broader community, is the commitment to provide answers to both practical and esoteric questions. The social contract that perceptual and vision science, in particular, have made with society is patently reductive. Society's support for a purely phenomenological psychology would probably be as constrained as that allotted to art history, for example, if that was all that was offered in return by perceptual science.

However much of a commitment perceptual science has made to reductionism, it is necessary to at least consider whether intractable questions exist. I believe that this consideration is long overdue. There are known bounds and limits constraining the range of questions that can be answered by science in general, and some extraordinarily serious ones for perceptual science in particular. It is well known—indeed, it can be rigorously proven— that there are mathematical problems that can easily be stated, but for which no solution exists. Computer scientists know that some problems are noncomputable in a practical sense even if not theoretically prohibited. There are the boundaries established by the nature of nature as expressed in some of its most fundamental laws. Physicists appreciate that perpetual motion machines, speeds faster than light, and time travel machines do not exist outside of the fictional literature of parascience. The Second Law of Thermodynamics reminds us that eggs cannot be unscrambled. I argue in the next chapter that a neural interaction explanation of mental processes is like both scrambling and unscrambling eggs. Structure and information are lost in the former case that cannot be retrieved in the latter.

The existence of boundaries and limits in the physical and biological sciences, along with the indisputable successes of these other sciences, produces a focus of internal conceptual conflict for the perceptual sciences. The resolution of this conflict has to come from the realization that some questions are easier to ask than to answer, and there is good reason to assume that perceptual scientists, in particular, are poking at the very border of the unanswerable. No amount of human drive or ambition or surprising new technical developments can overcome these fundamental limits on problem solving.

Previous Successes

Another driving force in the seduction of contemporary perceptual scientists as neuroreductionists is the fact that neurophysiology, and especially the study of individual neurons, has already enjoyed some tremendous successes. I have previously mentioned a few of the most notable discoveries in this field. Now I must clarify the nature of some of these successes to explain why they have so often misled with regard to other seemingly related issues. The major problem is that most previous successes in which neural explanations seem to have been achieved have been concerned with the transmission aspects of neuronal function. We know a lot about how information is transduced and encoded in the peripheral portions of the nervous system. However, this is not the same issue as the question of psychoneural equivalence: Where and how does a pattern of nervous activity become the same thing as the mental process? The confusion of the transmission aspects of the visual system with the psychoneurally equivalent representation aspects is one of the most overlooked and serious issues confronting any proponent of neuroreductionism.

We have learned an enormous amount about the constituent components of the visual nervous system at all levels. Many of these cells are in the sensory pathways. Neurophysiology is particularly easy to study in the domain of sensory mechanisms simply because responses there are anchored to easily measured and standardized parameters of the physical stimulus. We know precisely where and when a stimulus occurs and its exact quality and quantity because of independent physical measurements. Sensory neural responses are, therefore, synchronized with the four great parameters of the perceptual responses—space, time, quality, and quantity—in other words, where, when, what, and how much? This is why we have made so much progress in studying the transmission aspects of vision and the other senses. Other mental processes are far more challenging to examine. It would, for example, be far more difficult to synchronize something like "admiration" with a particular stimulus or neural response even if you could fortuitously find the place in the nervous system in which its psychoneural equivalent is located.

Progress in the neurophysiology of individual neurons has stimulated an inordinate belief in the plausibility of correctly linking neural responses to perceptual responses beyond the most peripheral levels. The reasons for this belief are several. First, cellular neurophysiology, which as I have noted is the science of the individual neuron, has focused our attention on the cell as the locus of all kinds of mentation. The *pontifical neuron*, the *cardinal cell*, the *grandmother cell*, and last but certainly not least, the *Neuron Doctrine* (see Barlow, 1995, for a recent exposition of this point of view) are all phrases that imply the priority of these individual units as the basis of perceptual representation. The basic argument in all of these theories is that single neurons (or small numbers of neurons) are capable of representing what may be very complex concepts.

The flaw in this argument is that the true neuron doctrine—the statement that the nervous system is made up of cells demarcated from each other by bilipid membranes, each with its own nucleus (and other metabolic inclusions), and communicating by specialized chemical or electrical messengers—is a structural theory and not a functional one! What we know about neurons mainly concerns their individual structure, irritability, and metabolic functions. What we do not know very much about is their role in processing information, not as individual neurons, but as components of the huge networks that most likely are the foundations of thought, perception, and all of the other experiences we collectively call mind.

In other words, the classic neuron doctrine, emphasizing the nature of the single cell, is actually quite neutral with regard to the nature of the polycellular basis of psychoneural equivalence. The classic neuron doctrine deals with the physical nature of the nervous system in the same way that the study of bricks deals with the nature of the components of a building. It is not the nature of the brick that is critical (of course, it sets some limits); it is the way the bricks are organized into a coherent and interlocking structure. You can build a lot of different kinds of buildings out of the same carload of bricks! Conversely, a floor plan tells you little about the nature of the building material. The difficulty is that most knowledge of neurons is analogous to knowledge of individual bricks, but that the real problem is that of their organization—the floor plan.

Nowadays, a few neuroscientists tend to agree that the individual neuron is actually of minimal consequence for the encoding of mental processes. Some have even come to accept the idea that it is the statistics of populations of very large numbers of neurons that is the critical issue. The action of an ensemble of neurons is now acceptable as the psychoneural equivalent to at least some of my colleagues. It is even accepted by many that this population may fluctuate, with a different sample of neurons involved at different times in a single mental activity. Conversely, individual cells may vary their role in a population with no effect on the global perceptual experience of the organism. The point is that the single cell is not capable of representing anything other than a very broad range of whatever stimulus parameter to which it responds. Perceptual precision depends on a large sample from which emerges something comparable to, but not necessarily the same as, a statistical average.

Success in observing the patterns of activity of single neurons has also created another misimpression: the idea that a higher level neuron that responds to some aspect of the stimulus that was not explicitly encoded by lower level neurons makes it, the higher level one, in some sense, special. This is also a manifestation of our misemphasis on the role of single cells in producing mental experiences. The fact that a parameter of the stimulus is represented in the responses of a single cell at the level of V1 or V2 does not mean that that same information was not encoded at lower levels by populations of other cells. This is a very subtle but, as we shall see, a very influential point, the misunderstanding of which was also engendered by the focusing of our attention on single cells.

Selection of Evidence

Another powerful and compelling force toward accepting neurophysiological and cognitive reductionist strategies is the enormous amount of evidence that is available. We have so much data on the responses of individual neurons, and for that matter the perceptual responses of individual people, that it is possible to find almost anything that one needs to support virtually any reasonably plausible theory. The number of journals in the field of neurophysiology grows annually and the number of potentially related articles must now be enormous. The very complexity of the field produces a widely diverse set of findings. With the generally accepted requirement for significant statistical tests of significance at the .05 level, certainly a substantial amount of data is published that is in the spurious 5% category. Such spurious data aside, there is always a substantial opportunity for the raw results of an experiment to be misunderstood for something other than what they really are.

There is, furthermore, an even more subtle factor that must be considered when one is looking for the sources of support for any particular contemporary theory. That additional factor is the self-fulfilling prophesy. All of us tend to seek support for our own theories. How important this factor is cannot be exactly quantified, but certainly the selection of experiments to be run, the paradigm to be used, and the expectations of what the results should be bias the data considerably. Few scientific studies, indeed, are run with rigorous double-blind techniques, and often this can lead to tendentious and unbalanced sets of results. It is sometimes the case that these erroneous results are subsequently caught (see, e.g., the Stryker and Sherk, 1975, account of the biases involved in experiments purporting to show that experience was necessary for the development of orientation columns reported by Blakemore & Cooper, 1970, and by Spinelli, Hirsch, Phelps, & Metzler, 1972). It is unfortunate, however, that sometimes these corrective studies cannot find their way into the literature and the original tale becomes a reified part of the science's general culture, as expressed in its textbooks.

In a similar vein, one of the most often used techniques of psychology, the double dissociation paradigm, has often led to curious distortions of the way in which we view psychological processes and functions. G. C. Van Orden, B. F. Pennington, and G. O. Stone (personal communication, 1996) considered the implications of this technique and the ways in which its application can become a self-fulfilling prophecy of the explanations we formulate of mental and brain processes in a promising manuscript entitled

What do double dissociations prove? Inductive methods and theories in psychology.

The double dissociation idea is based on a comparison of two findings. It is assumed that if activations of two different operations or structures produce different results, then the operations or structures are the loci of the respective results. For example, Van Orden, Pennington, and Stone were especially interested in lexical processing. As an example of the fallacy involved in the double dissociation paradigm, they report the cases of two patients, one of whom has a lesion in one brain area and loses syntax, but does not lose semantic meaning of individual words. The other has a lesion in a different area and loses semantic meaning, but still can produce syntactically correct sentences. The initial conclusion from this comparison is that the first patient has a damaged syntax "center" and the other has a damaged semantics "center.

Van Orden and his colleagues pointed out, however, that there are many logical flaws to this argument. For example, the acceptance of the two-center conclusion depends on an a priori judgment that something corresponding to anatomical "centers" and cognitive components actually exists. The double dissociation technique, they suggested, tends to support the a priori hypothesis, whatever hypothesis is initially suggested, to the exclusion of others that are equally plausible. Rather than two centers, it might well have been the case that there was a single center with high interacting functions or some other form of nonlinear organization.

In other words, Van Orden, Pennington, and Stone (personal communication, 1996) argued that the double dissociation procedure simply tends to confirm whatever hypothesis one begins with and produce false positive results. They wrote about this popular method of searching for the mental architecture:

> The tautology of the double dissociation logic illustrates the circular fallacy in all contemporary logics that discover the causal basis of behavior. These include the subtractive methods popular in mainstream cognitive psychology, neuroimaging studies, developmental psychology, and most other areas of psychological inquiry.

They also noted that the popular double dissociation technique violates the well-known proscription against accepting a hypothesis, a situation that can lead to tautological reasoning. Rejection of the null hypothesis is, as is well known, a more appropriate form of inference.

The abundance of evidence and the tautology of the self-fulfilling theory expressed by Van Orden, Pennington, and Stone permits investigators to make an unconscious selection of whatever it is that they wish to find. Van Orden and his colleagues go on to show how even as simple an a priori premise as the idea that different components exist can lead to fallacious theoretical outcomes in their chosen field, language processing.

Van Orden and Papp (in press) went on to develop this idea by arguing that brain scan methods, also dependent on certain preassumptions and a subtractive methodology, are equally fallible. They argued that (a) the technique assumes a neural system with interacting centers but no feedback and (b) the technique assumes the existence of a cognitive system with independent and isolatable functional modules. Van Orden and Papp suggested that neither of these criteria is "likely."

Although I speak to this point later, it should be noted now that their ideas generalize to the more profound notion championed here: There is no way to permeate the barrier that exists between brain and mind from psychophysical studies.

Economic, Political, and Other Practical Considerations

There are some other very tangible and practical reasons for the past transformation of what is fundamentally a phenomenological, descriptive perceptual science into one that has all too often yearned for an ontological reductionism as its standard philosophy. Perceptual scientists have long been on the outside of the medical–industrial complex. The National Institutes of Health and other medicine-related granting agencies and their political supporters in the Congress, as well as the general community, have tended to look on the purely molar psychological studies as not being of very great promise for the solution of applied, medical problems. Clinical psychology is also in a continuous war with psychiatry and has generally lost the battles. How very useful it would be, then, to cloak perceptual science in a biological-cum-medical garb for grants, fame, and name.

I am sure that this is not *the* driving force for individual perceptual psychologists, but some of the organizations that have represented scientific psychology have gone to great lengths to justify experimental psychology by wrapping it in the cloak of a medical model. The issue is, of course, complex, and certainly striving for medical relevance is not the sole force driving intellectual neuroreductionism. However, in a world that so highly rewards the technical and applied side of science, it can be an appreciable contributor.

A curious side issue is that the new biochemically oriented psychiatry is, from the point of view of many scientists, totally atheoretical. We know almost nothing of the ways in which psychotropic drugs act to change behavior at the detailed network level. We know something about their metabolic effects on individual membrane receptors or whole neurons, but what they do to affect the organization of the brain and to serve as therapies for mental illness remains as mysterious and opaque today as it was to the first witch doctors who had their clients smoke or ingest some plant, fungus, or hippopotamus dung. Most new psychotropic drugs have been discovered by chance. Many seem to have uncontrolled side effects or a variability of action that enhances our uncertainty about exactly what they are doing.

In summary, by dressing up perceptual psychology in the languages of biochemistry or neurophysiology, this predominantly mental science has been brought into the same arena as some other contemporary sciences in a way that is both socially relevant and well funded.

A MINITAXONOMY

Over the years that I have discussed matters of the kind that I am writing about in this book, I have found that much, if not most, of the disagreement between contending sides is based on differences in the meaning of certain key words. Therefore, throughout this book I try to clarify the meaning of some of these words and terms in the hope that at least some of the semantic confusion can be ameliorated. It has been the experience of most of us that some of the most vigorous arguments have ended suddenly when one or another of the participants suddenly said, "Oh, is that what you mean by that word! I thought we were talking about something else. I got it."

The following section is the first of several that I place in this book to help clarify my use of some of these important words.

Structures and Functions

The following meanings are intended to hold throughout this book:

- *Mechanism, structure,* and *operator:* All of these terms refer to a component or part of a system that does something to information.
- *Process, operation, transform,* and *function:* All of these terms refer to what is done to information by one or another of the already mentioned mechanisms, structures, or operators.

The general distinction drawn here is between structure and function.

Experimental Psychology

Experimental psychology is the empirical, data-driven science of transformations between stimuli and response, constrained by the intrapersonal privacy of mental events to measurements of interpersonally communicable behavior. Some experimental psychologists are mainly mentalist cognitivists; some are behaviorists. The key idea distinguishing between the two schools of thought is the degree to which each group accepts the premise that it is possible to infer underlying neural and cognitive processes by observing overt behavior.

Cognitivism or Cognitive Science

The most recent instantiation of experimental psychology is *cognitivism* or *cognitive science*. Although it is difficult to identify a single founder of the field, certainly the early works of Miller, Galanter, and Pribram (1960) and Neisser (1967) were influential in the reshaping of the field. Cognitivism is characterized by beliefs that reduction from behavior to the components of mental processes is an obtainable goal. Cognitivism, like behaviorism, accepts the reality of mental processes and neural mechanisms, but diverges from behaviorism in supporting the premise that behavioral data can be used to specify their nature. Cognitivists are implicitly, if not explicitly, reductionists as they search for models of the underlying mental architecture.

Behaviorism

A school of experimental psychology currently out of fashion, *behaviorism* is characterized by the belief that the scientific exploration of mental behavior is constrained to interpersonally communicated behaviors. Introspective reports, although also interpersonally communicable, are eschewed as being too far removed from the actual mental processes and too polluted by irrelevant processes. Most modern behaviorists, like their cognitive counterparts, accept the notion that mental processes and experiences occur and are real and that some equivalent brain state must correspond to each cognitive process and each mental state. However, they deny that behavior can be used as a means of inferring the nature of the internal events. Behaviorists prefer to keep their theories limited to the same level as their data and are implicitly, if not explicitly, antireductionists.

Mental States

Mental states are internal events that inherently can only be "witnessed" or experienced by the individual. Their existence can be signaled to others either verbally or physically (two kinds of behavior), but there is no way of ascertaining whether their true, let alone precise, nature has been communicated. That is, they are intrapersonally private and cannot be directly examined by another person. Obviously, behavior and mental state can be disassociated; this is the basis of the profession of acting and the source of some difficulty when one encounters sociopathological personality types. On the other hand, the ability to disassociate mental states and behavior can also alleviate a substantial amount of human conflict.

Mental states or psychological experiences come in a wide variety (percepts, feelings, motives, learning, etc.). Mental states are inadequately described, at best, by a host of ill-defined descriptive terms collectively categorized as *emotions* (e.g., *rage* and *love*) or *percepts* (e.g., *red* and *loud*). Because mental states can only be measured indirectly through behavioral measures and introspective reports, the problem of linkage between behavior and mental state is as challenging as the effort to link mental states and brain states.

Behavior

The term *behavior* includes those responses made by an organism that can be interpersonally witnessed and reliably measured by an outside observer. Behaviors may include anything from speech, other motor responses, or even glandular, physiological, or metabolic processes.

Reduction

In addition to Robinson's (1995) taxonomy, reduction is defined as an analysis of a system into its components. Churchland and Sejnowski (1989) defined reductions as "explanations of phenomena described by one theory in terms of phenomena described by a more basic theory" (p. 15). In each case, the basic concept is the same—molar properties are deciphered in the terms of the constituent microelements. Obviously, there is a hierarchy of elements, each step of which is "micro" to the one above it.

Description

A *description* is a mathematical (or verbal or computational) representation of the functions, processes, or transformations carried out by a system that maps the course of events (i.e., the behavior) of that system. Process description is carried out in a way that is separable from assumptions and facts about the specific internal mechanisms that might effect the processes. I argue in the next chapter that most models and theories are, at best, descriptions no greater in explanatory content than an equation fitting a curve. Therefore, all formal models are neutral with regard to internal structure. Although such a curve may allow us to predict behavior, it cannot tell us anything specific about the infinity of plausible and possible analogous mechanisms that may account for that behavior. When dealing with complex theories that involve specific parameters or components, there is an illusion that we can say something about internal mechanisms. This illusion is just that, a fallacious conclusion, and does not mitigate this criticism. Even the most complex mathematical or formal theories are totally neutral with regard to internal mechanisms. (See Uttal, 1990, and chapter 2 for more on this point.)

Theory

Clearly, what is meant by a *theory* must change in the light of these more precise definitions of explanation and description. Theories are the heart of science in that they extrapolate beyond local data to general ideas. Theories may be microscopic or macroscopic. Thus, they act as syntheses and compilations, organizing and arranging knowledge. But if the argument I have presented is correct, they can only be process descriptions and not explanatory reductions in any situation that relies solely on behavioral data. Theories often introduce concepts such as charge, gravitation, emotions, and drives that can help to simplify and organize knowledge. When they do, however, they are describing relationships and not explaining the nature of the machinery that produces those energizing forces.

With these definitions in hand, my hope is that my readers are now somewhat better prepared to undertake this iconoclastic voyage to a modern view of the conceptual bases of contemporary perceptual science.

WHAT THIS BOOK IS ABOUT

This chapter has introduced some of the basic ideas that have influenced the way in which my personal scientific philosophy has developed. I have no illusions that all of the ideas presented here are popular points of view. Nevertheless, I feel deeply enough about some of these matters to have gone to the effort to put this book together. Without question, this is a critique of contemporary thinking about three very important topics. The first concerns the nature of models and theories. The second concerns neuroreductionism—a matter already introduced. The third concerns cognitive reductionism—the attempt to define the internal mental architecture.

In each of these fields I try to define exactly what I see as the basic philosophy and then to explain my view of how the activities in each of these fields must be reinterpreted. This is key to understanding my goals. I am not saying that the experimental research in any of these fields is inappropriate or incorrect in any sense of these words. My point is that a new look at modeling, biopsychological bridge building, and mental architecture unraveling is in order. I am not suggesting that research in each of these fields stop or even change course. I am suggesting that we consider that some possible misdirections and misinterpretations may have permeated these scientific fields. I note several times before this book concludes that the research that has been carried out in cognitive psychology, neurophysiology, experimental psychophysics, and theory and model building is elegant and informative and can stand by its own rights. My critique is aimed at what the data that have been forthcoming from each of these fields mean, and how far they can be extrapolated from the laboratory to a specific interpretation of the nature of the mind. I hope it is clear that my commitment to this scientific field is profound and I am not suggesting either suppression or repression. In fact, I believe that a reconsideration of the meaning of these three scientific approaches is necessary if perceptual science is to survive as an identifiable and coherent field of science.

This book has two parts. First, as I did in the previous four books in this series, I try to express the major principles that seem to me to summarize a logically consistent statement of thought in this field and some of the emerging logical and conceptual difficulties. This part of my critique constitutes the major portion of this work. Chapter 2 considers models and their use; chapter 3 reviews contemporary neuroreductionist efforts; and chapter 4 explores the problems encountered in the search for a mental architecture.

The second part consists of chapters 5 and 6. In chapter 5, I propose a future agenda for perceptual science. Given the criticisms that have been made in the body of this book, what must we do to reconceptualize and revitalize this important science? My view is that we must return to an earlier stage of scientific inquiry—a kind of behaviorism in which we deal with models in a new way and in which we eschew both neuroreductionism and cognitive reductionism. In chapter 6, I present a summary of my perspective of perceptual science in the form of a list of what I believe are its most important emerging principles.

Is my view correct or clouded by my own logical and conceptual errors? Only time will tell. For the present, let's now see how one perceptual scientist arrived at this neobehaviorist philosophy.

CHAPTER

2

BARRIERS BETWEEN THEORIES AND MECHANISMS[1]

WHAT ARE THEORIES AND WHAT DO THEY MEAN?

In this chapter, I explore the problem of the role of theories and models in relating perceptual processes to the underlying mechanisms. I ask: What do formal models of cognitive or perceptual processes mean? What can models do and what can they not do? The purpose of this chapter is to consider these questions for a wide variety of formal models—mathematical, computational, neural network, statistical, symbolic, and others that are just arriving on the scene.

Formal models and theories have been with us for some time. Mathematics and statistics have been used to describe cognitive processes throughout the history of experimental psychology. Historically, the first theories in this science, those of Weber and Fechner, were both formulated in the language of algebra and calculus. Computer models have been with us from virtually the first moment that digital computer technology became available (see, e.g., Farley & Clark, 1954, Rosenblatt, 1962, Selfridge, 1958, and Widrow, 1962, among others; and for a comprehensive review of the history of this field and the mathematical relationships among the various theories see Grossberg, 1988a, and Carpenter and Grossberg, 1991). The Anderson and Rosenfeld (1988) and Anderson, Pellionisz, and Rosenfeld (1990) com-

---

[1]This chapter is a revised and expanded version of an article previously published in *Perception and Psychophysics* (Uttal, 1990) and is used with the permission of the Psychonomics Society.

27

pendia of significant papers in neurocomputing are also good reviews of the history of one cluster of formal models. However, the recent impetus for the renewed interest in computer simulations and mathematical models of cognitive processes has been generated by, among others, the work of Anderson (1968), Grossberg (e.g., 1968, 1969, and as summarized in his 1982 and 1988b books), Marr's important book (1982), and one of the most influential works, the twin volumes by Rumelhart, McClelland, and the PDP Research Group (1986a) and McClelland, Rumelhart, and the PDP Research Group (1986). The past decade, in particular, has seen an explosion of interest in the development of formal models of perceptual processes (see, e.g., Watson, 1993, and Landy & Movshon, 1991).

Contemporary modeling efforts have already successfully produced formal analogs of many perceptual and other cognitive processes. Processes have been "simulated," "analogized," and "represented" by programs and mathematical formulas that perform behaviorally in much the same way as do the organic systems under study. Nevertheless, these impressive simulations must be evaluated in terms of what they mean, not just how well they fit functionally to the time course of some behavior. It is especially important that we consider what these models mean in terms of the underlying mechanisms and processes they purport to represent. This is an often overlooked epistemological aspect of many contemporary models.

In this chapter, I present an alternative interpretation of the relationships between formal models and the underlying biological reality—the neural substrate—on the one hand and the psychological reality—the cognitive processes—on the other. I examine some issues and ideas that speak to the validity, verification, and testability of formal models in an ontological reductionist sense. I am especially concerned with the question: What limits, if any, exist concerning what models can say about the internal workings of the mind on the one hand and the brain on the other?

Epistemological inquiries of this kind are necessary because formal models and their attendant neural and cognitive corollaries are often misinterpreted as valid reductionist explanations that realistically and effectively depict the actual workings of brain or cognitive mechanisms. I argue here that this is not the case. My thesis in this chapter is that models are very limited in what they can say beyond describing the course of the modeled processes. By *course*, I mean the variation of one measurement parameter or another over time or space.

I should point out that I am not concerned here, nor do I have any argument, with the mathematical details of how models work or what algorithmic functions must be carried out to simulate more or less accurately cognitive processes; that comes later in this book. Rather, I am concerned with what formal models may or may not have to say in their role as putative reductive "explanations" of the systems they analogize. The issue at hand is: What, in fundamental principle, can we expect of a formal model in terms of its ability to *explain* as opposed to its ability to *describe*?

The constrained, limited, and conservative answers I offer to this question may be familiar to some of my readers, but should not come as tremendous shocks or surprises to anyone. The concept that there might be specific limits to scientific measurement or achievement has wide currency in other scientific fields. As I pointed out in the previous chapter, physical and chemical sciences live comfortably (most of the time) with their limits, including indeterminacy principles, the speed of light constraint, the impossibility of perpetual motion, and the need for statistical summaries of large aggregations of particles. Unlike physicists, cognitive scientists of a reductionist bent sometimes behave as if they believe that their models can be conclusively explanatory and that it is only a matter of time, effort, and new technology before a full analysis of the mechanisms underlying brain–mind relationships will be forthcoming.

It is important that my readers appreciate in advance the essence of the epistemological argument I make in this chapter. What I am arguing here is that formal models cum theories of this genre can have nothing definitive to say about the physiological or logical mechanisms by means of which perceptual processes are carried out; they are neutral, in fundamental principle, with regard to internal mechanisms. I am also asserting that it is not simply a matter of technical refractoriness or the logistics of complexity, but one of fundamental principle that impedes our attempts to draw verifiable conclusions concerning internal workings from formal models.

The question of what models and theories mean has been at the core of the philosophy of science at least since the days of John Stuart Mill. Mill influenced subsequent scholars such as the very modern Ernst Mach, who asserted later that "Scientific investigations do not penetrate nature; they organize in economical fashion that which experience presents to us" (as quoted in Edwards, 1967, vol. III, p. 291).

These are virtually the same words used by a group of contemporary neuroreductionists—Sejnowski, Koch, and Churchland (1988)—when they suggested that models "should be considered a provisional framework for organizing possible ways of thinking about the nervous system" (p. 1305).

(In some later writings, as we see in the next chapter, these same authors do take a somewhat different stance when they support an extreme form of neuroreductionism called eliminativism.)

Mill may have been one of the earliest to explicitly raise concerns about explanation and reductionism, but he was only one early representative of the powerful tradition of antireductionism that has surfaced from time to time in philosophical thought. Many other scholars agree with McDonough (1991), a widely respected student of the work of Ludwig Wittgenstein, that:

Wittgenstein's view that philosophy must not advance theories or explanations, but must content itself with descriptions, is well known. His view that
even science is ultimately not explanatory, but merely descriptive, has been
less emphasized. . . . Science is non-explanatory in the sense that the point
must come where the processes cannot be further explained, and we are
forced to merely describe "concomittancies." (p. 237)

Recently, other philosophers of science have also analyzed the problem
of explanation and reductionism specifically in terms of the fundamental
nature of the relationship between mind and brain and have considered the
role formal (computational and neural network) models may play in explanation. Fodor (1968) made the same point about analogy that I am about to
make here. Speaking of a theorem-proving machine, he asserted: "the machine would be inadequate as an explanation of theorem proving insofar as
it does not do proofs in the same way as a human mathematician does
them" (p. 136). Later, Fodor (1981) pointed out that reduction is not necessarily the only strategy by means of which even the most physically oriented
science can be pursued. In words that are equivalent to those I used earlier,
he suggested that one can reasonably be a metaphysical monist (asserting that
mind emerges directly from brain processes) and still eschew neuroreductionism as methodologically valid with regard to one's practical epistemology.

Massaro (1986, 1988) also raised questions about the role played by
another kind of computational model, connectionism, in psychological theory. He notes that some connectionist models may be too powerful in the
same sense that I discuss in chapter 3 with regard to the application of
Fourier analysis to visual modeling. The general problem is that these techniques are at once too powerful (they can model virtually anything) and too
weak (they are, therefore, too general) to establish, by themselves, anything
specific about internal structure. Massaro's point argues against the applicability of a type of contemporary psychological theory that has gained a
wide but uncritical popularity in recent years. The point of some of my own
empirical research (Uttal, Baruch, & Allen, 1995a, 1995b, 1997) is the same,
but aimed at Fourier theory. Cutting (1987) raised the same problem for
another kind of model, group theory.

Neural network models have played an important role in perceptual
theory in recent years, but one that is constantly changing. In their earliest
forms, neural net models were thought of as networks of nodes that represented simulated neurons. Over the years, there has been a gradual and
subtle alteration in thinking about these models. Nowadays, the nodes are
thought of more as generalized functional units rather than as individual
neurons.

In the many applications that have been made of these models to engineering problems, there has been a gradual distancing from the biology of
the nervous system to the more general notion that parallel processors can

perform many interesting information processing functions that are essentially organized in a two-dimensional matrix. Many of the general parallel processing ideas developed as engineering tools to solve some practical problem are totally unanchored to the biology of psychology of organisms. Nor does there appear to be any sound reason why they should be so anchored. We use whatever tools we have available without always understanding everything about them. Massaro's warning that these models are too general must be kept in mind when engineering models are represented as psychological theories.

Nevertheless, Rumelhart, McClelland, and the PDP Research Group (1986a) argued for the utility of their modeling approach because models of the type they offer "hold out the hope of offering computationally sufficient and psychologically accurate mechanistic accounts of the phenomena of human cognition" (p. 11). In opposition, my point is that although sufficient to simulate the course of some processes, neither the detailed operations of PDP models nor of any other neural network approach can be shown to be also necessary and, thus, unique. Thus, there is no way that they can be verified as being psychologically "accurate" in any sense beyond that of description.

Of course, we do not find universal agreement about the connectionist ideas even among contemporary cognitive scientists. Vigorous criticisms have been made by such scholars as Fodor and Pylyshyn (1988) and Pinker and Prince (1988). Fodor and Pylyshyn severely criticized the connectionist idea as not actually being a neural network idea but simply another version of the representations characteristic of many other kinds of cognitive modeling. Although appreciating that the parallel and distributed processing networks invoked can do a "lot of computing," Fodor and Pylyshyn suggested that their theoretical role cannot be distinguished from some older statistical approaches. They went on to note that although the models themselves are interesting analogs, it is their meaning and significance that seem to be at the core of the controversy that surrounds them.

Pinker and Prince (1988) also criticized connectionism, but from the point of view of language models in particular. They argued that one of the main purported advantages of connectionist or "neural net" theories—that the rules of thought can be dispensed with when one uses such a net—is invalid in general and specifically for the recent connectionist model of language offered by Rumelhart and McClelland (1986b). Their critique of the connectionist approach is based on a long list of the failures of the model and the fact that these failures arise specifically out of the nature of the connectionist approach.

Philosophers have approached the issue of what models mean with similar caution. Dennett's (1981) "type intentionalism" theory, for example, asserts that "every mental event is some functional, physical event or other, and the types are captured not by any reductionist language, but by a regimentation of the very terms we ordinarily use" (p. xix). Dennett suggested that this point of view is a further development of an earlier "Turing machine functionalism"—the idea that although all mental states are physical, they need not be embodied in the same physical mechanism even if modeled by the same Turing algorithm. I interpret this to mean that different mechanisms having the same functions can be analyzed and interpreted in the terms of some physically neutral language (e.g., mathematics) that is neutral with regard to which of the possible underlying mechanisms is actually present.

Cummins (1983) made the same point in a different way. In distinguishing between instantiation and reduction, he noted that "Uniform instantiation is not sufficient for reduction, since a variety of modal truths will hold for the target property that do not hold of the instantiation" (p. 24).

In asserting that "connectionism is 'neutral' with regard to rationalism" (p. 323), Pfeifer and Verschure (1992) reflected the same sort of disassociation between this particular approach to theory and the actual underlying mechanisms that I mentioned earlier. My argument is that this caveat holds true for mathematics and model building in general. Although superficially reductionist and even neural, close examination reveals that these models are nothing more than descriptive analogies of the biological mechanisms. The argument that formal models are neutral with regard to the underlying mechanism is closely related to the argument that a neuroreductionistic theory is unlikely to be available in the future.

McGinn (1989) specifically addressed the classic form of the reduction issue when he asked, "Can we solve the mind–body problem?" His answer was clear and his reason strikes a familiar chord:

> I do not believe that we can ever specify what it is about the brain that is responsible for consciousness, but I am sure that whatever it is it is not inherently miraculous. The problem arises, I want to suggest, because we are cut off by our very cognitive constitution from achieving a conception of the natural property of the brain (or of consciousness) that accounts for the psychophysical link. (p. 350)

It is important to note that McGinn believed, as do many of us who have considered this problem, that the barrier that exists between cognition and/or mind, on the one hand, and neurophysiological models, on the other, is a matter of fundamental principle. It is not simply a shortage of available data or the absence of a critical technique, that is, an "in practice" barrier, rather it is one that could never be overcome no matter what technological developments lie ahead. How the brain and the mind are interrelated is unknowable to human beings as profoundly as the speed of light is unsurpassable or as a quantum state is not knowable without altering it.

Some who ask the same question about mind–body relations, although they agree with this idea in principle, cloud the issue with what are essentially irrelevant matters. For example, Klein (1992) suggested that the mind is not reducible to the body (i.e., the brain) because (a) they are "operating on different levels" and (b) "There are pragmatic and religious reasons to maintain the mind body split" (p. 237). With regard to (a), I believe that Klein confuses the descriptive languages of science and the observable parameters of experiments with the fundamental reality of mind and brain. With regard to (b), it seems to me that Klein has introduced variables that are completely irrelevant to the scientific problem at hand. As we shall see, there are far better reasons operating within the level of physical science and mathematics, that make the argument much more effectively and without the introduction of irrelevancies.

Others have expressed antireductionist views that are based on the same kind of concerns that I have presented here. They include Chalmers (1995), Jackson (1989), Nagel (1986), and Rakover (1986, 1990, 1992). Rakover's discussion in his 1992 article is particularly cogent and reviews in an interesting way the history of scientific psychology relevant to the mind-body problem.

Antireductionist views such as those are not unanimously held, of course. Other well-known scholars (most of whom are closely related to the neurophysiological or computational fields) have distinctly different, although evolving, views about the possibility of reductive explanation. For example, Churchland (1986), strongly arguing for the possibility of reduction from mind to brain, misinterpreted (from my point of view) the kinds of reasons that will be most compelling in countering the argument that there will ultimately be a verified neuroreductionist theory of mind. The "common theme," according to her, of current objections to mind-brain reduction is the fallacious argument that "mental states are not physical states" (p. 346). I agree with her on the inadequateness of any form of this argument. However, there are some much more powerful physical arguments for asserting that neuroreductionism is impossible without denying that mind is a process of a physical substrate. I write more of the "eliminativist materialist" school of thought she and others represent in a later chapter.

Interestingly, Churchland, who originally expressed a deep commitment to reductive explanation, went on shortly thereafter to express some concern about the possibility of such a radical reductionism. In a subsequent paper (Churchland & Sejnowski, 1988) she and her co-author suggested that although "Neurobiological data provide essential constraints on computational theories" (p. 744), it is also true that: "the possibility that cognition will be an open book once we understand the details of each and every neuron, its development, connectivity, and response properties, is likewise misconceived" (p. 745).

This cautious theme was further developed in their much more comprehensive book (Churchland & Sejnowski, 1992) in which they went on to modify the original cellular reductionist credo by invoking interacting neuronal systems:

> The overarching contention of this book is that knowledge of the molecular and cellular levels is essential, but on its own it is not enough, rich and thorough though it may be. Complex effects are the outcome of the dynamics of neural networks. (p. 4)

A remaining question, of course, is: Would even total knowledge of the nature of these networks be enough? The corollary query can also be added: Would it be too much to handle?

Psychologists have tangled with the same issue in their efforts to determine the mental architecture—the arrangement of the cognitive components of thought. Whether or not the internal representation can be determined by behavioral means has led to considerable controversy over the years. Anderson (1978) antedated many of the arguments made in this book in his criticism of cognitive reducibility. I have more to say about this version of the "meaning of models" debate later in chapter 4.

Clearly the problem of what computational, mathematical, neurophysiological, or, for that matter, any kind of models can and cannot accomplish is a very important topic that should be of deep concern to psychologists, computer scientists, and philosophers. It is the purpose of the rest of this chapter to present one opinion, based on my own personal point of view, that virtually all kinds of models are, in virtually all situations, incapable of the kind of ontological reductionism defined by Robinson (1995). I believe that this perspective is based on reasonably solid principles from other sources besides cognitive or perceptual science itself. I acknowledge that many of these arguments are indirect, but collectively they raise grave doubts about the ways in which our theories and models are currently interpreted. The following sections analyze some of these specific constraints on the power of theories and models.

SOME CONSTRAINTS ON THE POWER OF MODELS

Formal models are, in a sense, more elaborate "linking hypotheses" (Teller, 1984) in that they purport to describe a precise relationship between the formal structure of a computer program or mathematical algorithm and a cognitive process. Neuroreductionist, but noncomputational or nonmathematical, models attempt to relate neural and psychophysical findings. By showing similarity in process, the conjecture is that either kind of model can demonstrate similarity of mechanism. The following sections of this chapter suggest some reasons why these conjectures may not be valid.

The Combinatorial Explosion: Problems Arising
From Numerousness

Let us first consider the complexity of the brain in simple numerical terms. At low magnification, the nervous system appears as a wonderfully complex aggregate of a number of interacting centers and nuclei. Yet even at this relatively gross level (which is not the appropriate one at which to consider the psychoneural equivalents of perception or cognition), the degree of interconnectedness may be very large. There seems to be no question that it will be found to be even larger as anatomists and electrophysiologists track the connections among the ever-increasing number of centers now known to be involved in even as relatively straight forward visual processes. The works of Allman (1981), Kaas (1978), Van Essen (1985), and, for an excellent summary, Zeki (1993) illustrate this complexity. Allman (1981) noted that more than 14 visual areas have already been discovered in the brain of the owl monkey; Van Essen (1985) provided a map (facing his p. 268) of the macaque cortex suggesting that as many as 40 regions may have some visual function. Van Essen went on to note that although the human brain has not yet been mapped in as detailed a manner, if the same kind of structural organization holds as in simpler primates, there is room for "literally dozens of visual areas in the human brain" (p. 283). This number was moderated later to about 30 (Felleman & Van Essen, 1991).

The situation is made even more complicated by the intricate series of interconnections among these many visual regions. Van Essen (1985) listed 92 distinct interconnecting pathways among these visual areas in the macaque that have been reported by neuroanatomists working on visual brain anatomy. Even newer statements (Felleman & Van Essen, 1991) list 318 known intercenter connections.

The question one must ask in the context of this very complicated system is: Is it plausible to carry out an analysis of a system of this complexity (30 or 40 areas interconnected by as many as 300 tracts)? One way to approach this question is to assume, as a first approximation, that the interconnecting pathways are simple—that is, to consider them to be homogeneous communication channels conveying a collective positive or negative valence in the manner of electrostatic charge or gravitational force. Realistically, however, it must be remembered that the system of visually involved nuclei is not so simply organized; the areas that are connected seem to communicate by means of reciprocal, multichannel tracts consisting of many complexly encoded independent fibers. However, the proposed simplification allows us to initially consider this problem in a manner analogous to the multibody problems of mechanics and physics.

Just consider the problem of defining the hierarchical structure of the various centers now known to be involved in vision in the primate cortex. Hilgetag, O'Neill, and Young (1996), in what I believe is an article of equal importance to Moore's (1956) classic work, showed that it is impossible to determine the hierarchical organization of the many parts of the visual brain from currently available information. They proved that there is an enormous number of equally likely hierarchies possible given the limited and idealized classification of the connection types. Yet the simple trichotomy of connection types (up, down, lateral) they used is almost certainly an oversimplification given the variety of neuronal fiber types and functions within the intercenter pathways. If they are correct in their analysis and in their conclusions, the arrangement of the various visual centers responsive to motion would be indeterminate from the available data. Even more important, as Hilgetag et al. (1996) went on to say, "further data, if classified by the presently understood criteria, would still not specify the exact ordering of cortical stations in the visual system" (p. 777).

The results of a few other comparisons are not encouraging about the prospects of any enterprise to analyze such a system successfully. Astronomers have taught us that, in general, a deterministic, exact solution is not available for even as small a system as three mutually interacting bodies (unless one of the three has negligible mass or external forces dominate the gravitational forces of all three bodies) given current methods of analysis. This classic proposition was shown to be true, in general, a hundred years ago by Henri Poincaré. Therefore, it would not be possible, in principle, to deal with a problem of the complexity of the 30 or 40 centers of the visual brain in such a direct manner if the organizational analogy I draw between brain nuclei and planetary bodies is appropriate. The system of simultaneous equations describing this "multibody" interaction would be much too complicated to be solved directly by even a very powerful computer.

Astronomers, on the other hand, have developed some methods for dealing with interacting objects when their number is very large (>200) by considering their discrete forces as the inseparable elements of a continuous field of force. Thus, large numbers of interacting forces can be thought of as contributing collectively to a field with a density that can be specified at all of the points in a space. It is this potential density function that then becomes the critical factor in the multidimensional calculations that are used for this kind of analysis. In this manner, quite satisfactory approximate solutions to the multiple interactions of the forces from the many point-like objects that collectively produced the hypothetical potential field can be determined, and the overall behavior of the system estimated (Greengard, 1988; Kellogg, 1953).

There are difficulties even with this kind of approximation, however. The mathematical procedure for producing an approximate global solution to a multibody problem of this magnitude requires that the forces exerted by and the behavior of the individual objects be submerged into those of the field by approximating the total effect of each point in a discrete mesh and then interpolating to each interior location in the mesh. Furthermore, many attempts at approximate field solutions to the multibody problem do not work when the number of objects is less than 200 and the density of the objects becomes too low for a field to be simulated. In the intermediate case ($3 < n < 200$), the only available solution to the multibody problem is that of actual physical or numerical simulation. In other words, the system must actually be constructed in the form of a computer program (or some kind of mechanical analog) and then allowed to run its course as certain perturbing inputs are applied to it. Depending on the nature of the system, this approach can sometimes provide a useful solution, but computability usually depends greatly on the uniformity and simplicity of the network and on interconnection forces that can be represented by relatively simple functions. Otherwise, the situation becomes analogous to the general three- or n-body problem and can only be represented by an unmanageable and almost certainly unsolvable system of equations.

Hence, although it may be possible to describe statistically what happens to a complex ensemble of objects (e.g., the collection of stars in a galaxy or the totality of neurons in a cortical nucleus), the behavior of the individual element (i.e., the individual star or the individual neuron) is not specifiable. Thus, just as is the case with the pressure of gas in a rigid container, the free-running electroencephalograph, the impulsive stimulus-evoked brain potential, or the behavior of a social system, the behavior of the components cannot be deduced from the ensemble activity of the entire system. In all such cases, the various involved sciences turn to measures of the molar attributes (e.g., pressure, electroencephalograph [EEG] voltage, social movements, psychological phenomena) to describe the ensemble's behavior. (By molar, I allude to those attributes of the system taken as a whole apart from the properties of its components.) All such approaches suffer from an inability to reduce those molar attributes to the behavior of the individual components simply because there are so many of them and the number of possible interactions grows rapidly as even a few additional components are added. Even then, the statistical model of gases must assume that all particles are identical and that they only interact weakly. This would be a further constraint to describing the nature of the components or to projecting up from their behavior to that of the whole system. The implication of this discussion is that no full analysis of even a moderately complex network, such as that composed of the modest number of the cortical centers, is possible.

The problem of complexity has been discussed so far in the context of the 30 or 40 centers of the brain's visual system. Yet even at this modest level of complexity, the task of analyzing the behavior of the entire system seems to be just as intractable as a rigorous model of, for example, the dynamics of the solar system. The problem of neural interactions becomes far more combinatorially explosive when networks of the individual neurons that compose these nuclei are considered. The unsolvable network of 40 nuclei connected by 300 or so tracts is replaced by an even more challenging one consisting of as many as 10^{13} neurons, each of which is potentially connected to a thousand or more of its fellows in a way that usually appears to the neurophysiologist to be disorderly and irregular.

It is difficult enough to calculate, even more so to conceptualize, the number of plausible neural subnetworks of 10^{13} neurons and perhaps as many as 10^{16} possible connections that may be present in the central nervous system. We just do not know very much about the size of a psychologically interesting neural array.

For the sake of discussion, however, let us assume that 10^6 neurons make up a network that is "interesting" in the sense that it constitutes an autonomous module capable of some plausible and useful element of cognitive information processing. Combinatorial mathematics then can be used to show that the number of possible networks of $n = 10^{13}$ elements taken $m = 10^6$ at a time must be very large. Specifically, the approximation formula $(ne/m)^m$ estimates the number of combinations of n elements taken m at a time. Ignoring the small constant e, there are approximately 10^7 raised to the 10^6 power different possible combinations, obviously a huge and intractable number.

I appreciate that this way of estimating the complexity of the nervous system is not completely satisfactory. However, it does give an idea of the enormous number of possible "mechanisms" that may exist in the brain. The point is that, for all practical purposes, there are innumerable combinations of as few as a million neurons possible in even small sections of the brain. The situation is even further complicated by the fact that we do not know which group of 10^6 neurons should be examined. The problem here is that with so many alternatives, it is unlikely that any neurophysiological investigation could unravel the network and no model could ever bring order to the specific underlying neuronal mechanisms of perceptual function. Redundant circuits, as well as simple numerousness, would always obscure the brain's true organizational details. Interestingly, ideas of extreme redundancy and multiple instantiation also suggest that we should be able to find virtually anything sought in the nervous system with electrophysiological tools. "Simple" cells, "Fourier" cells, "Gabor" cells, and a host of others yet to come should all be present in some form simply because they perform functions that can be described by the background mathematics. Thus, one of the great problems of this science is that we will probably always be able to find any new type of neuron as it becomes popular because of developments in other sciences.

The enormity of the combinatorial problem faced in dealing with realistic neural networks is understood by mathematicians but is usually ignored by neuroreductionist-oriented cognitive scientists. Mathematicians like Stockmeyer and Chandra (1979), for example, in an illuminating consideration of the size of computational algorithms, noted the existence of "simple" combinatorial problems that, although they involve only a few elements ($n \approx 64$ as exemplified by certain versions of the traveling salesman problem) and are demonstrably solvable in principle, would necessitate a "computer as large as the universe running for at least as long as the age of the universe" for their solution. Thus, they are asserting that although this computer might have as many as 10^{126} logical elements—a number approximately equal to the number of protons in the universe—it still would not be able to solve some problems encountered in even simple games in anything corresponding to a reasonable amount of time in a complete and rigorous manner.

Stockmeyer and Chandra's point should not be misunderstood. They are not asserting that such combinatorial problems are infinite or unsolvable in principle, but rather that, even though some problems of this genre are finite and solvable in principle, they remain unsolvable in practice: The computational algorithms required to evaluate the many possible descendent possibilities of even the simple sequential process typified by a board game are beyond the power of any conceivable computer.

It seems clear that the nervous system is an example of a "game" much more complex than the ones Stockmeyer and Chandra describe. Therefore, a computational analysis or model based on the simulated interaction of its discrete parts is patently impossible to achieve. The only exception to this generalization, and the basis of the few past successes in neural modeling, occurs when the system is very simple. When very severe constraints, such as an almost crystalline regularity and totally regular and simple interactions (as exemplified by invertebrate eyes), are imposed, then some analyses are possible.

Thus, the few really successful (and truly neural) network theories depend a great deal on the presence of regularity and repetition of the elements in the network for their successes. The algebraic model of the *Limulus* eye, such as the classic Ratliff and Hartline model (1959; see also, Ratliff, 1965), developed to simulate contour intensification (a neurophysiological analog of the perceived Mach band), and the differential equations of some of the more modern versions (e.g., those used by Cohen & Grossberg, 1984, to simulate boundaries and features as well as other more complex features) are all analyses that assume uniform arrangement of the constituent model neurons. The behavior of one neuron is prototypical of all of those in the network and the kinds of interactions are common to all cells. The details of the connections within the network define the behavior of the whole system. It was the presence of such a homogeneous and regular network that permitted Ratliff and Hartline (1959) to simulate the spatial visual illusion known as the Mach band by observing the response of a single neuron while moving a light source over a stationary *Limulus* retina. Unfortunately, this success was also the source of a great deal of unjustified optimism that these early accomplishments could be generalized to the irregular networks that are typical of the vertebrate nervous system.

For those interested in the present stage of development of modern neural net theory, there is probably no better discussion of the family of relationships among various neural network models of many cognitive processes than Grossberg's (1988a) elegant exposition of the principles and history of this field. It is important reading for everyone interested in this field, whether or not one agrees with the direction taken by neural network theoreticians.

The point of this discussion is that a general analysis of the brain at the level of networks of individual neurons is algorithmically unlikely because of its enormous complexity and numerousness. Nevertheless, if we were to ask, what is the critical level of informational interaction, the level at which cognition is most likely encoded?, the answer would most likely have to be phrased in the terminology of this intractable network of these wonderful cells.

Mathematics, Brain, and Nature Are One-Way Systems: Entropy Cannot Be Reversed to Order in Closed Systems

Nature is governed by fundamental laws that some of us feel contraindicate some of the goals of neuroreductionists and computational modelers. One of these fundamental propositions is the Second Law of Thermodynamics, which, in the domain of physics, can be stated as follows: No body can give up heat to a body of higher temperature. In the domain of information theory, a counterpart of this law is: Isolated systems tend toward a state of greater randomness than the one in which they currently reside.

One major implication of this fundamental law of nature is that there is a directionality to time. That is, the flow of events cannot be reversed to its origins. In other words, although it is very easy to mix the batter for a cake, you cannot "unmix" it. This has led the Second Law of Thermodynamics to be referred to as "time's arrow" by such scholars as Blum (1951).

It is not well appreciated, but the Second Law has not yet been rigorously proven by physicists. Nevertheless, this fundamental physical principle is widely accepted; few reputable scientists would waste their time developing a perpetual motion machine, one of the thermodynamically forbidden but ardently sought goals of parascience. I now argue that this principle has a psychobiological corollary. That corollary is: The molar behavior of a complex system (like the brain) cannot be analyzed or reduced to its logical and elemental neuronal underpinnings. The degree of complexity at which this corollary becomes operative for the nervous systems is uncer¹ n, of course, but what I say later about chaos may speak directly to that sue.

If correct, the corollary of psychoneural nonanalyzability would hold, it should be noted, even though there is no question that brain–mind systems can be created and can develop. I hope it is clear that I am not arguing that a brain cannot grow, develop, and ultimately produce conscious awareness. The conjecture I pose here is that thermodynamics implies that although simple laws can lead to complex behavior, the behavior of the complex system is not reducible to the large number of expressions of those simple laws and the microscopic interactions that generated it. To do so would be akin to unscrambling eggs or the unmixing of that cake batter I just mentioned.

The behavior of familiar physical systems provides support for this conjecture. As I pointed out earlier, when observing the behavior of a gas we cannot say anything about either the original or current state of all of its component particles. To observe the current state of an individual particle we would have to turn to local measurements of position and velocity. Although this can be done (within the limits of the Heisenberg uncertainty principle) for an isolated individual particle, it is obviously an impossible task for all of the particles in a container for reasons of numerousness that have nothing to do with Heisenberg's famous law.

Even if it were possible to measure a large enough sample of such current states, it still would not be possible to reverse the process and compute the original states of the component particles. It is not just a matter of simple numerousness (of the particles) playing havoc with any attempt to detail the attributes of the individual particles. It is also impossible to go from even a complete knowledge of all of the current individual states (a total impossibility) back to the beginning. The problem is that there will always be a vast number of possible alternative pathways from "then" to "now" and, also, an innumerable number of initial conditions that could evolve into the current state of a system of component particles. This would be so even if we did not have to deal with the numerousness problem, per se; this difficulty would obtain for even a very small number of components. The discussion of chaos theory to be presented later in this chapter elaborates on this point.

Thermodynamics, thus, suggests that the hoped-for informational analytic bridge may not exist between microscopic and macroscopic levels of even modestly complex ensemble systems. The psychological implication of this argument is that it is not a priori true that the attributes of one level of a complex system are analyzable or reducible into the language and symbology of another level, even though there is no doubt that the macro system is the sum of the actions of the microsystem's components. Specifically, the Second Law of Thermodynamics raises doubts about our ability to go from behavior or from molar physiological processes to the details of the arrangement of the neural elements that underlie those processes.

I cannot close this section without acknowledging that this thermodynamic argument is not a rigorous proof of the nonreducibility conjecture. It does raise a doubt, however, about some of the analytic goals of psychobiology and perceptual neuroscience, as well as about the models that are used to describe either behavioral or brain responses. It is but one element of the argument I present here. My hope is that all of the issues I raise will collectively lead us to a more thoughtful consideration of the true significance of the models we generate to describe brain and mind. My assertion at this point is that all models, regardless of their nature, can only be descriptive and can never be analytic or reductive for combinatorial and thermodynamic reasons. This lays the foundation for a more extreme suggestion: You can generate as many hypotheses as you please concerning internal structure, but they cannot be tested or validated by experiments that only consider input–output relationships. This is the topic of the next section of this chapter.

The Black Box: Problems Arising If the Brain Is a Closed Automaton—Moore's Theorem

Can we hope to reduce cognitive processes to their underlying neural mechanisms? Can we use mathematics to uniquely determine cognitive internal structures from external observations of the molar functions we call behavior? These are two of the intimately related questions with which this section is concerned. I deal here with another aspect of these perplexities—the difficulty that engineers refer to as the "black box" problem. The issue here is straightforward. How much can be learned about the internal structure and mechanisms of a closed system that can be examined only by stimulating it with controlled inputs and careful recording of the outputs? There is no doubt that one can easily describe the overall transform of the closed system. How much further one can go in determining the nature of the internal architecture or the internal machinery, mechanics, and processes than producing a description or deriving a functional law of the transformation between the input and the output is yet to be determined.

Obviously, there are some impediments. We have already seen how some of the classic techniques of psychological research are deeply flawed on a statistical or logical basis. The Van Orden, Pennington, and Stone (personal communication, 1996) critique of the double dissociation method discussed in chapter 1 suggests that what has hitherto been generally acceptable may be, in fact, inappropriate.

Exactly this kind of reduction from observed behavior to brain functions has, of course, been one of the major goals of psychological research for most of its history, if not the major goal. From the beginning, natural scientists have tried to link experiences and behaviors with a variety of brain mechanisms by invoking whatever was the technology of the times as a guide. I now examine the closely related, but slightly different, assumption that models and theories that describe behavior are capable of saying anything about, much less precisely determining, the nature of the internal mechanisms of a very special black box, the human brain.

Curiously, this is one issue that can be examined from the point of view of a rigorously mathematical proof. One of the most compelling arguments against the idea that we can reduce the externally observed behavior of a system to its internal mechanisms is to be found in the work of Moore (1956). Moore's theorem has long been overlooked, but it is of such fundamental importance to the topic of reductionism and modeling that it must be considered here in some depth.

E. F. Moore is a mathematician who has worked in the field of finite automata theory. A *finite automaton* is specifically defined as a device that is deterministic (as opposed to probabilistic, random, or stochastic) and has a finite number of internal states, a finite number of possible input "symbols," and a finite number of output symbols. One of Moore's (1956) theorems (Theorem 2) is directly related to the argument made here that the reductive (as opposed to the descriptive) aspects of formal theories cannot, in principle, be tested, verified, or validated by input–output methods. Specifically, Moore said:

> *Theorem* 2: Given any machine S and any multiple experiment performed on S, there exist other machines experimentally distinguishable from S for which the original experiment would have had the same outcome. (p. 140)

Moore went on to assert: "This result means that it will never be possible to perform experiments on a completely unknown machine which will suffice to identify it from among a class of all sequential machines" (1956, p. 140).

It is certainly debatable whether or not Moore's theorem is applicable to the modeling of human neural and cognitive processes. However, the brain does meet all of the definitional criteria of an automaton that were mentioned previously. Therefore, it seems that the mind–brain can be considered to be a finite automaton. Some may argue that the brain is so complex that it is beyond a reasonable extension of the rubric of "automaton." Certainly, we would all agree that even if very large numbers of states and neurons are involved, the number is finite. Another concern, which is really outside the realm of this discussion, is that the word *automaton* does not fit the human mind–brain complex for nonscientific and traditionally dualistic reasons. This argument is totally irrelevant. It is based on a popular definition, rather than the formal one that Moore proposed.

Hence, Moore's theorem, given its applicability to the class of systems to which we humans seem to belong, places severe constraints on some of the work currently carried out by theoretical and experimental psychologists and cognitive modelers—constraints of which these scholars may be unaware. It is particularly limiting for those cognitive scientists who attempt to understand, measure, and define the exact nature of the mental architecture—the internal, representational, and functional mechanisms—by behavioral means alone. Those who feel that neurophysiology may somehow overcome this difficulty by "opening the black box" need only refer back a few pages to my discussion of the enormous number of neurons and combinations of neurons involved in cognitive processes for relief from this equally fallacious misunderstanding.

Of course, on issues as fundamental as this, not all agree with the black box limitation. Control system engineers refer to an approach called Realization Theory. This mathematical tool is supposed to be able to infer internal structure from input–output relations alone. However, as so often happens when one encounters this kind of counterargument, a closer examination of the methodology indicates that it is, in actual fact, far from being a compelling counterexample. Astute Realization theorists appreciate that there are always innumerable alternative structures. The reason for the nonunique product of Realization Theory is that it is based on some very constraining assumptions. These assumptions limit its application so much that it can be seen to be irrelevant to the behavior–brain issue. First, it works only with linear systems. The very nonlinear nature of both human mental states and the interactions within a neural network would, therefore, prohibit its application a priori in the way suggested by control system engineers.

Second, severe constraints are imposed on the kinds of solutions to the problem of internal structure that can be obtained by the application of Realization Theory. Specifically, the solutions that can be obtained must be based on the criterion that they will be the simplest and most economical. This is analogous to the minimum energy principles that are applied in developing many solutions to mechanical problems. Criteria of simplicity and economy like this may be useful in developing some notion of an ideal system. However, they are not necessarily the way that a mechanical system must be engineered by some less than fully competent engineer or by a more than ordinarily potent evolutionary process. Furthermore, there is no need for simplicity and economy when one is talking about the brain. The vast number of neurons provides ample opportunity for instantiations that are both redundant and uneconomical. Indeed, criteria other than simplicity and economy might be the ones the that guided the evolution of the brain. Adaptability, redundancy, stability, and self-correction may all take priority over other criteria. Thus, the existence of Realization Theory, however useful as it may be in the designation of some plausible internal mechanism, does not represent a challenge to Moore's theorem or the black box limitation.

Moore's theorem, although stated very formally, is not a totally novel concept and should not surprise perceptual scientists. It is another way to express the behaviorist, operational, positivist philosophy. The basic barrier to determining internal mechanisms implicit in Moore's theorem is also reflected in some of the classic arguments in peripheral sensory coding theory. One of the clearest and best known examples is the long-lasting controversy concerning the nature of the cone photochemicals—an issue dating from the time of a simpler kind of psychophysics. The problem concerned the nature of the three photochemicals. Were they broadly tuned and widely spaced along the spectral axis? Were they narrowly tuned and bunched together? Were they broadly tuned and narrowly spaced? No one of these possibilities could be confirmed and none could be rejected on basis of the psychophysical data alone. All could be manipulated in a way that would reproduce the findings of trichromatic color vision experiments. In this relatively simple situation, the nature of the internal photochemical mechanisms could not be determined. The problem waited for electrophysiological and spectrophotometric techniques for its ultimate resolution of moderate width and broad but overlapping spacing along the wavelength axis. How much simpler a problem this was than the ones confronted by cognitive psychologists when they attempt to determine the mental architecture of "attention," for example. Obviously, although they had never heard of Moore or his theorem, color vision scientists had been functioning in accord with it. Searchers for the solution of the much more complicated problem of the underlying mental architecture should be.

If we take it seriously (and I think we should take it very seriously), Moore's theoretical challenge to the analyzability of automata may mean that, for reasons of the most fundamental principle (as opposed to the practical problems of combinatorial numerousness or complexity), we can never decide between alternative mental architectural models for any cognitive process. It may also mean that the neural structure of the system is opaque to the tools of psychophysical research. If his theorem is right and if it can be validly generalized to human mentation, then many of psychology's reductive goals become patently unobtainable and their pursuit ill-advised.

Indeed, psychology's situation may be even worse than that of Moore's generalized automaton. In the case of mental experiences, we do not have direct access to what are arguably the most immediate outputs of the system—the mental responses or percepts themselves. Visual perception, for example, is a private experience that is not directly sharable with others. Ideally, science deals with the explicitly measurable, yet in our science it is only an indirect indicator—overt behavior—that is measured. The underlying cognitive or neural processes, the true target mechanisms for the reductionist, are, therefore, doubly inaccessible. In practice, of course, all sciences suffer from this same disability and the ideal is never achieved.

Moore's theorem supports a different kind of philosophical characterization of perceptual science than the one popular today. It suggests that
this science may be tackled better by means of a behaviorist epistemology
than by a reductionist approach. It can do so without denying the existence
of mind or cognition or whatever other term one would like to use to
describe mental phenomena. It also does not reject the fundamental metaphysical principle of psychobiology: that mind is a brain process. Instead,
it suggests that we will always have to be satisfied with some kind of a
descriptive neobehaviorism in which it is accepted that psychological processes cannot be reduced to the microscopic details of neural nets or a set
of simple component cognitive functions.

To make this point crystal clear, I assert as a corollary to Moore's theorem that: *No psychological, psychophysical, or behavioral experiment can ever
say anything definitive about the internal workings of the mind or nervous
system. It can only describe the course of the process, not what mechanisms
account for it.* Given that much of the reasoning that supports experimental
psychology has been based on its reductive efforts, this strong statement
deserves considerable attention and much more discussion than it has
enjoyed to date. This premise provides one of the strongest arguments for
a change in our approach to experimental psychology in general and perceptual science in particular. This new approach is none other than a new
kind of an old friend—behaviorism. I expand on what I believe are the
properties that should characterize this new behaviorism in chapter 5.

The intrapersonal privacy of cognitive processing and the implication
that some kind of positivistic behaviorism may be required to rationalize
this science make up a serious matter. It is both another way of expressing
the engineer's "black box" proscription and a reflection of the potential
impact of Moore's theorem. The formalisms of this very important theorem
have a very direct impact on more familiar aspects of perceptual science.
However expressed, this theorem asserts that it is not possible to uniquely
determine the internal mechanisms of a closed system (the brain) by input–
output (behavioral) analyses alone. It can be argued that the specific internal
mechanism can be defined by looking inside the black box. However, even
that strategy may not be sufficient to attain perceptual science's goals, as
explained in the next section, in which I consider the implications of contemporary chaos theory for neuroreduction and cognitive reductionism.

Problems Arising When Deterministic Systems
Give Rise to Apparent Randomness

If it follows from Moore's theorem and other considerations that it is necessary to look inside the black box to identify specific mechanisms, does
this mean that we will always be able to understand the inner workings of
a mechanism should we actually be able to take the top off? Specifically,

does neurophysiology–the interventional approach that literally takes the top off–provide a means of crossing the black box barrier? The answer to this question also has to be: No! We have already considered several reasons why this negative conclusion is inevitable–complexity, numerousness, the combinatorial explosion on the one hand and thermodynamics on the other. However, complexity and numerousness are just practical problems. It is not inconceivable that some day we might invent an ultrafast transform or a supercomputer that will allow us to overcome even that handicap. The achievable goals of modeling and reductionism are, however, far more constrained than is implied by the practical barrier imposed by relatively uncomplicated, although numerically overwhelming, combinatorics. I suggest that the necessary original information (i.e., the initial state of the components of the system and the history, in terms of both time and organizational space, of their interactions) that led to a particular outcome is not just too ponderous to grasp, but actually no longer exists in the present state of any system of the complexity being considered here. In other words, it is not just difficult to understand the details of the current state and history of a system like the brain, it is impossible! The constraint on reductionism that I now consider, chaos theory, is, like the thermodynamic argument, more a matter of fundamental principle than of practical concern.

That a fundamental barrier to reductionism exists is the message of chaos theory–an important new development in the study of nonlinear systems like the brain. Chaos theory supports the conjecture that, for fundamental reasons, the behavior of such systems may be unpredictable in the future, irreducible to their underlying mechanisms at the moment, and irreversible to the past. If these implications of chaos theory are verified, additional support is given to the argument that between mind and mechanism, as well as between theory and mechanism, there exists a two-way barrier that is insurmountable, not just challenging. If this is true, we can neither reduce the molar to the microscopic nor predict the molar from the microscopic.

In brief, contemporary chaos theory may be interpreted as arguing that our world is governed by the following rules:

1. Deterministic molecular laws may direct and control the current state, as well as the evolution, of very complex behavior based on the myriad properties and interactions of very simple components.

2. This complex set of deterministic interactions, however, may result in a system that is chaotic and apparently random because of the pyramiding of small uncertainties. Thus, it may not be possible, in principle, to predict the future state of a modestly complex system even knowing the "full" details of its initial state (Grebogi, Ott, & Yorke, 1987).

3. The apparently random chaotic system does not exhibit a pure form of randomness, however. It may still produce organized behavior at a mac-

roscopic level. The point is that any examination of the arrangement of the microscopic components of the system may display apparent randomness (albeit not true randomness) in spite of that overall molar order.

4. Neither the apparently random behavior of the ensemble of microscopic elements nor the ordered global or molar behavior of the overall system may be reversible to their initial state origins or reducible to current state of the components. This is closely related to the thermodynamic irreversibility idea discussed earlier in this chapter. In this case, however, irreversibility arises because the information describing the interactions that led to the final state from the initial state has actually been lost. It is lost not just because there is no possibility of maintaining the history of the many small interactions and uncertainties, but also because small uncertainties have snowballed into a state in which the information literally no longer exists. In other words, the barrier to reduction is not just a practical matter, it is a matter of fundamental principle.

5. Chaos theory may be very useful in helping to locate and identify global forces operating on the system that are otherwise hidden. "Regular," "strange," or "chaotic" *attractors* (i.e., global forces emerging from the organization of the system that act to direct its molar behavior, analogous to the potential fields used in solving *n*-body problems) may be discerned in very complex, nonlinear systems. It may be possible to predict global outcomes (such as the shapes of snowflakes or the dripping of water from a faucet or even human cognitive processes) based on these attractors. However, it must be appreciated that in this case chaos theory deals with the molar outcome and not with the microscopic details of the underlying structure.

There is a very important concept—apparent randomness—embedded in these rules of chaos theory that should be made explicit. We must distinguish between a dichotomy, in this case, of a system that is *truly or completely random* and one that is *apparently random*. The brain is obviously not completely random—our mental and physical realities constitute an existence proof that the apparent chaotic confusion of microscopic neural activity often leads to organized, coherent macroscopic behavior. There is, nevertheless, an apparent randomness about the intricate pattern of microscopic cellular activity that underlies that organization. When we examine a subsystem of the brain that includes even a moderately small number of interacting neurons (not the behavior of an individual neuron that may be very regularly related to the stimulus), we often find a disorder that cannot be distinguished from true randomness in spite of the system's molar functionality.

There is a reason for this apparent randomness when the operation of many cells are observed simultaneously. It is to be found in another one of those very important but long overlooked reports that has much to say to reductionists of all stripes. Cox and Smith (1954) pointed out that when the activities of a number of periodic (i.e., highly regular) pulse generators were combined, the pooled output appeared to be random (i.e., perfectly irregular). That is, when one examined the combined output of several periodic generators, the combination tended toward an irregular pattern that was statistically no different from the output of a random generator. Their proof of this statement is rigorous. The implication of such a proof for neuroreductionism is that analysis into components is not possible even in the idealized case of perfectly periodic pulse generators. The corollary is that the problem is even worse in the case of the nonperiodic signals emanating from neurons. How, then, can one ever hope to understand the detailed logic of a perceptually interesting neural network, even given the possible appearance of some super array of microelectrodes? It is also entirely possible that the problem may even be exacerbated as one goes from one to a hundred or even a thousand ganged microelectrodes.

Cox and Smith's work antedated contemporary chaos theory by many years, but its message is the same. Intractable complexity of an entire system can arise from simplicity of the individual components in a way that makes it impossible to go backward from overall system function to the details of component activity. Regularity can give rise to randomness, or the appearance of randomness, in a way that makes the result immune to any kind of analysis.

Chaos theory, therefore, is essentially a theory of macroscopic function and, like psychophysics, is antireductionist in essence. It deals with macroscopic "attractors" and forces and not with the microdetails of the organization of a system. It deals with nonlinear systems, perhaps better than any other approach to that complex set of problems, but in a holistic manner. Farmer, one of the leaders in the development of chaos theory, was quoted by Gleick (1987) as saying:

> The trend in science, and physics in particular, has been towards reductionism, a constant breaking things down into bitty pieces. What people are finally realizing is that that process has a dead end to it. Scientists are much more interested in the idea that the whole can be greater than the sum of the parts. (p. 134)

Chaos theory, thus, suggests another source of difficulty and raises another fundamental barrier to understanding complex systems, even when an enclosing "black box" can be "opened" to internal examination. These ideas have been elaborated by Crutchfield, Farmer, Packard, and Shaw (1986), among others, in an especially clear discussion in which they explicitly stated the implications of chaos theory for prediction, in addition to its implications for reductionism. According to them, chaos theory "implies new fundamental limits on the ability to make predictions." They also argued, as I do here, that microscopic measurements are not always extrapolatable to detailed macroscopic outcomes. Although these authors went on to assert that some classes of random processes may actually be opened to a deeper understanding using the mathematics of chaos theory, their thesis should be read as implying that there will be fundamental limits emerging from such an analysis that will forever constrain our ability to understand the detailed mechanics of the turbulent breakup of smoke, the weather, the erratics of fluid motion, or the operation of a very large number of neurons in a cognitive process. In each of these cases, they argue that the system is so complicated that it must basically be considered to be random at the microscopic level—thus precluding a top-down reductionist analysis as well as bottom-up predictions. Although chaos theory suggests that it is possible to designate some global attributes that integrate these apparently random microscopic states into some kind of a useful statistical measure (e.g., pressure, the ratio of turbulent to laminar flow, the electroencephalograph, or perceptual phenomena), reduction to the activity of individual elements is impossible according to chaos theory!

Most of the constraints on reductionism that I previously discussed (with the exception of thermodynamics) emphasized complexity and suggested limits on analyzability in practice. Chaos theory now adds to the argument that there may be even more serious limits in principle. These systems are not just complex and multivariate, they are apparently random—that is, intrinsically unanalyzable at the microscopic level. Therefore, the expectation that some new computer or other new technology will allow us to achieve neuroreductionism is as futile as the quest for a perpetual motion machine.

The Crutchfield, Farmer, Packard, and Shaw discussion of chaos is not just mathematical esoterica. It is directly relevant and specifically damning to some of the implicit programmatic goals of both neuroreductionist and mathematical or computational theorists of cognition. This interpretation is crystal clear in the following excerpt from their work:

> Chaos brings a new challenge to the reductionist view that a system can be understood by breaking it down and studying each piece. This view has been prevalent in science in part because there are so many systems for which the behavior of the whole is the sum of its parts. Chaos demonstrates, however, that a system can have complicated behavior that emerges as a consequence of simple, nonlinear interaction of only a few components.
>
> The problem is becoming acute in a wide range of scientific disciplines, from describing microscopic physics to modeling macroscopic behavior of biological organisms. The ability to obtain detailed knowledge of a system's structure has undergone a tremendous advance in recent years, but the ability to integrate this knowledge has been stymied by the lack of a proper concep-

tual framework within which to describe qualitative behavior. *For example, even with a complete map of the nervous system of a simple organism, such as the nematode studied by Sidney Brenner of the University of Cambridge, the organism's behavior cannot be deduced.* Similarly, the hope that physics could be complete with an increasingly detailed understanding of fundamental physical forces and constituents is unfounded. *The interaction of components on one scale can lead to complex global behavior on a larger scale that in general cannot be deduced from knowledge of the individual components.* (p. 56, italics added)

Models Are Only Abstractions of Full Reality

In the context of establishing what a model means, it should be established just what a model is. Trivially, a model, whether made of neuromimes, mathematical terms, or plaster, is a reduced portrait or representation of something that is more complex, richer in detail, different in size, or existent at a different time. Like any other partial representation of an object, a model is less than that which it represents. This is its raison d'être. The model or the map—the reduced representation—is more convenient for reasons of scale or the very lack of details found in the real entity. A map does not include all of the information inherent in the real world that it models, and this is its great advantage. It can be carried from place to place, laid on a table, even folded, unlike the real landscape. Similarly, mathematical, computational, and even neural models, no matter how precisely they may predict function, do not include all of the details of the real systems they portray. Both maps and formal models are of necessity incomplete and partial.

There is, however, a reverse side to this generality. Sometimes models may superimpose their own properties on our concept of the object being modeled. Hence, the model of the object may reflect a property that the object does not actually possess, or it may ignore a constraint that is present in the real world. In this sense, therefore, the model may be more (rather than less) than the reality.

This line of thought has practical implications for psychophysical research. In some cases the model of a phenomenon is so incomplete that it does not operate under the same constraints as does the human subject. The model may predict an unconstrained or ideal performance level that is never achieved (or achievable) by the subject. A clear example of this kind of discrepancy is found in the work of Barlow (1978), in which it was shown that subjects performed only half as well as an ideal model predicted they should in a texture discrimination task. As another example, Braje, Tjan, and Legge (1995) and Tjan, Braje, Legge, and Kersten (1995) reported that their model of a ideal observer for the recognition of objects was far more efficient than the human. Efficiencies of the human were as low as only a few percent of those predicted by the model. Obviously, inefficiencies of one kind or another may be operative in the real situation of the human observer that are not taken into account by these models.

The other kind of discrepancy between a model and reality may predict a lower level of human performance than that actually achievable. This occurs when subjects are able to take advantage of some attribute of the stimulus that has not been programmed into the model, but that allows the human to exceed the "ideal." My laboratory has encountered such a situation in work reported by Uttal, Davis, Welke, and Kakarala (1988). We used a simple three-dimensional surface-fitting process to model the ability of a subject to reconstruct the shape of a surface from a very sparse sample of dots randomly positioned (on that surface). The mathematics of the situation is straightforward. It is patently impossible to fit or recognize the exact stereoscopic surface with fewer than five dots if the surface is a quadric and fewer than seven dots if the surface is a cubic. Nevertheless, our subjects performed significantly better than chance (12.5%), correctly naming one of the eight forms with as few as two dots (24%)—an impossible achievement if it was not based on constraints imposed by earlier experience with the limited set of forms, and much better than that with three and four dots (40% and 50%, respectively).

A similar result was obtained in a slightly different field of perceptual research, one in which motion rather than disparity was used as a cue for three-dimensional form. Braunstein, Hoffman, Shapiro, Andersen, and Bennett (1987) also found their subjects doing better than predicted by their mathematical model. Under a rigidity constraint programmed into their model, subjects should have required three sequential views of four points to perceive the shape of a rotating dotted form. Their subjects, however, were able to do so with either fewer points or fewer views. Without a doubt, the subjects in these experiments made use of other information that was not incorporated into the models. Clearly, the models that expected too little in both of these cases are as inadequate as models (e.g., those proposed by Barlow, 1978, or Tjan and Braje and their colleagues) that expect too much of the human visual system.

In the former case, the predictions of the model exceeded the performance due to the fact that the model did not incorporate some constraint to which the human was subject. In the latter case the human exceeded the model's predictions because the human "knew something" that the model did not. In other words, the human was able to apply some constraint that was not programmed into the model. In both cases, the incompleteness of the model is the critical factor in the underestimation or overestimation of human performance. In retrospect, all of these research groups were able to partially explain their respective discrepancies and thereby improve their models.

However interesting these details may be, the salient point in the present context is that a model is not the same as the reality it represents. This is such a simple truism that it is surprising how often it is forgotten. No matter how good they are, there will always be some residual difference between our models and reality. This discrepancy can also be interpreted as representing a barrier to explanation and a limit on the degree to which a model can be tested and verified. Of course, the goal of theory is to reduce these discrepancies, but the remaining uncertainty concerns whether or not any model can actually close the gap between itself and the realities of complexity of the magnitude with which we are concerned here. Some of the arguments presented earlier suggest that both in practice and in principle they may not be able to do so.

Perception Is Inferential: A Deterministic, Algorithmic Model May Simply Not Be Relevant or Realistic

Another possible difficulty with formal theories of any kind of cognitive process is that the tool used to implement the program and/or the mathematics in these simulations is often either a highly deterministic entity—the digital computer—or a system of equally deterministic analytic equations. These methods and tools of analysis are characterized by a highly deductive mode of operation.

Whether they are serial or parallel, electronic or optical, computer systems are designed to operate in a precisely causal and rigidly deterministic manner. Given a particular set of initial conditions, the final outcome will always be the same. That is, each subsequent state is the outcome of a precisely determined transformation of a preceding state. This mode of operation may be quite suitable to describe what happens in the peripheral parts of a sensory system that are more concerned with the communication of sensory information than with the transformation of that information into perceptual experience. It is not equally clear that it is appropriate for the more intertwined components of the central nervous system, in which determinism may well be hidden in complexity. Of course, it is possible to write a program that simulates a less rigid kind of system. However, even then, such models depend on the precise execution of program steps by the computer. Consider, for example, how careful one has to be to introduce an outside source of randomness to produce a true series of random numbers. Without such an outside source, random number generators often have cyclic or deterministic behavior that may be very difficult to detect. On the contrary, the failure of a single deterministic instruction usually leads not just to variable behavior, but to total catastrophe in a computer program.

If anything is well established in psychology, it is that the higher levels of human cognition do not operate in this strictly deterministic fashion, but by a much softer, fuzzier, inductive kind of logic only loosely determined by the stimulus conditions. The perceiving brain seems to use processes (of which we have but the barest understanding) of inference, interpretation, and a kind of high-level adaptive logic that are not of the same genre as the rules governing the algorithmic, deterministic computer or the analytical forms of mathematics usually applied in this domain. Such a set of inferential rules may be simulated to some degree on a computer, but it is very difficult to make the generalization from one type of problem area to another. Nevertheless, this process is prototypical of human cognition and occurs in what seems to be an effortless manner.

In his discussions of the failure of generalization and pyramiding in artificial intelligence (AI) studies, Dreyfus (1972, 1992) pointed out that most current AI systems can only improve by adding program components and not by generalizing older ones to new universes of discourse. His work also has implications for the formal modeling of cognitive processes, because no current model seems to be able to generalize beyond the particular microuniverse for which it was developed. Even the highly touted neural net models are more or less restricted to the specific problems for which they were designed. The ability to adapt to new stimulus situations and to generalize to novel conditions should certainly be a hallmark of any model that presents itself as a valid explanation of organic mentation. However, such an ability is not yet exhibited by our contemporary AI techniques. Indeed, a recent cutback in activity in this field suggests a loss of the scientific community's confidence in the traditional AI enterprise. The implications of the discrepancies between our modeling and tools and human cognitive (and therefore neural) logic is that perhaps our tools are even less appropriate than had previously been appreciated.

This is by no means a new issue, although older discussions may have been cloaked in other terminologies. Whether thought is inferential or mediated (i.e., rationalist) as opposed to deterministic (i.e., empiricist) has concerned psychologists and philosophers for centuries. The kind of indirect, mediated cognition that is now generally accepted to characterize our mentation has, in one previous incarnation, been known as *unconscious inference*, a term proposed by Helmholtz (1925). It is also of the same genre as the formal and rigorous statement of inference made by Bennett, Hoffman, and Prakash (1989). One thesis of their important work is that perception is not only inferential, but also that it is not, in general, either deductively valid or unbiased. Absence of deductive validity would mean that the rules of standard logic (and presumably the rules of both mathematics and computational logic) do not hold with regard to the mechanisms underlying our thoughts and perceptions. To mimic the real world of cognition accurately, our models should be inferential and rationalist; unfortunately, they have tended to be determinist and empiricist.

My point here is that no artificial intelligence, computational, or connectionist model seems even to come close to operating with the same kind of logic as does generalized human intelligence. All of the algorithmic and deterministic strategies that characterize current theoretical efforts are different in a fundamental way from the adaptive and inferential processes likely to be executed by the brain. According to this point of view, virtually all computational models are not even adequate first approximations to the underlying logical mechanisms of cognition they purport to represent. I am referring here to their fundamental axiomatic roots, not just to some simple mimicking of the modeled process. Thus, a priori, they must be invalid as ontological explanations of mental processes, however well they describe the behavior.

None of this should be interpreted to mean that complex, adaptive, inferential behavior cannot emerge from the concatenation of elements that are individually deterministic. Chaos theory has made it clear that such a thing can happen regardless of its own limits as a model. Indeed, consciousness (i.e., our own self-awareness) is itself an existence proof of that hypothesis. But no one has yet shown any satisfactory bridges between deterministic neural elements and inferential thought of the kind that could bridge that gap, and many of the issues raised so far also add to the doubt that such a quest would be successful.

The Cumulative Microcosm Does Not Equal the Macrocosm

There is no denying the enormous accomplishments of neurochemists and neurobiologists in understanding the components or, as computer engineers call it, the "technology" of the cognitive engine between our ears. We have enjoyed a revolution in the last half century in both neurochemistry and neurophysiology. However, as I noted earlier, all of this elegant knowledge may be irrelevant to understanding cognitive processes because it tells us little about the essential level of psychoneural equivalence—the details of the interneuronal interactions among the networks of neurons that are the psychoneural equivalents of mind. Nevertheless, physiologists and biochemists working in the neurosciences at this microcosmic level often claim that their studies have molar cognitive or behavioral implications. Furthermore, cognitive psychologists propose that their models provide insight into the mental architecture. Perceptual psychologists, in particular, claim that their findings have neural implications. A more critical look at these assertions (discussed in greater detail in the next two chapters) suggests that they are unjustified. Neurochemical discoveries of how a synapse works or of the ionic mechanisms involved in the propagation of the action potential, although stupendous achievements in their own right, are more comparable to studies of the materials of which a transistor is made. However exciting, these findings are not relevant to the unraveling of the logical systems into which neurons are organized. The argument presented here is that this level of system interconnectivity, of information manipulation, is the essential level of action accounting for how the brain "secretes" mind. It is not the nature of the neural parts that is important any more than the type of transistor defines the computer's function.

Neurophysiological studies, by practical necessity, deal only with the interconnections of a very small number of neurons—far less than would be sufficient to explain the simplest cognitive process by even the most conservative estimates. Psychological studies are neutral with regard to internal mechanisms, as we have already seen. None of these approaches deals directly with the essential nature of cognitive processes. The essential level is that of the very complex, intricate, and tangled interconnections of the neural network.

The point is that cognition arises out of the organization of these components, not out of their metabolic characteristics or their local means of communication. The biochemical and cellular physiological properties of the components of a neural network are totally irrelevant to its informational attributes beyond what constraints may be imposed by conduction speed or recovery time.

Understanding the metabolism of neurons or their underlying biochemistry, therefore, is not tantamount to or even directly related to achieving understanding of cognition; that understanding can only come from the discovery of the laws governing "reasonably" large interacting ensembles of neurons. As we have seen, combinatorics, thermodynamics, and chaos theory suggest that such an analysis of psychologically significant networks may not be a realizable goal. Therefore, molar behavioral approaches may be the only route to understanding cognitive functions.

It is interesting to note, therefore, the enthusiasm for what may prove to be a useless technology. There have been many reports that arrays consisting of several hundred microelectrodes have been developed. I have no doubt that this technological tour de force has been accomplished. But, the question remains: For what can they now be used? If Cox and Smith (1954) are correct, then all that can be observed by this array is an apparent randomness. This method, therefore, is unlikely to give us insight into the logical laws by means of which the essential neural network operates. The neural network, the appropriate level of analysis, may be opaque to empirical examination at the very level at which we must be seeking the mind.

Surprisingly, given these assertions, there remains a substantial controversy concerning how much we really know about the salient cellular interactions, mechanisms, and forces that describe complex neural interactions. Does that knowledge presently exist? Some (e.g., Hawkins & Kandel, 1984) have considered this issue. Hawkins, Kandel, and their colleagues have made many other important contributions to our understanding of some simple kinds of learning in invertebrates. They have elucidated possible neural circuits in the sea hare *Aplysia* responsible for conditioning and habituation, and have even made contributions to our understanding of the kinds of chemical processes that explain changes in synaptic conductivity and might, therefore, mediate changes in these networks associated with experience. But, contrary to some others in the field, Hawkins and Kandel were extremely constrained in their interpretation of their results. They wrote:

> We do not provide any data suggesting that higher orders of conditioning must necessarily emerge from the basic cellular mechanisms of more elementary forms of learning. Nor would we argue that participation of the cellular mechanisms that we have outlined here in higher orders of conditioning would provide evidence for their role in yet more sophisticated types of learning. (p. 389)

Thus, even beyond the problems associated with the study of extremely large numbers of small interactions, it can be argued that we do not yet know the specific nature of the microscopic rules of interaction in the relevant vertebrate neuronal systems. The critical combination and interaction rules of neurons are still undiscovered, if not undiscoverable. This may be a surmountable challenge in the future; in principle, electrophysiologists can be expected to make progress in this direction. It is yet to be established, however, whether they can do so in practice for any vertebrate central nervous system given the variability of the neural structure from specimen to specimen, from species to species, as well as the possibility of redundant and overlapping encodings of the same process.

The germane question here is not, what do we know?, but rather, what can we know? It is not yet clear that we can know what is needed or that past progress is really what it seemed to have been at first glance, when extrapolated from the neurophysiological to the cognitive domains.

If one looks at the past history of neural net modeling it is clear that only in the simplest cases, using relatively regular neural nets such as the *Limulus* eye or the cerebellum, was any simulation successful. Even then, the theoretical accomplishments are rare. Many so-called "neural net" theories, although perfectly good descriptions of some cognitive process, are based on neural (as opposed to generalized parallel) networks in only the loosest sense. Often they merely represent discrete embodiments of mathematical (i.e., descriptive) formula and are actually neutral with regard to internal mechanisms. In other cases, very simple networks consisting of only a few neurons are used to simulate the function of the much more complex networks that almost certainly must be instantiated in real organisms (see, e.g., Anderson, 1972; Grossberg, 1982). These simple systems often do a creditable job of simulating or imitating some of the molar process aspects of a cognitive or perceptual transformation, but it is conceivable, if not likely, that they do so by vastly different logics than those used by the enormous ramifications of neurons in the brain. Theories or models using such regular or minimal systems need not operate by means of the same rules that a complex, irregular system consisting of many idiosyncratically interconnected components does, even though the behaviors of the two kinds of systems may be superficially the same.

Similarly, models that seek some solution to the mind–brain relationship in terms of synchronous or synchronizing activity (e.g., Freeman, 1995) ignore the real problem of the details of the neuronal interaction. Neither a few sample neurons nor any waveband of the electroencephalogram is operating (and I would suggest could operate) at the essential level of network interactions.

This is, of course, the terrible problem. It is the ensemble of details that leads from brain to mind. The molar measures lose the details, whereas the cumulative study of the details is prohibitive because there are so many of them. In a nutshell, this may be the reason why a true (as opposed to a superficial) neuroreductionism is not possible.

Although I have taken a stand on the matter in previous paragraphs, it must be acknowledged that it is not yet definitively established what is the most appropriate level of analysis critical for understanding the perceptual or cognitive information processing aspects of the brain. Networks of individual central neurons seem to me to be the most obvious and likely choice of the fundamental and salient level. As we have seen, however, even the simplest perceptual process may involve so many neurons that we must consider it to be a part of a chaotic (apparently random) system in the sense described earlier. Are the rules the same at all levels of anatomic organization and magnification? Are the laws the same at all levels at which the brain–mind is examined? It has been suggested that the two general domains at which science operates—those of the macroscopic, human scale one and the microscopic, invisible one—operate under the influence of laws that may be quite different. Prigogine (1980) reminded us of Eddington's (1928) suggestion that there are primary laws that control the behavior of individual particles and secondary laws that regulate the behavior of ensembles. Of course, this may only be a reflection of the practical combinatorial difficulty of computing the results of a large number of interactions or of the limits of contemporary theory. It may also imply a misinterpretation of a quantitative change for a qualitative one (i.e., concatenated multiple interactions may only appear to be different in kind from the individual interactions).

On the other hand, perhaps Eddington also had an insight into something more fundamental that is also reflected in thermodynamics, chaos theory, psychology, and all of the other sciences that deal with complex systems arising from the interaction of myriad components and operating in the macroscopic world. Perhaps, even though there may be no difference in quality in some absolute sense, there are differences in the ways we must approach problems at the two different levels. These differences between the different laws operating at different levels may "only" be the practical outcome of complexity and nonlinearity—but this would make them no less real in terms of the epistemology governing our studies.

I will not pursue this speculation further, but whatever the future may hold, the bridges that we wish to build between the neurophysiological microcosm and the behavioral macrocosm certainly do not yet exist: We have not yet been able to build satisfactory explanations of Eddington's "secondary" laws in terms of the "primary" ones, if in fact they can be connected. Neither brain actions nor statistical mechanics have been reduced to simple deterministic laws. Chaos theory and combinatorics suggest that the search for some of these bridges may be a search for a chimera; from a more realistic point of view, such a reduction may be unobtainable.

Mathematics Is Descriptive, Not Reductive

Finally, I want to elaborate on a point made briefly in the introduction to this section of this chapter. Mathematics is an enormously powerful tool, but it is not omnipotent. The insights into natural phenomena given to us by classical analytical methods as well as by contemporary computational techniques have been profound. Nevertheless, it is important to keep clear just what can be done with mathematics and what cannot.

It is a well-appreciated fact among students of quantum physics that there are some solutions to differential equations that are physically meaningless. That is, some of the solutions of equations purporting to model physical systems have no significance but are merely superfluous and extraneous baggage emerging from the mathematics rather than from the physics of the real world being described by that particular notation. This same fact is part of the understanding of even newer theories of the physical world such as string theory, as I noted in chapter 1. Therefore, all parts of a mathematical model may not be relevant to the system being modeled. In the same way, mathematical or computational models (or neural models couched in mathematical terms) may also fall victim to this same difficulty and denote mechanisms that are not likely to be found within the brain.

A closely related, but often forgotten, property of mathematics is that this powerful technique is intrinsically nonreductive. That is, mathematics is neutral with regard to specific underlying mechanisms. This powerful system of thought can work in situations in which the premises that govern the physical reality are totally distinct and separable from those governing the mathematical manipulations.

A closely related and very important point was made by Casti (1996). He suggested that our dependence on a mathematics that is "unreal" (because mathematics is a representation of reality rather than reality itself) in many cases actually "hampers our ability to answer questions about the natural world" (p. 103). Even though problems such as those posed by the certain board games or the "protein folding" task are extremely difficult to solve mathematically, we accomplish the former and nature accomplishes the latter with what seems to be the greatest of ease. Casti's point is that, however useful and powerful, mathematics can add superfluous difficulty to problems that can be solved quite easily by other means—for example, induction or simulation.

Another example of the assertion that mathematics may add superfluous meaning or difficulty is the all-too-powerful Fourier analytical method. It is sometimes overlooked by enthusiasts that Fourier-type analyses allow the reduction of any one-, two-, or three-dimensional pattern to sets of super-positionable orthogonal (usually sinusoidal) functions. This form of analysis can succeed even though there is nothing that corresponds to sinusoidal generating mechanisms in the physical system being analyzed. Indeed, the great power of the Fourier method is that any function, regardless of its actual underlying mechanism, can be analyzed as if it was the actual physical result of the superposition of the outputs of a set of real orthogonal function generators. This property permits the selective filtering or enhancement of specific spatial frequency components. Such transformations allow us to modulate any image in a controlled and known fashion or to solve mathematical problems that cannot be solved in any other way.

This strength, however, is also the source of the great weakness of Fourier analysis when it comes to its role in explanation and reduction. I return to consider what I call the "Fourier fallacy" more fully in chapter 3.

Other instances of the premises of mathematics being separable from those of the system being described are trivially evident in any kind of curve-fitting algorithm. All that is required for a perfect fit of a model to a mechanism is that there be sufficient degrees of freedom in the mathematics to accommodate the functional behavior of the data being approximated. The history of learning theory, in particular, is filled with examples of mathematical models selected with just enough degrees of freedom to represent whatever function was under consideration at the moment. The various parameters in the models took on a physical and reductionist realism that is hard to accept in retrospect.

To make the point, consider that there is no reason to assume that a polynomial equation (to pick a trivial example) that fits some process is actually physically instantiated as a sum of a series in the physical system. One has only to work briefly with analog computers to appreciate the fact that the assumptions about process and mechanism are separable and distinct, and that the relation between analogs is not the same as that between homologs.

A related issue is that since we actually know virtually nothing about the logical mechanisms that are used by the nervous system, spurious analogs may mislead seductively. Many of our mathematical models produce descriptions, but few would baldly accept the idea that specific mechanisms such as Marr's (1982) "Laplacian of a Gaussian" zero-crossing operators actually exist in the brain. My opinion is that what he was actually saying and what must ultimately be meant by such computational models is that certain stimulus features are important in human vision *and* that mechanisms (of which we know very little, but which are also sensitive to these features) may perform functions that are analogous to those human visual operators.

Of course, it is also possible that the zero crossings are not all that important and that we operate by manipulating completely different, but analogous, stimulus attributes. These attributes might include such properties as "overall configuration." Global arrangement properties would be processed by means of logical mechanisms that are totally different than those that would be invoked to process local features. The main problem with mathematics in this regard is that the available mathematics has been designed to serve mainly as an analytic tool for systems that can be taken apart—if it is local and feature oriented. We do not yet have the mathematical tools necessary for understanding highly parallel processing of whole objects. Yet it is virtually certain that such a globally sensitive neural logic is actually being executed in the brain. Given the kind of mathematics that is available, and the opacity of what is happening in the brain, it is not too surprising that many current theories stress the elements of stimuli rather than their organization during visual processing. Unfortunately, we must await a better mathematics and a better understanding of the logic of the brain to approach vision from a molar point of view. Of course, we are also haunted by the specter that such a problem can never be solved. That is the thesis of this chapter.

The indeterminate nature of mathematical representations was also discussed in a series of papers by Stewart and Pinkham (1991, 1994), and Stewart, Pinkham, Mancino, and Chomak (personal communication, 1997). Stewart and his colleagues approached the problem of visual acuity and contrast sensitivity by suggesting that these perceptual measures can be formulated as eigenfunction problems. In particular, their formulation involved the use of Hermite functions as the eigenfunctions. Their argument was that it is mathematically impossible to distinguish a feature detector (of any kind) from a Fourier spatial frequency channel or any other kind of potential analyzer. All can be produced by linear combinations of the Hermite functions.

Two conclusions can be drawn from this line of thought. The first conclusion is that the mathematics used in this case is absolutely neutral with regard to which specific mechanism is actually present in the brain. All operators are indistinguishable from each other within the terms of this model and, presumably, any other. Second, and extremely relevant to our understanding of the significance of neurophysiological data, if this eigenfunction model is appropriate, all types of neural analyzers should be observable in the nervous system if one looks for them. All are the result of observing combinations of even more primitive components—the Hermite functions—just as any picture in the spatial domain can be converted by Fourier analysis to sinusoids in the spatial frequency domain. In Stewart's personally communicated words, "Whatever you can say about a feature detector, you can also say about a similar Fourier detector." According to Stewart and his colleagues, combinations of low-order Hermite functions can look like line detectors, edge detectors, blob detectors, or even low-frequency gratings. Similarly, combinations of high-order ones look like gratings or even Gabor patches of high frequency. (How familiar this sequence is in the history of the neurophysiological investigation of the nervous system.)

It is important to emphasize that what I say in the present context for formal theories of the mind–brain is also true of all other forms of theory that aspire to play an explanatory, rather than a descriptive, role in science. All statistical models can also be challenged as being spurious if they are presented as reductive explanations. However, their fit and predictions are not spurious if description is all that is being attempted. Then either the fit is satisfactory or it is not. In this case, a precise criterion for choosing among the various alternative descriptive theories exists. Implications about internal mechanisms must be handled separately.

What, then, does mathematics do for us? My answer is that mathematics is a superb way of describing a system. It allows us to transform what is often an uninterpretable and qualitative scene into a quantitative, interpretable form. It often allows us to describe and extrapolate from the present and, thus, to predict the future course of a system. In some cases, it even allows us to determine the laws governing interactions among objects or transformations in their form. Mathematics can simplify, beautify, quantify, and, perhaps most important of all, force a precision of language and thinking on the theoretician that raises scientific inquiry from speculation to analysis. This latter attribute would be enough, even if mathematics had no other virtues, to guarantee its continued value to all kinds of intellectual pursuits, however compelling the arguments over its limits may be.

No mathematical procedure, however powerful, can peer deeply into a "black box" produced either because the system is really closed or because it is functionally closed by virtue of complexity of interaction or numerousness of its components. No formulation can create truth about internal structure from studies of the transformation that occur between input and output. In short, mathematics is so general that it is flawed in a fundamental way—we often tend to infer more than it implies. On the other hand, it can establish some fundamental constraints and limitations. Not unrelated to this point is the fact that mathematics can establish that some problems cannot be solved in a reasonable length of time or, for that matter, ever.

The conclusion to which we are directed by these considerations is that there may very well be a vast difference between real psychobiological mechanisms and the inferences that are sometimes drawn from formal models. What I am suggesting is that, in principle, computational, mathematical, or connectionist models can say nothing rigorous about the internal mechanical or structural reality of a system in an ontological reductionist sense—they are neutral in practice and principle—regardless of how perfectly they describe function or process. They may be elegant and fully descriptive, but they can never be explanatory in the reductive manner suggested by some contemporary theoreticians.

SUMMARY

In the preceding sections of this chapter, I discussed some of the reasons why it seems unlikely that that computational, neural network, and mathematical models can ever be tested and verified as valid reductive explanations of the internal workings of the nervous system or of the mind. Although these models may serve as powerful descriptions and ingenious heuristics, they are in a fundamental way neutral about the internal mechanisms of all kinds of cognition.

I do not think that these limitations are as ominous for perceptual scientists as they may at first seem or that my concerns are inordinately pessimistic for our science. The end of psychology, the neurosciences, or artificial intelligence research is not at hand: only a clarification and redefinition of what it is that we are about. Our colleagues in the physical sciences increasingly appreciate the limits of their models and theories and have flourished in spite of what are virtually the same kind of limits that should discipline our attitudes toward theories of mind. Indeed, some of the most significant contributions of the physical sciences have been their identifications of those limits. Physicists have modified their views about nature to incorporate indeterminativeness, uncertainty, and probability, rather than championing an older view of strict causation. They recognize the barriers that exist between a model and reality. They also appreciate the message of chaos theory expressed in Prigogine's (1980) words: "The future is not included in the past. Even in physics, as in sociology, only various possible 'scenarios' can be predicted" (p. xvii).

Some time ago mathematicians also came to appreciate the epistemological limits of their own enterprise. They have long known that there are some theorems that cannot be proven or are indeterminate, and they live comfortably with those limits in their activities. Why, then, should perceptual scientists not also accept the existence of similar constraints, limits, and indeterminacies in theories concerning their part of the world? We perceptual scientists deal with systems that are so much more complex and multivariate than are the ones dealt with by physicists that theoretical progress must necessarily be slower for us than for them. To suggest that we can achieve for the complex brain what physics could not achieve with as simple a mechanism as a three-body system is an inexcusable arrogance. To assume that the reductionist implications of a theory, which is at best a process analog, can be validated in terms of the brain's underlying architecture reflects a lack of understanding of how science works and some fundamental limits of models, neurophysiology, and psychophysics. Raising false hopes or setting theoretical goals that have already been proven to be unattainable (e.g., by automata, chaos, or computational theorems) reflects an ignorance of very relevant contemporary developments in related fields of science.

In conclusion, I want to anticipate and counter a major potential misinterpretation of the argument that is made in this chapter regarding the role of theories and models. By no means should it be interpreted as a pessimistic view of them, in general, nor of neuroscience, in particular. Both the empirical and theoretical strategies for studying brain and mind being pursued now are intrinsically timely and interesting in their own right. If properly interpreted and understood, the findings from these pursuits are among the finest accomplishments of contemporary science.

So far I have spoken mainly about what models do not mean and what they cannot do. There is a further set of important epistemological issues, however, that must also be confronted. These have to do with what these models do mean and what they can do. I have argued that the main thing they do is to describe function and molar behavior. This idea can be further particularized. Formal models are capable of precisely specifying the functional transformations that occur between the inputs and outputs of a system. They can quantify otherwise vague notions of the amount of information that can be processed. They can also allow us to test various alternative input conditions and determine whether the system is likely to respond in the same way to them. Indeed, they may allow us to predict the stability of a system that carries out the transformations that must occur.

There are other important reasons we should proceed with the exercise of formal modeling.

First, mathematical, computational, and neural net modeling, however limited, is vastly superior to the prequantitative, verbal, and imprecise speculations that characterized most earlier forms of psychological theorizing about cognitive processes. Formal models, constructed in the form of computer programs, mathematical equations, or even physical networks demand a precise definition of the salient rules that govern system function. They can, at least, distinguish between the plausible and the implausible, even if they do not allow us to distinguish between the plausible and the real. This kind of reasoning is, therefore, a huge leap forward toward the understanding we seek in terms of the precision of the language used as well as providing an exact functional description of the behavior of a complex system.

A second reason for proceeding with formal modeling is simply that this is all that is necessary for some purposes. In spite of the ideas presented here that an ontological reductive analysis of the brain is practically and theoretically impossible and that we cannot verify any model of cognition in a truly reductive manner (except in the most trivial cases of peripheral sensory communication), much can be done. There are other goals of formal modeling. We may wish only to imitate or describe some human information process. If so, all we really have to know is what kind of transformation occurs during the process and not necessarily how the nervous system does it. Thus, we can manufacture (in principle, if not in current fact) a perfectly good artificial intelligence system capable of performing useful visual functions, for example, by observing and modeling human vision, making informed assumptions (however unverifiable they may be) about what are, at best, plausible and analogous internal mechanisms, and writing a program using any one of a large number of functionally equivalent algorithms. The system so developed is not likely in the foreseeable future to perform with the same flexibility and competence as natural vision (although there is no obvious a priori reason why it cannot), but it may function at a perfectly satisfactory level for some practical task or give a perfectly good mathematical description of the relevant phenomenology to a perceptual scientist.

A third argument for formal modeling is that it is intellectually elegant and satisfying. It would be inappropriate to throw up our hands in despair because we can never achieve complete reductive explanation. Psychologists should note that the implications of the Second Law of Thermodynamics regarding the impossibility of a perpetual motion machine did not dissuade mechanical engineers from proceeding with their studies of internal combustion engines, nor did molecular numerousness deter physicists from studying gas dynamics. The analogy to psychology should be obvious. Interaction with nature in this manner has often produced heuristics that stimulate inventive solutions to problems in unexpected ways, even if they are not exactly the same ways a real system accomplishes the same task.

A fourth reason to pursue this work is that even though contemporary models may be better characterized as description than reductive explanation, description itself is of extreme value. Description may tell us about the historical course of a process and may allow us to extrapolate the course of events for the future. To be able to predict events, even though the underlying mechanism remains impenetrable, is itself a remarkable achievement.

Finally, however sharp the discontinuity between the knowable and the unknowable, we clearly have not come close to the limits of understanding to which I have alluded. We are progressing and improving our understanding of perception and other cognitive processes. There has been a constant closure on what I believe is the "truth" of the neural and logical basis of perception (if not cognition in general). We have progressed from electrotonic field theories (Koffka, 1935) to single-cell models (Barlow, 1972) to analytic function models (Marr, 1982) to parallel neural net theories (McClelland et al., 1986; Rumelhart et al., 1986; Uttal, 1975, 1981a) of how the brain works—and this progress is a harbinger of a trend in the right direction. The fact that a barrier may exist somewhere ahead should not deter us from striving to approach that barrier as closely as possible and, in many cases, it may be that the barrier need not be crossed. For example, knowing the position and momentum of all of the particles in a tank of gas adds little to our knowledge of a system already adequately described by the values of temperature and pressure. The need for detailed knowledge of the neural basis of mind may ultimately fall into this same category of superfluous, as well as unobtainable, knowledge.

On the other hand, the enumeration of these reasons for going ahead with this type of modeling should not obscure the central thesis of this chapter—that no formal model of any cognitive process is verifiable and validatable, or even testable with regard to internal mechanisms. As elegant as it may be, and as well as it may describe a process, no model can be uniquely validated as the true ontological reductive explanation of any cognitive process. The kinds of tests of necessity and sufficiency that scientists have always demanded are simply not available. Although this conclusion may be disappointing to some perceptual theoreticians, I believe it to be generally accepted throughout other areas of science, and in the long run it will help us on our way to the next phase of understanding of visual perception, free of the illusion that we "know" more than we actually do.

In the meantime, we must not forget that some of the less exciting and more mature responsibilities of perceptual science must still be satisfied. We must search out the facts, describe the phenomena, and quantify the processes and transformations of mind and behavior to provide the fundamental material required for the continued and fruitful pursuit of the formal modeling enterprise.

Theories and models of the kind we have discussed here are not the only strategies for attacking the problem of the mind–brain relationship. Two others are extremely popular in contemporary perceptual science. The first, already partially introduced in this chapter, is neuroreductionism—the effort to explain mental processes by reducing them to their neural underpinnings.

The second is the effort to detail the nature of the mental architecture, the mental components from which mind and behavior are built. These are the topics that are dealt with respectively in the next two chapters as I explore further the limits and deficiencies of reductionism. All of this is preparation for a positive statement of what a new perceptual science must look like in order to overcome the logical and empirical difficulties in the contemporary approach.

3

THE CASE AGAINST PERCEPTUAL NEUROREDUCTIONISM

In the past two or three decades, modern experimental psychology has become profoundly integrated into the neuroscience enterprise. Workers in cellular neurophysiology and perceptual science now move across the boundary between the two fields, hoping that understanding of the nature of the brain–mind relationship will ultimately be found. This chapter deals with the relationship between the two fields and, in particular, the issue of whether or not behavioral (specifically meaning "psychophysical") findings can be transmuted into information about the underlying neurophysiological mechanisms.

As essential as progress in the neurosciences is for many important, even socially critical, needs of humankind, there remain many unknowns about how the two fields can and, therefore, should logically interact. The purpose of this chapter is to consider some of the basic issues, premises, and expectations that arise when neuroscientists from either background compare neurophysiological and psychophysical findings. My goal is to examine critically and dispassionately an issue that has all too often been overlooked in the day-to-day excitement of some of the stunning new findings coming from experimental studies in either of the two fields.

The proposition that psychophysical data may be useful in defining the underlying neural mechanisms has wide currency in today's perceptual neuroscience. It is so ingrained in the *zeitgeist* that even raising this issue disturbs some reductionistically oriented scientists in both fields. Nevertheless, I believe that that an open general discussion of this matter is very important and all too long deferred.

The fundamental issue raised is: Do constraints, limits, and barriers exist that can bar us from building the logical and conceptual bridges between sensory and perceptual studies in psychological and neurophysiological laboratories, respectively? Of course, this is a corollary of the question asked about models in the previous chapter simply because neural explanations of psychophysical phenomena are themselves theoretical models. The point is that "when neurophysiological data are used to explain psychophysical findings, they become neurophysiological theories," in the prescient words of one colleague, Charles S. Harris. Nevertheless, the issue of potential limits to the neuroreductionist enterprise is important and it has sometimes been ignored in the rush of new findings and data.

In this chapter, I attempt to extract from the technical details of some sample studies what I see as the implicit, if not explicit, assumptions that underlay the authors' attempts to link neurophysiological and psychophysical findings. I consider whether these assumptions are justified given the ultracomplex nature of the processes, mechanisms, and phenomena considered in this joint neuroscientific enterprise. I announce at the outset that I will conclude that much of the logic is imperfect, a substantial amount is based on highly fragile data, and that the whole enterprise of psychophysical–neurophysiological bridge building is so flawed that it probably should be rejected in favor of a more realistic and plausible operational, positivist, behavioral approach.

To carry out such an analysis, we need to understand the goals and commitments made by neuroscientists of both persuasions when they undertake their laboratory research. It seems to me that the implicit promise made to society by many neurophysiologists (beyond the currently unpopular idea of knowledge and understanding for their own sake) is that their work on neurons not only will add to our understanding of how these wonderful cells work individually (an arcane pursuit of minimal interest to most nonscientists), but will also lead to a deeper understanding of the way in which the mind works. The hope is that we will ultimately know enough about the brain to modify behavior and heal mental illness, matters of considerable social importance. The implicit commitment is that, by understanding the operation of single neurons, we will be able to understand how the interactions of many neurons produce mental processes. The word *produce* used in this context is, of course, loaded with expectations and connotations that lie at the frontiers of both science and philosophy. We have to yet to solve this greatest of all scientific problems: How does conscious experience emerge from the action of a huge network of neurons?

Clearly, in the recent decades when the study of the brain has played such a prominent role in the national scientific agenda, the hope that physiological data would help us understand and cure mental illness has also given this particular subfield of the neurosciences a special impetus. The study of the function of the liver, skin, or musculature, even though each is an anatomically larger organ than the brain, has not attracted such attention and funding. There is something special about the brain that transcends the physiology of these other organs; of course that special role is the production of mind.

The work of cellular neurophysiologists may be characterized as a synthetic approach, driven as it is by tools such as microelectrodes that look generally at isolated points of the nervous system. The underlying premise is that if we first understand the nature of the parts and their simple interactions, understanding of the ensemble will surely follow as we work upward and concatenate the microstructures into macrosystems that can exhibit mental activity.

A comparable, but reverse, implicit promise is made by many experimental psychophysicists. Their work, driven as it is by the behavioral and molar measuring tools available to them, has to be characterized as an analytic approach. These scientists use tools that examine the overall or molar function of the nervous system's products—behavior and consciousness. They presuppose that the psychophysical methodology they use to examine the overall perceptual and cognitive processes of humans can provide clues to the mechanisms used by the nervous system as it transforms stimuli into perceptual and motor responses. An underlying premise of this research is that the molar or ensemble activity of a system retains traces of the interactions and mechanisms of the individual neural components. In this case, we go from the molar level to the microlevel of the component neuronal elements.

Neuroreductionism, as I set forth in chapters 1 and 2, is the general term for a body of theory that suggests that it is possible to explain molar perceptual processes in terms of the underlying neural mechanisms, either analytically or synthetically. The twin promises made by perceptual psychologists and neurophysiologists, respectively, have become central tenets of the neuroreductive enterprise.

Perceptual neuroreductionism, a specific application of the more general ontological reductionist approach discussed earlier, has become the modern instantiation of the classic study of the relationship between mind and body, or more specifically, mind and brain. It is in this persistently important arena that some contemporary philosophers and all experimental psychologists and neuroscientists have now converged on an axiomatic first principle: the fundamental monism that all kinds of mental activity are neither more nor less than the product of the extraordinary complexity of the brain's neuronal actions and interactions. The monism expressed in this grand first principle is nearly universally accepted by all in this field except for a few at or beyond the outermost fringes of science or a few others whose tolerance of internal inconsistency is unusually high. Of course, there are vastly more proponents of nonmonistic dualisms or pluralisms of many kinds, but these philosophies are outside the scope of this book as well as outside the boundaries of scientific discussion and examination.

Without question, materialistic monism, as a guiding first principle, is itself beset by internal controversies. To some, a rigid adherence to this principle may even be a means of removing the representation of psychological processes and phenomena from the discussion, if not denying the existence of the phenomena themselves. This extreme form of "eliminative materialism" (e.g., as expressed by P. M. Churchland, 1988, and P. S. Churchland, 1986) is the demon that Robinson (1995) was trying to exorcise in his article discussed in chapter 1. To others, including such identity theorists as Feigl (1960) and Armstrong (1962), both perceptions and brains are real. That I agree with this latter group of theorists should be absolutely clear by this point in this book. Simply put, perceptions are processes, and brains are the engines that carry out these processes.

The vocabulary used to describe the relationship between neural and mental responses is not at all clear in most of the literature in this field; precise definition of what is meant by the various kinds of relationships is absolutely necessary, yet rarely encountered. To help prevent some confusion and to clarify my use of the term, it is appropriate that I must now amplify my use of the term *psychoneural equivalence*. Psychoneural equivalence is the embodiment of the prime monistic premise of the neurosciences. A materialistic monist assumes that some mechanism of the brain and some process of the mind occur within a correlation that is so tight, both temporally and spatially, that each is "identical" to the other. The state of the brain mechanism becomes the equivalent of the mental act.

The metaphor that I use to make this point is of wheels and rotation. It makes no sense to assert that the rotation of the wheel is "unreal"; it makes even less sense to talk about rotation without a "wheel." This is what I mean by psychoneural equivalence. To exercise the metaphor a bit further: "Rotation" cannot be conceived of as occurring at some other place or at some other time than where and when the "wheel" exists. This means that some neural mechanism and/or process must be considered to be "equal" or identical to the mental process in the strongest sense. It is not just similar or concomitant, but the two are one and the same in the sense that one is the function of the other. In short, a materialist monist asserts that there are some parts of the brain at which the complexity of the information-processing activity becomes so great that conscious awareness emerges. That is, neural complexity at some place and some time *is* denotatively identical to mental experience.

The word *is* in this case is a very strong relation implying equality and sameness in a way that transcends "correlation" or "similarity" by many degrees of robustness. The activity of these regions is both necessary and sufficient for sentience and other mental phenomena to appear. When the relationship is so strong that function of the neural net *is* mind, then the two are psychoneural equivalents of each other.

Of course, psychoneural equivalence is not all that the brain does. There are other places in the brain and lower levels of the nervous system that do not achieve the necessary level of complexity to produce anything like those awarenesses we call *mind*. Some neural mechanisms merely serve as transmission channels for the signals from the transducers. Neither the transmitted signals nor the channels through which they pass are equivalent to, nor are they the locus of, the perceptual experience. They are necessary precursors for the experience to occur, but they are not sufficient for that experience.

The key idea here is that activity in the lower levels of the nervous system (probably including some cortical regions) that convey all of this information is not sufficient to produce the experience. If the higher levels, where the true psychoneurally equivalent mechanisms are presumably located, were removed from the brain, no amount of activity in the lower transmission centers would produce a perceptual experience. However, if the necessary information could be inserted directly into the isolated higher centers in some way, perceptual experiences presumably would occur. Although this may seem like a bit of physio-anatomical magic, in fact the production of vivid, if disorganized, perceptual experiences by direct electrical stimulation of the cerebral cortex is a time-honored procedure in physiological psychology and neurosurgery (Penfield, 1958).

There is little controversy among contemporary neuroscientists of all persuasions concerning the ontological first principle, materialistic monism; they agree that mind is a brain function, nothing more, nothing less. However, ontology is not the whole story. The epistemological perplexity has also already been introduced. Even if we all adhere to the monistic ontology, can we hope to reduce mental phenomena to neural phenomena?

The issue is further complicated by the fact that the same question can also be formulated in the opposite direction: Can mental phenomena be predicted from knowledge of the neuronal components? The contending sides in this argument are not equal in number, by any means. A clear majority asserts that neuroreductionism is likely to succeed without limit, given enough time. They argue that whatever has not yet been accomplished is constrained only by the absence of a better microelectrode, an improved computational engine, or some other eventually to be developed tool. The claim is that given enough time, anything is possible; the assertion is that only pessimists would suggest that there are fundamental barriers to knowledge without limit. On the other hand, a small but increasing number of neuroscientists, among whom I include myself, profess that neuroreductionism is limited by major logical, theoretical, and conceptual difficulties, barriers, and obstacles, as well as by mathematical and technical computational ones.

The issues under discussion, however, are not just philosophical esoterica. They have direct relevance to the psychophysical methodology used in perceptual science. It is, for example, unfortunate that so few vision scientists have read or remember the few eloquent pages (144–160) of G. S. Brindley's (1960) book on the visual pathway. Brindley distinguishes between two kinds of observations—Class A and Class B. Class A observations are those that are essentially pure discriminations of identity or equality. In other words, the Class A experiment is based simply on the question: Are two stimuli identical or different? It requires but the simplest kind of mental judgment on the part of the observer. Class B observations, on the other hand, are those that require something more than this basic judgment of identity or difference. They require observers to go beyond a simple discrimination to apply some metric of quantity, quality, time, or space. Brindley believed that, in general, Class B observations "have mostly been used unsatisfactorily" as data for the justification of what he called "psycho-physical linking hypotheses" and to which I now refer as neuroreductionist theories.

Brindley's point is that only the simplest judgments can be accepted as Class A observations. Virtually all other types of responses that require much more complex cognitive processes affect and modulate the perceptual experience. I believe that what Brindley was calling to our attention was that Class A observations are the only ones in which the theoretician can be even modestly assured that the higher levels of the nervous system are neutral and only minimally imposing their own characteristics on the resulting perception. When attention is involved, when qualitative estimates must be made, or when searches must be carried out in which common features have to be abstracted, the situation is simply too polluted with the involved properties of the "higher levels" to trust what is being reported as representing anything specific about the neural mechanisms of the lower levels. Unfortunately, all too many psychological studies are so confounded. One must decide whether the confusion is of interest itself, or whether one has to redesign the experiment to use a technique that will provide Class A data.

More recently, Teller (1980, 1984) effectively reminded us of Brindley's foresight in anticipating the rush of uncritical and ambitious neuroreductionism in which we now find ourselves entangled. Her call (Teller, 1984) that neuroreductionists should go out of their way to detail exactly what their linking hypotheses are is extremely pertinent. As we see later in this chapter, the connections drawn are often unacceptable simply because the underlying assumptions are clouded, ill-defined, and even logically inconsistent.

The perceptual neuroreductionism issue is also clouded by the fact that there are several questions concerning the relationship between mental and neural functions that sometimes overlap, are often confused, and in which different amounts of progress are likely to be made. For example, currently there is a substantial amount of excitement surrounding the use of positron emission tomography (PET) and functional magnetic resonance imaging (fMRI) devices to examine the locus of brain activity in an observer who is performing different perceptual, cognitive, or motor tasks. Many experiments using this tool are asking, and seem to be answering, an important question: What parts of the brain are active during particular mental processes? This is an example of what I have previously have referred to as the *localization* question (Uttal, 1978a). The quest to answer this question is a respectable scientific enterprise. It follows in the footsteps of the great tradition of the brain extirpators who cut, poisoned, and froze portions of the brain in attempts to find out what parts were centers for various perceptual-motor functions. This interventional approach—selective destruction of portions of the brain—foundered in the 1960s and 1970s when both the experiments and the observed interactions became so complex that the cost-benefit ratio of the yielded knowledge was no longer acceptable to the scientific community.

The new noninterventional tools such as PET and the fMRI have opened new avenues of attack on the localization issue. I believe the localization question to be a valid one and that it may yield understanding about the areas of the brain that are activated during well defined mental processes. However, it is not without its problems and difficulties, many of which have been ignored by its advocates.

There have, nevertheless, been exciting and interesting developments in the quest to localize cognitive functions in the brain. A comprehensive overview can be found in Gazzaniga's (1995) heroically edited volume *The Cognitive Neurosciences*. An outstanding example of what can be done with this method is the work of Sereno, Dale, Reppas, Kwong, Belliveau, Brady, Rosen, and Tootell (1995), who have been able to demarcate the borders between the several visual areas (V1, V2, VP, V3, and V4) of the human brain. I am also very much impressed by the impact PET imaging techniques have on our knowledge of what areas of the brain are involved in vision. The work of Ungerleider (1995) is also notable in targeting some of the areas of the human brain that may be involved in visual memory and learning. Ungerleider has even been able to identify distinctive areas that seem to be involved in different human visual learning tasks.

As enthusiastic as I am about the ability of the imaging techniques to answer some aspects of the localization question, I should point out that they are not without their critics. The approach seems direct and simple, but it is not. There are several fundamental assumptions built into it that leave some residual doubt about even the best designed experiments that purport to locate cognitive functions and brain areas. Practitioners of this field make two important assumption from the start.

1. Van Orden, Pennington, and Stone (personal communication, 1996) suggested that the first assumption is the localization of function itself. It is assumed that there exist demarcatable regions of the brain that have sepa-

rate functions—that is, that there are isolatable regions in the brain that carry out neural processes that map onto psychological processes. The possibility that all mental functions are actually the result of an integrated pattern of activity with many, if not all, of the brain regions involved in even simple acts is usually not considered as an alternative.

2. The second fundamental assumption is that the psychological processes themselves are also separate and isolatable enough to be localized. This assumption is based on the idea that the words that we have for cognitive processes adequately map the underlying mental activity. As I discuss later, many of our psychological processes seem to be more reflections of our experimental technique than of any psychobiological reality.

Van Orden, Pennington, and Stone (personal communication, 1996) and Van Orden and Papp (in press) also considered the differencing technique that is the basis of brain imaging studies of cognitive localization. The basic idea is that a region is considered the locale of a mental function to the degree that its activity is different in two different images—one taken while the cognitive act is under way and one while it is not. They believed this technique is conceptually the same as the double dissociation technique they criticized in other contexts. Van Orden and his colleagues suggested that this technique, once again, can be a self-fulfilling prophecy. The assumption that components exist leads inexorably, and incorrectly, to the false positive conclusion that they (the hypothetical components) are localized in regions where differential activity is indicated. Indeed, when one considers the difference procedure, any activity present both when the task is being carried out and when it is not would be invisible. Therefore, any specially "hot" region showing up in the difference image could represent only a small part of the total activity and suggest localization when, in fact, none existed.

Van Orden and Papp (in press) also identified another a priori assumption that can lead to mistaken theories about the localization of function in the brain when one uses the PET and fMRI techniques. That additional confounding assumption is that only feed-forward projections occur between the involved brain centers. That assumption, as they pointed out, is almost certainly incorrect—feedback in the central nervous system is as well known as is feed-forward. Such reciprocal interactions raise serious doubts and can invalidate any conclusions concerning the localization of any supposed cognitive components in the brain.

There is another important issue here. That is that a difference image showing areas that are active when a certain cognitive function is carried out does not provide compelling evidence that this highlighted activity is essential to the function. It may be ancillary, correlated, and even concomitant, but still not be the region subserving the cognitive function. For example, the highlighted area might simply be indicating the release from inhibition of some area that was suppressed previously. Obviously there are serious conceptual problems that have not been thoroughly thought through concerning the significance of these imaging studies.

The difficulties with the brain imaging studies suggest some problems that might have existed with the older brain extirpation approach that transcend economic and practical concerns. Perhaps there are deeper reasons why that direct interventional approach does not flourish today. One possibility is that it was logically flawed in the same fundamental way as some of the other reductionist strategies.

Nevertheless, whatever the outcome of the localization controversy, and whatever progress may be made in that domain, it must be understood that the issue of localization is not the essential question in perceptual neuroreductionism. The essential part of the brain–mind relationship, from my point of view, is not a question of *where* in the brain something is happening (a *macroscopic* question). Rather, it is: What interactions are occurring among the neuronal components at that location that are the necessary and sufficient psychoneural equivalents or codes or representations of perceptual and other mental responses?

The question of the details of the logical information processing network, which must be asked at a much more *microscopic* level, is the essential one. It is "essential" in the sense that it is the details of the interactions in some localized or dispersed neuronal network that must be the actual equivalent of mind. Mind, this point of view asserts, is the result of the detailed interactions of the neural network and not of the result of the molar activity of the various centers. Unfortunately, so many of our new tools are capable of looking only at the cumulative, macroscopic response that we tend to forget this point.

Place, of course, may be a part of the neural code for some attributes of perception; Mueller's specific energy of nerves is a fundamental law that still holds. However, the location of a cluster of neurons per se is not the essential part of its role as the psychoneural equivalent. Perception, like all other mental processes, must arise out of cumulative network origins. That is, the mind emerges as a result of the collective details of the interconnection pattern of many neurons.

Although of considerable interest in their own right, the more macroscopic approaches using PET or fMRI scanning techniques obviously bear their own baggage of problems, uncertainties, and difficulties. Furthermore, as I have just asserted, they are not aimed at answering this essential issue. To say otherwise would be the equivalent of saying that the essence of a computer is the part of the box in which it is mounted or the daughter board on which the CPU chip resides—or, to make the point even more blatant, where the chip is located. Quite to the contrary, I think it is self-evident that the crucial aspects of the computer, as of the brain–mind, are instantiated in the logical details of the interconnections and interactions among the component units from which it is built. At this point the analogy between the physical sciences and the neurosciences becomes the tightest. But it also at this point that the combinatorial, thermodynamic, and chaotic constraints described in chapter 2 are most evident in the neurosciences.

The many questions concerning the microscopic, neuronal basis of mind (as opposed to the macroscopic localization issues) can be collected under the rubric of *representation*. The macroscopic localization problem is probably solvable to some degree. The representation problem, I now argue, is much more challenging and, in most cases, is completely intractable. I also contend that the psychophysical method alone can never be sufficient to resolve the neural representation problem. Furthermore, even when coupled with what may superficially seem to be relevant neurophysiological data, there always remains a substantial doubt about the linkage between the two domains. This caveat holds true if one is theorizing "down" from psychophysical results and findings or "up" from neurophysiological data. The obstacle in each direction is quite distinct. Bottom-up analyses fail for a very practical set of reasons mainly associated with the large numbers that very quickly emerge in that kind of combinatorial exercise. Top-down analyses fail because of the loss of detailed information as order turns to chaos.

In the top-down case, the constraint also arises out of a fundamental issue that I have already alluded to in chapter 2 as the black box problem. I also pointed out that there exists a formal proof from automata theory (Moore, 1956) for this "problem." Moore showed that no matter how many experiments one may do on the transformations that occur between a stimulus and the elicited response, there will always remain an infinite number of alternative mechanisms that can produce the same input–output relation.

Moore's theorem is an example of what I mean by an "in-principle" barrier. It is not a temporary technical difficulty arising form the fact that we simply do not have the appropriate tools to do the job. Rather, it is the equivalent of the unachievable goals of exceeding the speed of light or engineering a perpetual motion machine. It is something that cannot be done, no matter how much time and how powerful the tool, because of fundamental limits.

In the bottom-up case, the problem is, on the other hand, mainly a practical matter. The number of neural interactions that must be involved in even the simplest thought can become very large very quickly. Clearly, no conceivable analysis tool is likely to be forthcoming that will permit us to simulate it, much less explain it in microscopic detail. Nevertheless, the problem is only one of sheer number. Thus, the barriers encountered in a foray into perceptual neuroreductionism may be matters both of basic principle and of simple combinatorial impracticality.

It is the thesis of this chapter that there are many such misinterpretations concerning the limits of the neuroreductionist enterprise. Much of what tends to be classified as bridge building between psychophysics and neurophysiology might better be referred to as "neuromythology"—a term probably first introduced by S. S. Stevens and most recently used by Green (1991). This term refers to the fact that many quasi-theoretical statements concerning the bridges between neurophysiology and psychophysics are logically unsubstantiated, poorly justified empirically, and more likely examples of wish fulfillment than hard science. Some are just ingenious speculative attempts to tell a plausible and interesting story. Nakayama (1990), for example, wove a tale of perceptual neuroreductionism that even he acknowledged "will probably resist verification or falsification" (p. 411). However stimulating this may be for cocktail conversations at national vision meetings, it is hardly a testable theory in the sense demanded by Popper's (1959) "falsibility criterion." Such plausible and interesting "stories" are much too large a part of what is offered up as serious neuroreductionism by contemporary perceptual scientists. However charming and inventive, they provide only illusory bridges to psychobiological reality.

In the remainder of this chapter, I consider the values and difficulties of the perceptual neuroreductionist approach by reviewing a few selected samples taken from the current literature of visual perception.

SOME CONTEMPORARY APPROACHES

In this section, my goal is to examine samples of the current literature to determine exactly what it is that a few of the contemporary crop of perceptual neuroreductionists are doing as they attempt to link psychophysical findings to neurophysiological results. I am interested in examining the details of their linking hypotheses and the logic of their arguments as well as detecting any hesitations or cautions in their own language describing these links. Sometimes their own cautious phraseology suggests that some of these scientists share, to at least some degree, my conviction that some of the bridges that are being built lack a robust logical foundation.

There are many different ways in which the putative psychoneural bridges are built; different scientists use different strategies. It is, therefore, useful to develop once again a minitaxonomy of the several strategies used in contemporary attempts to link psychophysical results to neurophysiological mechanisms. For example, the following classes exemplify the main neuroreductionist assumptions used by some of my fellow perceptual scientists in recent years.

1. A strong assumption: Some researchers suggest that their psychophysical tests directly specify the nature of the underlying neural mecha-

nisms. Phrases such as "psychophysical evidence for a neural mechanism underlying" are typical of this approach. This is a form of argument that implies that unique traces of specific neural mechanisms can be found in psychophysical responses. This is, of course, a very strong assumption and although not often explicitly expressed, it is the foundation of many neuroreductionist approaches. I argue that this kind of leap from psychophysical data to neurophysiological mechanisms is totally fallacious.

2. A modest assumption: Other researchers suggest that their psychophysical findings are "not inconsistent with" or "support" neurophysiological data obtained elsewhere. This is a form of argument by analogy. It is a less strong assumption, but one still fraught with logical difficulty.

3. A weak assumption: Still others suggest that their findings are supportive of nothing more than a general localization of a putative neural mechanism. For example, psychophysical results are sometimes involved to determine whether a particular perceptual process is mediated by "early, low-level" visual processes or "more central, high-level" mechanisms. Although this is even a weaker version of the linking assumption, even this idea is dependent on what are often misinterpreted psychophysical or neurophysiological data.

4. A linguistic assumption: In some cases, the neuronal terminology has simply been transposed to what seem to be analogous perceptual terminology. For example, the psychophysically defined "perceptive" field is proposed to be the equivalent or reflection of the neurophysiologically defined "receptive" field. Here, the issue is mainly semantic and seems to have led to the use of a single word to describe quite different mechanisms and processes. The end result is a profound misunderstanding of the nature of the neural representation of perceptual phenomena.

5. A heuristic assumption: On the other hand, perceptual data has been frequently and quite successfully used as a source of ideas and heuristics on which to base new experimental thrusts in neurophysiology. (This, incidentally, is an approach with which I agree.) Indeed, a considerable portion of modern neurophysiology has been stimulated to search for the mechanisms of what were originally discovered in the form of perceptual phenomena. Although they are not always found, this basis for an exploration is probably as good as any other. Demonstrations of unusual visual phenomena (i.e., visual illusions) have often been excellent sources of speculative new ideas for neurophysiological research.

Similarly, neurophysiology has often served as the source of new ideas for builders of perceptual theories. Neural net models, based on one of the incontrovertible generalities of brain organization—parallel processing—have played an important role in modeling perceptual phenomena. In recent years, the universally accepted general principle of parallelization, emerging more from the theoretical than the empirical study of neural networks, has even become the basis of a substantial amount of straightforward engineering work. It is important not to overplay this theme, however. Most of the stimulation for engineers has come from broad general principles of neurophysiology such as parallel processing itself, rather than the details of the network. Beyond that general heuristic, engineers usually depend on techniques and algorithms that had their origins in their own history.

One has to be cautious about the transfer of general principles from any science to the explanation of perceptual phenomena. History has clearly demonstrated that whatever technology is available and popular is quickly transformed into a theory of the relation between mind and brain. Pneumatic, hydraulic, and telephonic models all had their heydays. The current most influential technologies stimulating perceptual theory, of course, are computers and neurophysiology. Ideas and concepts from neurophysiology, in particular, have the added advantage of being indisputably associated with mental processes. That the brain is responsible for all of our perceptual phenomena is not a contentious issue here; rather, the argument is whether or not the details of this association can be unraveled, explained, and understood in a way that transcends simple metaphors, analogies, or even scientific puns.

Because of the very critical stance that I have taken with regard to the grand issue of neuroreductionism, it is important for me to point out that the individual studies that I critique in the following sections are chosen not because they represent vulnerable, weak examples of this kind of science, but because they exemplify some of the best of their genre. They are examples of high-quality research that has a noticeable impact in our collective search for reductionist bridges between psychophysical and neurophysiological findings. No matter how much I may disagree with some of the assumptions their authors may make and some of the implications they draw from their experimental work, I hope that the authors of each of these articles appreciate that my choice of their work is based on the fact that, in my opinion, they are formidable contributors to current perceptual science.

It is also important for me to point out once again that I am not challenging the importance of either independent neurophysiological or psychophysical research. One has only to look at the relevant neurophysiological journals in which studies of visual neurons are presented to appreciate the grandeur and excitement of new discoveries in that field. Similarly, the psychophysical study of visual phenomena has resulted in equally impressive discoveries about how we see. My criticisms in this chapter are aimed solely at what seem to me to be the fanciful bridges that are being built between the two domains.

Studies That Purport to Assay the Underlying
Neurophysiology Directly

Dresp and Bonnet's Studies of Illusory Contours

As a starting point, consider the work of Dresp and Bonnet (1991, 1993, 1995), who extensively studied the psychophysics of illusory or subjective contours. Illusory contours, originally brought to the attention of psychological science by Kaniza (1955, 1974), are particularly interesting because they reflect the perceptual outcome of stimuli that have no real physical existence. Rather, these illusory or subjective contours are "suggested by," "inferred from," or "interpolated from" the arrangement of other components of the stimulus scene. An excellent recent review of the general nature of the illusory contour phenomena can be found in Lesher (1995).

I have put quotation marks around the terms *suggested by*, *inferred from*, and *interpolated from* because one of the most interesting controversies surrounding these remarkable illusions is—What causes them? The two extreme answers to this question can be summed up as follows:

1. The subjective contours are created by some kind of an unconscious cognitive process functioning at relatively high levels of the visual system.
2. The subjective contours are created by the properties of neurons and neural nets functioning at relatively low levels of the visual system.

The first argument, of course, would be extremely difficult if not impossible to submit to neurophysiological substantiation. The second argument, it is suggested, depends on the demonstration of correlated neuronal responses that track the psychophysics of the subjective contours at the earliest levels of the visual nervous system. To understand the issues involved, let us consider in detail exactly what is known, or believed to be known, about the psychophysics and neurophysiology of subjective or anomalous contours.

A typical psychophysical experiment by Dresp and Bonnet was designed to demonstrate that there is the same kind of supportive interaction between illusory and real contours as there is between two real, subthreshold, lines or contours. The latter phenomenon was originally described by Kulikowski and King-Smith (1977), who called this phenomenon *subthreshold summation*. When added together, one of the two real lines became visible. This suggested some kind of a interaction of neural responses in the visual pathway between two encoded real stimuli that would otherwise have been individually invisible.

Dresp and Bonnet (1995) then went on to show that real subthreshold stimulus lines and illusory suprathreshold contour lines also interacted. The effect they observed was that a perceived (i.e., suprathreshold) subjective contour acted to reduce the threshold for the detection of a real, but subthreshold, line in the same manner that a real, and also subthreshold, line stimulus did in the Kulikowski and King-Smith experiment. The implication of this observation is that the illusory and real stimuli were interacting in the same way and, presumably, in the same mechanism.

This experiment was accompanied by what was presented as an effective control to overcome one obvious confounding possibility. It was necessary to show that it wasn't just the additional configural information about where the subthreshold real target was likely to be that was provided by the subjective contour that was producing the effect. It was necessary to also prove that the induced subjective contour itself accounted for the lowered threshold. This was, it was reported, accomplished by using a V-shaped stimulus that suggested where the real subthreshold line was likely to be but that did not itself produce the illusory contour. This stimulus, the authors reported, did not increase the detectability of the subthreshold line to the same degree as did the stimulus producing the illusory contour. Therefore, it was concluded by Dresp and Bonnet that there is a "functional equivalence" of the two forms of perceived lines (illusory and real).

While there is little doubt that the findings from their experiments and their conclusions concerning the perceptual interactions between the real and illusory contours are solid, Dresp and Bonnet's interpretations become problematical when they extrapolate from their psychophysical results to possible neural mechanisms for the phenomena. By equating their psychophysical findings with data from "wet" neurophysiological laboratories, they were making judgments about the involved mechanisms that I believe were not justified. In particular, Dresp and Bonnet noted that their findings were "functionally equivalent" or "consistent" with records obtained from the Von der Heydt and Peterhans (1989) study of neurons in the V2 regions of the rhesus monkeys. It was there that Von der Heydt and Peterhans reported responses from neurons that seemed to be sensitive to the same suggestive stimuli that produced the illusory contours as well as to real contours.

Dresp and Bonnet concluded from this similarity of the psychophysical and neurophysiological data that the locus of the subjective contour effect was in this early portion of the visual pathway—V2. Notwithstanding certain other matters that I deal with shortly, the main problem for a reader is, what did Dresp and Bonnet mean by the phrases "functional equivalent" (p. 1071), the "locus of the subjective contour effect," or "are consistent with" (p. 1078)? Although these terms are inadequately defined by them, I believe that they were attributing the perceptual phenomena to this peripheral level of processing. In other words, Dresp and Bonnet seemed to be accepting not only a correlation, but the psychoneural equivalence of the V2 neurons' responses and the perceptual phenomenon. Specifically, they were localizing the observed psychophysical interaction effects in V2.

There are at least four questions that can be raised concerning this association between these psychophysical and neurophysiological findings and Dresp and Bonnet's conclusion that the subjective contour effect is accounted for by a low-level visual process.

1. Is it appropriate to compare the Dresp and Bonnet and the Kulikowski and King-Smith findings?

2. Is it appropriate to compare the Von der Heydt and Peterhans neurophysiological results and the Dresp and Bonnet psychophysical findings?

3. Exactly what do the terms *functional equivalence of* and *are consistent with* mean in this context?

4. Are the neurophysiological findings themselves really as compelling as they seemed to be at first glance?

With regard to question 1 on whether the two psychophysical studies (Kulikowski & King-Smith, 1977; Dresp & Bonnet, 1995) were really equivalent, there were, in fact, some aspects of the two studies that should alert us to be cautious before accepting the logic of this argument. In fact, there is a major difference between these two psychophysical studies that substantially mitigates the power of the comparison.

It is important to keep in mind that the supporting or enhancing subjective contours that lowered the threshold of the target lines in Dresp and Bonnet's study were, as they pointed out, actually perceived. In the Kulikowski and King-Smith study, however, both the real supportive and real target stimuli were individually below threshold and were not perceived. Their influence on each other was exerted below their respective individual thresholds. In this case, the argument for a pure low-level interaction is much stronger. In the Dresp and Bonnet case, the subthreshold target stimuli are contaminated by information of a different kind—localizing signposts that say "look here!" produced by the suprathreshold subjective contours. Thus, there is a very real possibility that at least some high-level cognitive factors (e.g., the focusing of attention or the alteration of the criterion level) may be contributing to the results of their experiment. The point is that the two experiments may not be measuring the same thing in spite of what initially may seem to be paradigmatic similarities.

Therefore, we must ask: Are these two psychophysical experiments really assaying the same process? Dresp and Bonnet asserted that they are, and this is a basic assumption underlying their work. But the stimulus conditions are in fact quite different, as I have just shown. In the Dresp and Bonnet (visible) subjective contour case the door has been opened by the suprathreshold visibility of the subjective contours to cognitive and judgmental influences that are not available in the case of the real, but invisible stimulus in the Kulikowski and King-Smith experiment. The finding that there is a similar supportive role played by both real and illusory stimuli, respectively, in the two studies is not necessarily based on a true equivalence of the two processes. Although there is a rough correspondence, the difference between the perceived enhancing stimulus in their study and the unperceived enhancing stimulus in the Kulikowski and King-Smith one is a major confound in the Dresp and Bonnet discussion.

Does the auxiliary control experiment carried out by Dresp and Bonnet completely negate this criticism? Of course, there is no definitive answer to this question, but although ruling out one possible source of high-level contamination of their results, their control experiment is not completely convincing. Its validation depends on the judgment of the subjects that they saw no subjective contours. No control can rule out all possible contaminations. Was there any way that Dresp and Bonnet could have made their study and the Kulikowski and King-Smith study more comparable? Probably not; the concept of an invisible subjective contour is a difficult one with which to deal. However, they might well have tried to see if the influence of very-low-contrast Kaniza triangles was comparable to higher contrast ones. Is this asking too much? Not really! Forced-choice experimental designs (Pollack, 1972) have shown that a stimulus driven to the point of invisibility in a metacontrast type experiment can still affect the detection of other stimuli. The problem is that reported invisibility may not be the same as functional invisibility.

Needless to say, this problem of obscure confounds is not a difficulty unique to Dresp and Bonnet's work; it is a continuing problem in the interpretation of psychophysical findings (as well as in comparing psychophysical and neurophysiological findings in many other studies). Experimental conditions, although superficially similar, are often quite different when examined in detail. Anyone who has delved in psychophysical experimentation knows that small differences in experimental design can often produce large differences in results. Yet, all too often, superficial functional similarities are used as the bases for comparisons when, in fact, the differences greatly outweigh those similarities. Biologists and paleoanthropologists have long dealt with the problem of confusing anatomic analogies arising as a result of convergent evolution with embryologically defined homologies. The neurosciences apparently are far behind in being able to discriminate the similar from the identical.

Now let's turn our attention to the set of conceptual and logical questions that emerge when the Dresp and Bonnet psychophysical findings are compared to the Von der Heydt and Peterhans (1989) study. Before we consider this question in detail, it is important to describe exactly what was done in the Von der Heydt and Peterhans laboratory. In brief, the major finding of their work in this context was that 44% of the 103 neurons they studied in the V2 area of the monkey's cerebral cortex were responsive to the properties, such as orientation and width, of the subjective contours perceived by humans when they were presented with the same stimuli. Only 1 of 60 neurons observed in V1 behaved in this manner. The interpretation they made of this finding was that the neural signals from both real and illusory contours seemed to be activating these V2 neurons. Von der Heydt and Peterhans went on to elaborate this basic idea by suggesting that the neurons whose responses they measured in V2 represented a convergence of information from two channels: one channel from oriented line and edge detectors in V1, sensitive to real lines and contours, and the other channel consisting of neuronal responses that exhibited sensitivity to a spatially distributed array of "end-stopped" lines spread over a large receptive field.

It is critical, as we pursue this discussion, to understand the distinction between their observations and their interpretations. The hypothesis of the convergence of the "end-stopped" channel on the V2 neurons is really a theoretical statement that is invoked to explain an observation; it is not the observation itself. The observation itself said only that a reasonably high proportion of V2 neurons seems to be responsive to some of the properties (e.g., orientation) of the subjective contour in humans. The extrapolation beyond that observation is clearly an example of the transmutation of neurophysiological data into neurophysiological theory, a process that is all too often overlooked by the perceptual scientists who use neurophysiological theory, as opposed to observations, as explanations for their observed phenomena.

There is also a further problem. It may be that the neural responses observed in the Von der Heydt and Peterhans (1989) study were not exactly the same for the subjective contours as for real lines. They stated:

> Thus, edges and anomalous contours are equivalent in some cells but not in others, and for each orientation there seem to be many different types of cells. . . . Although the orientation tuning was generally very similar for bars/edges and anomalous-contour stimuli, we have also seen significant differences that are difficult to interpret. (p. 1745)

Thus, there remains considerable doubt concerning the assumption of psychophysical–neurophysiological equivalence made in the Dresp and Bonnet article. This is in addition to the psychophysical–psychophysical comparison made by them with the Kulikowski and King-Smith data. Because both of these comparisons are so basic to the entire argument of neural and psychophysical "consistency," we are left with a considerable degree of uncertainty about the validity of the between-domain comparisons they have made.

This brings us to the crux of the difficulty with this type of between-domain comparison and the second question posed earlier. Let us assume, for the sake of discussion, that the respective psychophysical and neurophysiological studies had both been impeccably executed and their respective interpretations of the equivalences of real and illusory stimuli were acceptable. Would the observations that neurons in V2 were sensitive to both real and illusory contours mean that it is here that the *psychoneural equivalence* of neural and perceptual responses occurs, in the strong sense of the term that I defined earlier?

I believe that Dresp and Bonnet are suggesting that this processing site—V2—in some special way does transform the stimulus to produce the coded version of a response that is subsequently perceived as a subjective contour. It should be noted, however, that their suggestion is based on the idea that it is here that single neurons are first found that explicitly respond in a way that is comparable to the perceptual response—the subjective contour. The issue now arises: Is there any special role of the first single neuron to explicitly code this visual process? Is this an acceptable criterion for specifying the functional equivalence, much less the psychoneural equivalence, of the psychophysical and neurophysiological responses? My conclusion is that the answer to this questions must be "No." The reason for this negative conclusion emerges from a basic idea of neural coding. Even though subjective contours may be explicitly encoded in the responses of a single neuron in V2, it must be remembered that they are also implicitly encoded by some less obvious codes in the retina, the lateral geniculate body, V1, and at all other levels of the visual system beyond V2 by distributed populations of neurons. If they were not, the experience would not occur. In other words, the information necessary to elicit the response is available every place from the retina onward, albeit in a distributed and multicellular form. An appropriate decoding mechanism would, therefore, be able to find a correlation between neural responses at any level of the nervous system and the perceptual experience of the subjective or illusory or anomalous contour. If such a correlation were not available at any place in the chain, then the response could not occur.

My point is that the fact that there are single neurons in V2 that seem to respond to certain attributes of the stimuli that produce subjective contours gives them no special role in the nervous system. What we are actually observing is a prejudice for the role of a single neuron, in spite of the incontrovertible fact that a distributed population is also completely capable of encoding the same information. It may be encoded in a form that is difficult to measure and that eludes the sensitivity of a single microelectrode, but the necessary information had to be present at all levels of the visual system or the perceptual response could not occur.

It seems to me that the single-neuron doctrine, the idea that individual neurons are responsible for the encoding of perceptual experiences, has become the guiding, albeit hidden, assumption in both Dresp and Bonnet's and Von der Heydt and Peterhans' chains of logic. This is hardly surprising and certainly not unusual given the environment driving so much of our data—the single point in space explored at the tip of the microelectrode. Given this initial assumption, it is understandable how certain conclusions can, indeed must, follow. However, such a chain of logic, flawed at its most primitive levels, may actually beg the umbrella question: Are single neurons or population statistics the actual psychoneural equivalent of perceptual phenomena?

It seems to me that a further unjustified and unsubstantiated logical leap has been made by Dresp and Bonnet (1995). That leap was that the responses in the V2 neurons measured by Von der Heydt and Peterhans are actually the psychoneural equivalents of the perceptual experience. That is, I believe that they are assuming that wherever a coded response in a single neuron correlates with the stimulus, that place is the locus of the experience. However, that certainly is not a necessary assumption. As we have seen, no correlating code at any level has any special significance. Some kind of representative code at each level is necessary for transmission to a higher level for interpretation. A code at each level is necessary without being sufficient for the perceptual experience to occur. Spatial convergence on a single neuron has no special significance. Indeed, modern views lean toward the view that it is the ensemble activity or statistics of large numbers of neurons that is the real code for experience. Therefore, it is equally plausible, if not more so, to assume that temporally synchronized activity in spatially separated portions of the nervous system may interact to produce a common result, even when no single neuron or locus defines by itself the perceived experience.

An easily understood analogy that sharpens the fragile nature of the logic on which the bridge between neurophysiology and psychophysics has been built by Dresp and Bonnet may be found in the field of color vision. Opponent color codes are well known to be used by single neurons at the second (and higher) levels of the afferent visual chain. This, of course, cannot be interpreted to mean that information defining color experience does not exist in the first-order neurons—the receptors. The same information must be present at both levels, although in the form of different codes.

Similarly, the fact that there are psychophysical experiments (Hurvich & Jameson, 1955, 1957) that reflect the presence of opponent color perceptual properties does not mean that the opponent bipolar mechanisms of the retina or higher levels are the psychoneural equivalents of the phenomena. Even given the indisputable facts that their psychophysical experiments demonstrate the opponent nature of color vision and that we have known for years that some neurons in the retina are opponent in their nature (Tomita, 1965), no one suggests that retinal bipolar or ganglion neurons are the psychoneurally equivalent loci of color experience. Rather, they are just way stations at which information from the receptors is modified and transformed, and from which it is communicated to higher levels of the nervous system where it is subsequently interpreted. This analogy emphasizes that although the same information can be encoded in different ways and although transformed information can and does leave traces in our visual experience that can be assayed by psychophysical tests, the lower levels are not necessarily or even likely to be the psychoneurally equivalent mechanisms.

The point is that, just as we would be hard pressed to argue that these opponent type neurons are the necessary and sufficient conditions for color experience, it is difficult to assume that the presence of a neural correlate of the subjective contour in V2 is the psychoneural equivalent of either a subjective or a real contour. It is but a way station on the path to the higher levels of the visual nervous system where either this information is decoded and interpreted, or where it arrives at a level of further processing that is sufficiently complex to be the true equivalent of our perception of a contour.

This discussion would be incomplete if I did not consider another possible meaning of the term *functionally equivalent*. It is possible that the various processing steps in the neural pathway are capable of introducing modifications of the afferent signals that will ultimately result in veridical perceptions or illusions. Thus, for example, the trivariant psychophysics of color additivity exists because of the absorption spectra of the cone receptors. Furthermore, opponent color cancellation is a phenomenon that is at least partially due to recoding by the bipolar neurons. And, finally, it is possible that we see subjective contours because of the sensitivity of the V2 neurons to the stimulus clues that create these illusions. From that point on, the "message" expressed in the illusion is a property of the transmitted signal until it arrives at the central loci where psychoneural equivalence actually occurs. The perceptual trace of each of the processing steps, this argument goes, is the result of that peripheral transformation, and psychophysical experiments are capable of assaying the effects of even very peripheral neural transformations. But the perceptual awareness itself does not occur peripherally.

This is a possible scenario, but it still raises difficult conceptual questions. Are all neural codes assayable in this manner? When is a neural transformation an information-bearing and perceptually effective code? When is it an irrelevant concomitant response that has no subsequent effect? Is every neural response perceptually significant? Where is the final site at which the transformed and modified coded information achieves psychoneural equivalence?

Given the many attributes of a visual stimulus that are encoded by the several different neural languages at the many levels of the nervous system, it is problematical how a perceptual experience could be solely attributed to a specific peripheral level. It may be that it is more appropriate to consider V1 and even some of the immediately succeeding levels (V2 and V3) as parts of the "peripheral" transmission system. The fact that there are so many ways in which cognitive experience can modulate our perception of both real and subjective contour perception also suggests that signal modulation may be a better description of the implications of Dresp and Bonnet's work than any assertion that V2 is the locus of the perceptual phenomena they describe.

There is, however, one final matter that must be raised, the fourth question I posed some pages earlier: Are the neurophysiological data themselves solid? Lesher (1995), in a comprehensive review, pointed out that the data reported by Von der Heydt and Peterhans are currently thought to be much more equivocal than was originally suggested. Indeed, Redies, Crook, and Creutzfeld (1986), using cats rather than rhesus monkeys, found a considerably different pattern of neuronal responses in those animals. Feline neurons that seemed to be responding to illusory contours occurred in both V1 and V2. However, there was only a small proportion of such neurons and they were all complex types. More recently, and even more surprisingly, Grosof, Shapley, and Hawken (1993) found responses in V1 of the rhesus monkey that seemed to respond to linear (as opposed to curved) subjective contour stimuli. The situation is similar, but different enough to suggest that assuming an identity of the neural and perceptual responses may be premature.

Another problem raised by this inconsistent pattern of neurophysiological results goes far beyond a matter of incorrect or missampled data, or experimental variation between species. Let us assume, for the sake of argument, that the data are sound and that neurons in some part of the nervous system actually do respond to the physical stimuli that also produce the subjective contour in humans. The remaining question is: Have these investigators misinterpreted the nature of the stimulus (as opposed to the response) sufficiently such that the critical attribute of the stimulus they believe is driving the neural response is not, in fact, the salient one? In other words, even if the same physical stimulus pattern is both exciting a neuron in the cerebral cortex of a monkey and producing a reported subjective response in a human, can one be sure that the same attribute of the stimulus is the critical one for both kinds of responses?

There is a long history of reinterpretation of what neural responses mean. The simple, complex, and hypercomplex neurons of the early Hubel and Wiesel reports have taken on new meaning as new ideas and experimental data have accumulated. Some of these same neurons have been newly interpreted as spatial frequency or Gabor filter-sensitive elements, for example. I also discuss later how the roles of the classic "face" and "monkey's hand" neurons have been reinterpreted. My discussion of Stewart and Pinkham's work later in this chapter is also directly relevant to this issue. They suggest, as discussed later, that each and every previously reported selectively sensitive neuron type can be observed in the visual system because all are the result of a more fundamental coding scheme.

The point is that neurophysiological data are not without their own interpretive and theoretical baggage. When a stimulus is characterized as being able to produce a perceived subjective contour in human perception, the neurophysiological experimenter concentrates on those aspects of the stimulus. However, there are other ways that the same stimulus can be described. For example, a stimulus described as a set of misaligned lines can be distinguished from one designated as a set of end-stopped lines. A neuron that responded to the sum of the responses to several such end-stopped lines would produce a neural response on the basis of that attribute of the stimulus, but that property still could be completely oblivious to the human; the human might be responding to the other property. In other words, the stimulus itself has been anthropomorphized and categorized on the basis of our responses; some other measure of that same stimulus may be an even more effective neural stimulant, but without a corresponding perceptual response.

This discussion initially concentrated on the logical and methodological differences involved in comparing neural and psychophysical responses to stimuli that produce illusory contours in humans. It went on to note that the neurophysiological data are not that robust. They vary from species to species and from interpretation to interpretation. The tradition of "explaining" psychophysical phenomena in terms of neural responses is so strong these days that we may be all too uncritical in our evaluation of both the logic of the experiments and the nature of the neural responses. Unequivocally, the psychophysical phenomena do occur. What remains uncertain is how these neural responses in V2 are involved in the production of those perceptual responses.

Lesher (1995) summed up the uncertainty that surrounds this entire issue:

> To establish the role that neurons play in illusory contour perception, additional parametric studies of inducing stimulus structure must be undertaken—of the effective grating overlap and gap, response to edge inducers, and responses to curved illusory contours. (p. 298)

Obviously, there is still much to be done in determining the nature of the relationship between the responses of V2 neurons (or any others) and these fascinating subjective phenomena. In the absence of a complete and final exposition, I believe that we have committed our science to a theoretical position that is anatomically much too peripheral. Some additional reasons for believing this to be the case are discussed in the next section.

Some Thoughts on Low- Versus High-Level Visual Processing

Recently, the locus question has been particularized to controversies between the possible "low-level" or "high-level" origins of certain perceptual phenomena. To some, *low-level* previously meant retinal. In recent years, however, it has come to mean all of the visual pathway from the retina up to and including some of the early cortical regions. With this new definition, low-level has come to be associated with the closely related ideas of automatic, preattentive, and precognitive visual information processing. These low-level mechanisms, it has been proposed, are sufficiently well localized and straightforward that the observation of a correlation between some neural activity and some perceptual experience should be sufficient to support the claim that the phenomenon is "mediated" or "explained" by the neural mechanisms themselves.

High-level, on the other hand, has always been associated with the attentive, cognitive activities of the highest cortical regions. It is here, presumably, that the neural network is so intricately arranged that it is essentially intractable to a neuron-by-neuron experimental analysis. "High-level" neurophysiology has thus somewhat uncritically become synonymous in some lexicons with "cognitive." This identity is based on the idea that complex visual functions involving interpretation, reasoning, or judgment (i.e., "cognitive" functions) must be mediated by visual regions far up the ascending pathway.

The sine qua non of a high-level process is its cognitive penetrability—the modulation of the perceptual experience by the symbolic, logical, or semantic content of the stimulus, as opposed to the raw physical attributes of the stimulus. Cognitive penetration is not a purely psychological concept. It has also been reported to have a neurophysiological correlate at higher cortical levels. Maunsell (1995) summed up the value of this process as follows:

> By filtering out irrelevant signals and adding information about objects whose presence is remembered or inferred, the cortex creates an edited representation of the visual world that is dynamically modified to suit the immediate goals of the viewer. (p. 764)

There is no question, of course, that the activity of neurons at the highest cortical levels can be affected by attention. To postulate otherwise would separate cognition from brain function and require a rejection of the entire monistic foundation of psychobiological science, and much of the empirical basis of cognitive psychology. A new set of problems and questions arises, however, when we seek attentive effects on neurons at the lower and more peripheral levels of the nervous system.

The effort to compare cellular neurophysiological recordings observed at relatively low levels of the visual system with certain perceptual phenomena continues apace in spite of the fact that many such phenomena are demonstrably cognitively penetrated. There are several ways that such correlations can be interpreted. I have already discussed two—the assumption that the relatively low-level activity is the actual psychoneural locus, and the assumption that the activity is only a coded representation being transmitted to the higher levels where it is interpreted as a perceptual experience.

A third assumption has attracted an increasing number of neuroreductionistically oriented perceptual scientists. That is that there is centrifugal activity from the high-level regions projected back down to the low-level regions. This centrifugal or feedback activity is presumed to originate in the far reaches of the cortex, but to be transmitted to low levels where it modulates the activity of V1 or V2 neurons, for example. This feedback idea is used to justify the presence of the correlated activity at low levels in cases in which it seems, for other reasons, that the "cause" of the activity should have been subsumed under the collection of high-level neural processes we classify as *cognitive*. Centrifugal feedback of this kind also has the advantage of unloading what would otherwise be substantial requirements for very complex visual processing from the low levels of the brain.

The feed-backward operation of this centrifugal neural information flow has also been suggested to play a much more peculiar role in imagery—perception that is not driven by the immediate physical stimulus, but rather by endogenous sources. The suggestion is that we are able to "see" the geometrical arrangement of patterns that are created by high-level imagery only because of centrifugal activation of low-level, retinotopically mapped mechanisms! This is an extraordinary and highly unusual suggestion. It suggests that we are able to unscramble high-level symbolic codes back to the retinotopic images that generated them. Although going from a isomorphic or retinotopic map to a symbolic (i.e., heavily encoded and transformed) representation seems plausible, going from symbol to map is highly implausible and probably a violation of many of the principles of chaos and thermodynamics discussed in chapter 2.

The attempt to explain "cognitive penetration" in terms of feedback to retinotopically mapped regions is but another example of what I believe is one of the most misleading enterprises in modern neuroreductionism—the persistent tendency to seek peripheral or low-level explanations for what seem more likely to be the result of very-high-level neural transformations. What we have learned recently is that all visual phenomena are much more complex than our early unidimensional "sensory" models suggested. We now know that even color and brightness, long thought to be most heavily influenced by the simple physics of the stimulus, depend on the spatial relationships of the components of a scene (Gilchrist, 1977; Land, 1959a, 1959b, 1977) as well as on expectations of a more cognitive kind (Adelson, 1993). I believe, however, that all of these evidences of cognitive penetration argue for central, rather than peripheral, processing. Now let's see how one investigator coped with this problem.

Watanabe's Study of Occluded Objects

In this section we deal with an experimental report (Watanabe, 1995) that grapples with the task of distinguishing between possible low-level and high-level loci for an important perceptual phenomenon—the McCullough effect (McCullough, 1965) and some new observations made by Watanabe concerning spatial occlusion and object orientation. The McCullough effect is one of those few seminal findings that has created long-term consternation, excitement, and challenge for perceptual science for several reasons. First, it is a color–spatial contingent effect. That is, the color response of induced afterimages is not unidimensionally determined, but depends both on the chromaticity of a conditioning visual stimulus and its spatial arrangement. Second, understanding the phenomenon is further complicated by the fact that the effect can be elicited by illusory perceptions as well as by real stimulus spatial patterns. Third, the issue is purported to be associated with the activity of neurons at "low-levels" that seem (from some points of view) to be behaving in much the same manner as the McCullough perceptual effect itself.

Watanabe showed that illusory contours could be invoked by occluding objects with orientations that could only be inferred but that were not physically present in the stimulus. These inferred orientations produced the McCullough effect just as well as if the orientation information had been given by real stimuli. His description of the perceptual outcome of the experiment is a solid contribution to the perceptual literature. To me, however, it seems that this is one case in which the equivalence of the illusory stimulus and the real stimulus suggests an interpretative or cognitively penetrated (and by this I specifically mean high cortical level) explanation of the phenomena. Watanabe believed otherwise.

Watanabe (1995) suggested that the effects he measured were determined by a common low-level neural mechanism that was simultaneously involved in transparency, occlusion, illusory contours, and the McCullough effect. Such interactions among the various perceptual responses to a multidimensional stimulus are in the spirit of much contemporary perceptual research and are not a matter of controversy. Watanabe, however, then attempted to build a bridge between his findings and some related neuropsychological data; at this point theoretical difficulties arise.

Watanabe specifically argued that the locus of the McCullough effect was in V1. He cited reports by Humphrey, Goodale, and Gursey (1991) and Savoy and Gabrieli (1991) as supporting evidence for this physiological–anatomical conjecture. On the basis of findings that patients with lesions in certain areas of the cerebral cortex could still produce the McCullough effect, Watanabe concluded that the neural responses corresponding to the perception both of occluded edges and of orientation and the McCullough effect occurred "quite early in the visual pathway." To his credit, later in his paper Watanabe qualified this conjecture by expressing his willingness to accept the possibility that although the effect seems most likely to depend on processes occurring as early as V1, it is also possible that centrifugal feedback from more central regions of cortex may modify the observed peripheral neural activity. However, as noted earlier, this is also a matter of considerable contention.

Watanabe cited a number of other psychophysical results that he believed supported a relatively peripheral locus for the key mechanisms in the McCullough effect, including monocularity, retinal locus specificity, and wavelength (as opposed to color contrast) dependency. These are the stimulus properties to which neurons in V1 and V2 are known to be sensitive. He argued that therefore the McCullough effect must also be that peripheral. What is missing is a discussion of some of the other data that support a high-level locus, including the reports of an extraordinary long persistence of the phenomenon (e.g., Jones & Holding, 1975). Of course, there is also the general matter of the neutrality of psychophysical phenomena in determining the underlying neural locus or mechanism of some phenomenon.

Therefore, two questions must be asked about Watanabe's neuroreductionist explanation of his psychophysical findings. The first is: Do the psychophysical results say anything compelling about the locus of the phenomenon? One of the main points of this present book is that psychophysical results, like mathematical or computational models, are completely neutral with regard to internal mechanisms. Psychophysical tests can only suggest plausible mechanisms from among what is virtually an uncountable number of equally plausible alternatives. Therefore, the answer to this question has to be, "No."

The second question is: What credence can be given to findings from neuropsychological patients in support of a specific locus for these phenomena? Watanabe's argument mainly depends on an acceptance of data from brain-injured patients to support a peripheral explanation of his psychophysical observations. However, the typical clinical, neuropsychological result is idiosyncratic and uncontrolled. The brain is simply too complex with its large number of interconnected areas, centers, and nuclei to justify the use of such results as arguments that attempt to localize particular functions in particular structures. Again, readers may consult Van Orden, Pennington, and Stone's (personal communication, 1996) cogent criticism of such localization hypotheses. The Hilgetag, O'Neill, and Young (1996) discussion of the indeterminacy of cortical hierarchies outlined in chapter 2 is also relevant in this context.

I recall once visiting the Mayo Clinic in Rochester, Minnesota, some years ago and being escorted through the voluminous electroencephalograph (EEG) files of Reginald Bickford, a distinguished neurologist. These records were all depth recordings, collected with electrodes that had been embedded in patients' brains. The files filled a huge room that had once been a human centrifuge facility used by the U.S. Air Force. Bickford was very honest in pointing out that after a long career of collecting these records he was unsure what they meant—each was so special and so unique that he was not able to draw general conclusions from this vast database.

Bickford's data make up only one extreme example of the difficulty that students of the brain have had in unraveling what is going on at high levels. I believe that human and animal neuropsychological studies, whether the lesions examined are experimentally or accidentally produced, are beset by enormous interpretive problems. Recovery of function, redundant areas, imprecision of lesion boundaries, transection of transmissions pathways, and such interactive relations as inhibition of inhibition (simulating excitation) all mitigate theoretical implications when cortical damage is used as a clue to the locus of cognitive function. Therefore, these neuropsychological case histories provide a very fragile platform on which to build modern and compelling theories of the brain mechanisms involved in psychophysical function.

Although Watanabe did argue that the McCullough effect is primarily a peripheral phenomenon, and that this suggests that his findings concerning orientation and occlusion are also the result of low-level mechanisms, he did acknowledge the fact that there must be some high-level influences. He said, "the McCullough effect [in this experiment] could not have occurred without the involvement of a subjective completion process" (Watanabe, 1995, p. 654).

I completely agree with this statement. However, the intended implication of Watanabe's entire study is that this subjective completion process is carried out peripherally. With this I cannot agree. Nevertheless, this too is a matter of conviction rather than rigorous proof, and it too is neutral with regard to the involved neural loci. Watanabe also cited the work of others who came to this same conclusion that the subjective organization of the stimulus affects the McCullough effect (Jenkins & Ross, 1977; Meyer & Phillips, 1980). To this argument can be added the discovery that imagery can affect the McCullough effect (Finke & Schmidt, 1978; Kaufman, May, & Kunen, 1981; Kunen & May, 1980). All of these studies suggest to me a high-level location for this phenomenon, and thus a high-level locus for the other phenomena described by Watanabe. The attempt to build a bridge from such complex perceptual phenomena to low-level (V1) neural mechanisms, therefore, is neither robust nor satisfying.

Spillmann, Ransom-Hogg, and Oehler's Conceptual
Transposition From Receptive to Perceptive Fields

Another approach to linking psychophysical and neurophysiological data is to transpose words and ideas directly, and, as pointed out later, often indiscriminately, from the neurophysiological to the psychophysical laboratory. For example, a well-known concept in neurophysiology is the *receptive field* of a neuron. This term refers to a very specific property of an individual neuron—the extent of the external world within which a presented stimulus can elicit a response in a neuron. Although the receptive field of an individual retinal receptor is very small, there is a general increase in the size of the receptive field as one ascends to higher and higher level neurons in the nervous system. The receptive field of such a neuron is typically much larger than the physical extent of the neuron's own arborization. Obviously, therefore, the measured receptive field is due to the convergence of a number of neurons onto the one from which recordings are made.

Based on this operationally defined neurophysiological concept—the receptive field—Spillman, Ransom-Hogg, and Oehler (1987) suggested the existence of a *perceptive field* that they claimed is directly related to the receptive field, but that is measured by psychophysical techniques. The psychophysically defined perceptive field, however, is a much more ambiguous concept than the receptive field, particularly when an attempt is made to build a bridge between the two ideas. The perceptive field is defined operationally (i.e., psychophysically) as the region of interaction around a particular point in the visual field. Unfortunately, the perceptive field is not anchored to a particular entity—a neuron. Logically, the process of identifying what are really two very distinct ideas (in terms of the operations used to define them) is the equivalent of trying to go from measurements of the molar activity of an entire system to the behavior of one constituent component. This, as was made clear in chapter 2, is at least difficult and probably impossible.

The problem is evident in both a horizontal and a vertical sense. Horizontally, each point on the visual stimulus scene is able to activate many of the interacting neurons whose visual fields overlap. Therefore, no point in the stimulus scene is encoded by the activity of any single neuron. Thus, by definition the perceptive field must be a measure of the activity of many neurons with many different receptive field sizes, and not a measure of any single neuron.

Vertically, the situation is even more complex because there are receptive fields of increasing sizes defined at virtually every level of the visual pathway. No one suggests that stimulation with any above-threshold stimulus activates only a single neuron at a single ascending level. Rather, vast numbers of neurons at all levels of the nervous system spring into action with the slightest perceivable stimulus. Which receptive field is then being compared with the perceptive field measurement? A central one? A peripheral one? An eccentric one? A foveal one? All of them? None of them? Given that there should be a wide range of receptive field types and sizes, would it not be expected that the receptive field at least at one level or in one position should match the psychophysical measurement? The question, of course, is: Given any measured psychophysically defined perceptive field, how could one fail to find a match some place in this vast array of neuronal elements across each level, or as one ascends the visual pathway?

In spite of these initial difficulties, ill-advised efforts are being made to define the properties of individual neurons on the basis of purported relationships between perceptive and receptive fields. Unfortunately, the data are gathered under such drastically different conditions and interpreted on such vastly different foundation premises that the term *perceptive field* itself becomes questionable. In some cases such measurements are simply equivalent to the resolving power of the entire visual system. In other situations, the perceptive field seems to be nothing more than a kind of conceptual pun, the physiological and perceptual words having very different operational meanings. The former is a measure of the external stimulus space (a region in space capable of affecting an isolated individual neuron); the latter is a molar, cumulative property of a huge number of neurons of varying receptive field sizes.

The target for this part of our discussion is the work of Spillmann, Ransom-Hogg, and Oehler (1987). They carried out an extensive study comparing the psychophysically measured perceptive field and a supposedly related physiologically defined receptive field. Spillmann and his colleagues used two psychophysical methods—the Hermann grid illusion (Hermann, 1870) and the Westheimer technique, in which the increment threshold is determined as a function of the diameter of a background field (Westheimer, 1965, 1967)—to measure the size of the perceptive field in both humans and monkeys. They observed that, in general, the psychophysical data agreed in both species. There was a similar increase in perceptive field size with retinal eccentricity. Comparable perceptive field sizes were somewhat larger in humans than in monkeys—but not out of line with the respective sizes of these two species. These psychophysical measurements do not pose any basis for disagreement or criticism. Indeed, they represent a useful contribution to our understanding of acuity and resolution differences across the retinas of two very interesting species.

However, the next step taken by Spillmann et al. (1987) was to compare these psychophysical results with the receptive field sizes of a certain class of retinal ganglion neurons—the broadband or M type neurons—in the monkey. They plotted these two measures—their psychophysical measures of the perceptive field and the neurophysiological measures of the receptive field of this particular neuron as originally reported by DeMonasterio and

Gouras (1975). The overlap of the two curves was presented by them as evidence that the receptive field size of these particular ganglion neurons accounts for the psychophysically measured perceptive field size.

As my readers may expect by now, I do not believe this argument is compelling. The apparent close correspondence of monkey perceptive and receptive field sizes is, from my point of view, a result of a spurious selection of neurophysiological data chosen from among a wide range of available receptive fields data and a fortuitous correspondence of them with molar psychological findings. There are several reasons for my position on this particular effort at neuroreductionism.

First, the specific ganglion neurons chosen for the comparison are only a small set of the many different types of neurons found not only in the retina, but also at many other levels of the visual system. We have to ask: Why are these particular neurons the ones to determine the psychophysical response?

Second, as Spillmann and his colleagues quite appropriately pointed out, there are a number of other psychophysical studies that also were supposed to measure the so-called perceptive field, but that produced considerably different values. These other, quite different, measures obviously would not have coincided with the particular neural values given by DeMonasterio and Gouras (1975), but might well have matched some others.

Spillmann et al. (1987) then made some very revealing comments:

> It is obvious that there are almost as many different curves as there are procedures. These differences cannot be attributed to the normal scatter of receptive field sizes (Hubel and Wiesel 1974; Peichl and Wassle 1979). Rather, they may point to cell types tuned to different stimulus sizes (Wilson and Bergen 1979; Watson 1982), or to mechanisms located at different levels of the visual system; or they may indicate that although some functions are suited for tapping perceptive fields and field centers, others are not. (p. 61)

This statement speaks directly to the issue that I have highlighted and that I believe they have chosen to ignore in the development of their neuroreductionist theory of the perceptive field. That is, why pick the M neurons of the retina as the neural correlate of the psychophysical phenomena they measured for any other reason than an almost accidental similarity of size? There are many other neurons that have different size receptive fields that do not agree with the measures made by Spillmann and his colleagues. Furthermore, there are so many different ways to measure the perceptive field that it is not at all clear exactly which one, if any single one, appropriately defines this global property of the visual system. If there are as many values for the perceptive field as there are measures, is there anything fundamentally useful about this concept? It seems more appropriate to assume that the nervous system performs many complex functions and that measures of this sort will be highly variable depending on not only the method used, but also the conditions of viewing. Indeed, the perceptive field seems to be more a measure of the psychophysical methods used than of any biological aspect of the system.

Given the residual doubts and absence of any unique and convincing association between psychophysics and neurophysiology in this case, I believe that the following statement by Spillmann et al. (1987) is unjustified:

> Because of their close correlation with single cell recordings and histological measurements, we conclude that these data support the concept of the perceptive field as a psychophysical correlate of the receptive field. (p. 61)

What is most disturbing is that the neuroreductionist approach of comparing selected psychophysical data to selected neurophysiological findings continues to be extremely popular. This is so in spite of the fact that such comparisons are often flawed by an almost ad hoc selection of both the relevant phenomena and neural structures.

Ishai and Sagi's Comparisons of Imagery and Perception

As we have seen, the results of psychophysical studies are often presented as evidence of the nature of the underlying neural mechanisms. The general strategy employed is analogy—a comparison of the measured responses of selected neural units and the characteristics of the perceptual response in selected experimental paradigms. Arguments by analogy are treacherous, however. I have previously pointed out that analogies, as well as mathematical or computer models and theories, are neutral with regard to the actual mechanisms that produce them. At best, the similarities can be suggestive; at worst they can be completely misleading and even place the theoretical discussion in the wrong context. Nevertheless, this version of the neuroreductionist enterprise continues.

For example, a recent study (Ishai & Sagi, 1995) illustrates the use of the analogical line of reasoning and clearly reveals some of the pitfalls that can endanger such an enterprise. Although these authors are careful in their discussion to limit the conclusions by asserting only that "Our data provide indirect support" (p. 1774), "Our results indicate" (p. 1774), and "It is possible" (p. 1774), the general thrust of their paper is that they have provided evidence for a common "mechanism" for imagined (i.e., stimulus-free) and perceived (i.e., stimulus-driven) visual experiences. Going even beyond that, they purported to locate the common mechanism in a particular part of the visual nervous system.

The basic paradigm used in their experiment is secondary to our consideration of the train of logic that allowed Ishai and Sagi to move from their results to the conclusion that low-level cortical areas are specifically involved in both the imagined and perceived experiences. However, there is a sufficient number of flaws in the design and execution of this experiment that it is necessary to consider their methodology in some detail.

The main psychophysical conclusion that Ishai and Sagi drew from their study was that the cognitive effects of imagined and perceived experiences are the same. Their method presented visual stimuli consisting of two peripheral components—Gabor patches—flanking another central Gabor patch. (A Gabor patch is a sinusoidally modulated stimulus that falls off in amplitude according to a Gaussian rule as one moves away from the center of the patch.) When the distance between the flanking patches and the target patch was small, the target patch was detected less well (i.e., the threshold was higher) than when it was presented alone. This is an example of masking or threshold elevation. When the separation was greater, however, the threshold was lowered and the detectability of the target patch was enhanced. The unique aspect of their work was that the experiment was carried out with both real and imagined Gabor flanking stimuli.

The surprise was their contention that their data revealed that both the imagined and real flankers exerted the same effect on the target Gabor patch. From my point of view, this conclusion is justified only if some extreme liberties are taken in interpreting their findings. Figure 3.1 is a reproduction of their Figure 2 from p. 1773 of Ishai and Sagi (1995). This figure compared the effect of varying the distance between the flanking Gabor patches and the target Gabor patch for both real and imagined flanking patches. They interpreted their results to show that both imagined and real flanking Gabor patches exhibit similar effects. To justify this conclusion by standard scientific methods, it would be necessary to show that the difference between (a) a control condition in which neither real nor imagined patches were used and the condition in which the effect of real patches was measured, on the one hand, was similar to the difference between (b) the control situation and the imagined conditions, on the other hand. Two experiments are necessary to prove this point. The control (no real or imagined flanking patches) must be compared to the conditions in which real patches were used and, even more important, the control must be compared to the condition in which the imagined patches were invoked.

However, one of these two necessary experiments—a simultaneous (i.e., the measurements are carried out in the same session) comparison of the control and the imagined data—was not carried out by Ishai and Sagi. The offered comparison of these two conditions was unfortunately based on findings from two different sessions, allowing all of the fluctuations that occur between sessions to potentially contaminate both their results and their conclusions. Their assertion that the control and imagined findings differed significantly is, therefore dubious. Without convincing evidence for

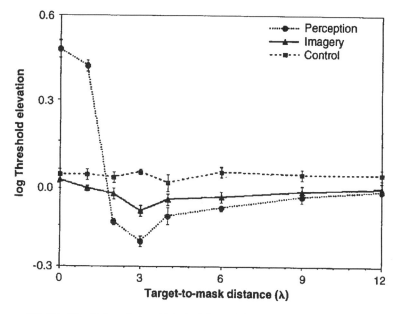

FIG. 3.1. The findings from which the Ishai and Sagi conclusions are drawn. The reader is referred to the text for discussion of this data set. Reprinted from Ishai and Sagi (1995). Common mechanisms of visual imagery and perception. *Science, 268,* 1171–1774. Copyright (1995), American Association for the Advancement of Science.

this basic fact, the rest of their explanation of their results becomes quite problematical.

There are other aspects of Ishai and Sagi's interpretation of the obtained data that are also subject to considerable criticism. The measured effect on the detection thresholds for the condition in which real Gabor patches were used is not monotonic. As we can see in Fig. 3.1, the curve plotting these data shows two distinctly different segments. First, there is a substantial reduction in sensitivity (thus, masking) that occurs when the real Gabor patches are very close to the target stimuli—distances measured to be equal to zero and one wavelength of the fundamental spatial frequency of the Gabor patches that were used. When the separation was greater than two wavelengths, there was, on the contrary, a reduction in the contrast threshold, indicating a higher degree of sensitivity in detecting the test stimuli—in other words, an enhancement in detectability or a lowering in the threshold. Thus, there clearly is a bipartite effect of the real masking stimuli—a masking followed by an enhancement in detectability. However, both the results for the control values and the results for the imagined patches were nearly flat lines. There was no indication of the reduction in sensitivity exhibited in the results for the real patches for the zero- and one-wavelength separations.

Both the "control" values and the data plotting the effects of the real stimuli were, appropriately, collected in the same sessions. The "control" values were also plotted along an axis denoted as "target-to-mask distance." However, the meaning of this parameter in the cases in which there were no flanking visual masks, either real or imagined (the defining property of the control condition), is problematical. The control results show only a slight suppression of sensitivity at all "target-to-mask distances." Because it was not clear how the "control" values (with no distance to be manipulated) could have been obtained, I made a personal inquiry to the authors. Their response was that the control values were measured in the same session in which the real stimuli were presented and the distance values assigned to each of them were simply those that had been used for the real stimuli. This is an acceptable, although unusual, way of distinguishing between the effects of the presence or absence of the flanking patches.

In the next part of Ishai and Sagi's experiment, the subjects were instructed to imagine the Gabor patches at appropriate distances. As I have just indicated, a different pattern of results occurred with the imagined flanking patches than with the real flanking patches. In the case of the imagined patches, there was no initial increase in the threshold for the zero and one Gabor wavelength "target to mask" distances. The curves plotting the data for the imagined patches (like that of the control patches) were flat as a function of the distance between the flankers and the target patches. Both the control and the imagined curves showed very little effect compared to the difference between either of them and the results for the real flanking patches. The slight difference between them, however, was reported by Ishai and Sagi to be "statistically significant"—a conclusion whose power is mitigated by the fact that the two sets of data were not collected in the same sessions. Indeed, both are so close to the baseline of no effect that it is even possible that they do not represent any positive effects of the imagined stimuli and the control conditions, respectively, but rather intersession differences of unknown origin. Thus, it is not even clear that there is a real difference between the imagined and the control conditions, a difference on which much of the argument made by Ishai and Sagi was subsequently based.

Considerable additional doubt about the validity of this central conclusion arises from the fact that differences between the imagined and the real patch conditions for some values of the "target-to-mask" distances are actually larger than the differences between the imagined and the control conditions. A significant statistical difference between the two curves for the imagined and real flanking conditions can only occur if the values for the zero and one Gabor Wavelength distance conditions are ignored. Their ex post facto justification for omitting these values given in a footnote—"This [difference] might be due to the fact that we used a simple detection task and stimuli that have no meaning, as opposed to common objects (such as lines and circles)" (p. 1774)–does not mitigate this criticism.

Let us assume, however, that all of these procedural difficulties can be accounted for and that there really is a similarity of the results for the imagined and the real flanking patch conditions. Let's now work through the train of logic that would then be required to justify the following three neuroreductionist conclusions drawn by Ishai and Sagi (1995):

1. The mechanisms for imagery and ordinary perception are the same.
2. Low levels of the cortex are involved in this phenomenon.
3. There exists a previously undetected kind of short-term memory that persists for about 5 min.

"The Mechanisms of Visual Imagery and Ordinary Perception Are Common?" Ishai and Sagi (1995) based their argument that there are common mechanisms involved in the visual experiences produced by either real or imagined flanking patches on the similarity in the observed response functions. As I have just shown, it is not entirely clear that the functions are, indeed, the same. However, suppose that we accept their conclusion for the purpose of continuing the discussion. The question is: Would similarity (or even identity) of these psychophysical functions be sufficiently strong evidence to justify the conclusion of a common underlying mechanism? Given what I have already asserted in previous chapters about psychophysical functions and models being indeterminate with regard to internal structure and mechanisms, the answer to this rhetorical question would certainly have to be "no" at the outset. But let's look at some other aspects of their discussion.

Argument on the basis of functional analogy makes the very strong, but unsupportable, assumption that similar behaviors or response patterns are necessarily reflections of similar mechanisms. The classic difficulty, once again, is that such reasoning confuses analogies with homologies. Although the fins of fishes and those of pinipeds are functionally similar, they do not arise from the same embryological origins. In a similar vein, no matter how similar the functions for the real and imagined patches described by Ishai and Sagi, the extrapolation from functional data to hypotheses concerning the underlying neural mechanisms is always treacherous unless substantiated by some kind of additional structural analysis.

In fact, when closely examined, it appears that many such comparisons between psychophysical and neurophysiological findings are examples of a similar kind of flawed analogical reasoning. Philosophers and scientists for ages have been both tantalized and perplexed by this kind of logic. Part of the perplexity arises from what I believe is a deep misunderstanding of the word *isomorphism*. Isomorphism (i.e., same shape), in an analogical sense, implies a similarity of form and function, but it does not necessarily imply an identity of mechanism. Two systems with completely different underlying mechanisms may exhibit common functional or process forms. The same mathematical functions, for example, can effectively describe both the behavior of an elastic spring and the oscillation of prey–predator populations. From that point of view they are functionally isomorphic analogies, but not mechanistic homologies. Similarly, models and theories are often superb analogs of they systems they represent. Indeed, the utility of a model depends on the degree to which it is analogous or isomorphic to the modeled system. But, as I pointed out in chapter 2, the kind of descriptive analogy that we call a model, mathematical or otherwise, is completely neutral with regard to the underlying structure. Similarly, psychophysical isomorphism is completely neutral with regard to the underlying mechanism.

This limitation of formal models is particularly salient when it comes to neuroreductionist enterprises of the kind we are discussing here. Even when the neural and psychophysical responses are isomorphic, even when they exhibit the same time course, these functional similarities do not guarantee that they represent the same mechanisms. This admonition is regularly ignored in many of the "bridging" studies so popular in perceptual science these days.

I pointed out in chapter 2 that analogical models that describe or represent the time course of some psychological or neurophysiological process can be very useful even if they are neutral with regard to the underlying mechanism. They can be used to predict future events, sometimes to an amazing degree. But they do this in an ontologically nonreductive sense and in complete conceptual isolation from the mechanics of the underlying system. This is the fallacy underlying the neuroreductionist proposition put forward by Ishai and Sagi. Even if one were willing to accept the comparability of their imagined and real masks, one could not extrapolate from that functional similarity to the idea of a common mechanism.

"There Are Low-Level Mechanisms Involved in Both Processes." Now let's turn to the second conclusion drawn by Ishai and Sagi (1995). They quite appropriately noted that the involvement of low-level mechanisms is still controversial and a major theoretical controversy in this field. Their cautious tone (e.g., "Our data provide indirect support," p. 1774, and "It is reasonable to assume," p. 1774) does honor to their scientific reserve. Nevertheless, like Watanabe, they asked us to accept their hypothesis that "the facilitory effect of visual imagery on perception was due to activation of the early representations" (p. 1774). To support this hypothesis, they noted that the psychophysical functions are orientation specific, retinal locus specific, and monocular (i.e., the effect did not transfer from one eye to the other). Thus, part of the argument by analogy they are building depends on these functional similarities between the psychophysical response characteristics and those of known V1 neurons.

If one were only asked to accept a relation between the psychophysical response to real stimuli and some neural activity in the low levels of the visual system (V1 and V2), the issue could be simply reduced to a confusion of the transmission aspects of the nervous system with its role as mediator of the psychoneurally equivalent representation. In the case of imagery, with no real stimuli presented to activate the low-level transmission pathways, the relationship between imagery and low-level visual functions is even more strained. The question then becomes: What role do the low-level mechanisms, such as those residing in V1 or V2, play in mental imagery? Another way to ask the same question is: Do imagined perceptual experiences, formed without external stimuli, activate low-level visual mechanisms, possibly by feedback from the higher levels to the lower ones?

This last question is an extremely complex issue and one for which there is a substantial amount of current disagreement. Miyashita (1995), in a commentary on Ishai and Sagi's (1995) report, literally begged the question by asserting that:

> Imagery experience requires a top-down mental operation, which activates backward projections. If an imagery task requires a reconstruction of the detailed local geometry of image (as counting the columns of the Pantheon) backward signals from higher order representations would reach topographically organized visual areas. (p. 1719)

This is an extraordinary suggestion that has mixed support in the scientific literature. I consider it to be among the more fanciful of recent neuroreductionist creations. The idea that a retinotopic image *can* be reconstructed in the lower cortical levels of the visual pathway as a result of high-level imagery strains credulity more than any other neuromythological proposition. (Perhaps its main contender for incredibility would be the equally strange idea that a retinotopic image *must* be reconstructed in V1 for an observer to see a form!) Although it is quite understandable and intuitive how a retinotopic image at some early level could be symbolically coded at some higher level, the inverse would require a reversal of the information flow that would violate many of the laws of thermodynamics and chaos that were discussed in chapter 2.

There are really two issues intertwined here. First, are the retinotopic, low-level representations the psychobiological mechanisms of imagery? Second, are the low-level retinotopic codes the result of centrifugal feedback from higher levels to the lowest levels? The idea that retinotopic neural codes were reconstructed during imagination is usually attributed to Kosslyn (1980; Kosslyn et al., 1993).

This controversy was the focus of a "debate" in a recent issue of the journal *Trends in Neuroscience*. In that series of arguments and counter arguments, Roland and Guly'as (1994) presented evidence against any role being played by "V1, V2, V3, VP, and possibly more" (p. 285) in visual imagery even though "Areas that are remote from the early visual areas, and that are located in the parieto-occipital and temporo-occipital regions of the brain are consistently active in visual imagery" (p. 286). Because these regions are also involved in memory retrieval, this makes a rational and reasonable alternative to the reactivation of retinotopic patterns in the lower levels of the cortex.

The other articles in this debate (Sakai & Miyashita, 1994; Kosslyn & Ochsner, 1994; Moscovitch, Behrmann, & Winocur, 1994) were generally opposed to the Roland and Guly'as critique (1994). Sakai and Miyashita offered a cognitive model that would permit such a system to work. Kosslyn and Oscher proposed an additive factors method (see our discussion of the double dissociation method earlier) and suggested that the tasks that Roland and Guly'as used were not valid imagery techniques or that individual difference between subjects might account for the differing results from different laboratories. Moscovitch et al. (1994) quite correctly suggested that "PET studies in normal people can only provide information about activation of early visual areas but do not demonstrate conclusively whether this activation is necessary for imagery" (p. 292). But they then went on to suggest that the only way to resolve this issue is to use human neuropsychological experiments, an approach that is also beset with many attendant uncertainties.

Roland and Guly'as (1994) responded in turn to each of these arguments, and added one additional and very interesting anatomical point. With regard to the centrifugal influences of high-level regions on low-level ones, they noted:

> Although anatomical back projections from non-retinotopically organized areas to lower, retinotopically organized areas exist in man, these back projections have a different target distribution from that of the forward projections with respect to both visual-field representations and enervation targets in different cortical layers. Thus, there is hardly any "machinery" in the visual cortex to materialize identical activation patterns of neuron populations in V1 and neighboring areas during visual perception and, by way of backward propagation, during visual imagery (as advocated by Kosslyn). (p. 296)

Of course, the controversy is not resolved by this exchange of opinion and interpretation of data, but a general point can be made concerning the arguments put forth by the critics of Roland and Guly'as. If retinotopic, low-level activity is assumed to be the necessary concomitant of imagery, then the mere demonstration of counterevidence, even if from a different imaging paradigm, does contraindicate the generality of the hypothesis and suggests that it should be rejected.

"There Is an Intermediate-Term (5 min) Memory That Is Mediated at a Low Level." Ishai and Sagi's hypothesis that there is a new, previously undetected kind of short-term memory also seems to be a post hoc explanation of some of their results; it also does not stand close scrutiny. Their "new memory" is suggested by the fact that if a period greater than 5 min is interposed between the presentation of the real target patch and imagined flanking patches, the elevation of the threshold does not obtain. Given the fragile nature of the phenomenon—as measured by them—this single experiment cannot be depended on to support the invention of another new memory. Indeed, the time course is sufficiently close to that observed in other kinds of short-term memory that even if the phenomenon could be replicated, there seems to be no reason to suggest something special and unique. In chapter 4, I discuss the difficulties involved in building a plausible mental or cognitive architecture. As discussed there, any supposition of a new memory type only adds to the general difficulties of defining the underlying mental architecture. Here, I am specifically concerned with the suggestion that an additional kind of memory exists.

I conclude my discussion of their work by noting that Ishai and Sagi (1995) presented an example of a very popular and trendy approach to neuroreductionist thinking. The empirical and theoretical flaws in their work are helpful in highlighting some of the logical problems that are encountered when attempts are made to build bridges between psychophysics and neurophysiology.

Psychophysics and Neurophysiology as Heuristics for Each Other

Both psychophysics and neurophysiology are respectable pursuits that need no justification beyond their intrinsic merit, elegance, and interest to their own scientific communities. Both enterprises can stand on their own and have already provided extraordinary contributions to our understanding of the world in which we live and of ourselves. In previous sections of this chapter, I highlighted a few case studies in which I believe that efforts to connect the two fields have exceeded reasonable scientific logic and standards. It is just because the problems encountered when one wishes to study the mind–brain complex are so profound and so important, that tentative and fragile associations are accepted that would not be sustained in a simpler and more directly accessible scientific arena.

But neuroreductionism comes in many forms, and there are ways in which psychophysics and neurophysiology can interact in a positive and productive manner. One useful way that poses few logical problems is simply the cross-fertilization of ideas and concepts that so often occurs in interdisciplinary science. This approach takes advantage of discoveries in either field to provide heuristic suggestions that can transfer interesting and otherwise unexpected ideas from one field to the other. Thus, neurophysiology can be a fruitful source of ideas that might lead to the discovery of psychophysical phenomena. Most notably, the early neurophysiological experiments of Hubel and Wiesel (1959) and Lettvin, Maturana, McCullough, and Pitts (1959) had a profound effect on subsequent perceptual research. Their findings opened the door to studies of the influence of spatiotemporally organized stimuli, as opposed to the simple wavelength and energy-dominated independent variables of previous years. As another example, the results of the later work of Hubel and Wiesel (1962, 1968, and many others) on moving oriented line, edge, and tongue-shaped sensitive neurons in the visual cortex of cats and monkeys stimulated a rush of psychophysical studies in the last couple of decades. It is difficult to pick up any issue of any modern journal concerned with vision or perception without finding articles that credit those classic neurophysiological studies as their intellectual source. Many of the most important psychophysical findings of recent years have been specifically stimulated by these very important contributions. It is important to appreciate, however, that these analogies need not be either explanatory theories or psychoneural equivalences.

The inverse strategy is to straightforwardly transfer the phenomena and results from psychophysics to new neurophysiological experimental designs. Many perceptual phenomena (e.g., the Mach band, the Hermann grid, the McCullough effect) have stimulated neurophysiologists to look for analogous mechanisms in "wet" preparations even though no definitive theoretical bridge from one to the other might yet exist. Sometimes the search is successful, sometimes not; very often the search produces a new finding simply because the problem was approached in a way that was conceptually more psychophysical than physiological. Indeed what we mean by the term *heuristic* is—Of or relating to a usually speculative formulation serving as a guide in the investigation or solution of a problem (*American Heritage Dictionary*). For example, the conceptual cross fertilization approach is the one that Saarinen and Levi (1995) followed in discussing the results of their experiments. In this study, they examined the improvement of Verneir acuity sensitivity with experience. They suggested that improvements in fine tuning of neuronal sensitivities might account for the selective learning that occurs in some tasks. They then offered what were candidly speculations about potential mechanisms that could conceivably account for the fine tuning and, thus, the improved performance.

Although this is a stimulating approach, it must be remembered that the mechanisms they proposed are not rigorously substantiated, nor did they claim them to be. Saarinen and Levi's heuristics, which incidentally ranged from central to peripheral mechanisms, were not specifically supported or rejected by their experimental results, nor did they propose that they should be. Rather, the heuristic speculations represented ingenious and plausible conceptual inventions, stimulated by the data of reasonable experiments. The authors did not make any attempt to identify them as rigorously supported "bridge theories," but simply dealt with them as sources of inspiration for future experiments.

I hope it is now clear that I am not suggesting that heuristic bridges between the neurophysiological and psychophysical domains are completely valueless in the evolution of a science as complex as ours. Like many other stimuli to invention, they provide an interesting and sometimes compelling source of new ideas. A heuristic is one source of new knowledge—an epistemological device—that has been accepted by some as perhaps more characteristic of human thought and learning than any strictly deductive procedure. In the absence of other more robust and rigorously substantiated intellectual bridges, a heuristic can provide a means of crossing an ideational gap by association, by analogy, or by others of the mysterious mental processes that account for so much of human intellectual progress. But, to reiterate, this kind of qualitative stimulation is not the same as an ontological reductionism.

Another way that a comparison of psychophysical and neurophysiological findings can be useful is by providing a means of excluding putative relationships. Although we can never confidently assert that results from these two domains are the true psychoneural equivalents of each other, it is sometimes possible to assert that some neural mechanisms can be excluded as possible mechanisms of a particular perceptual phenomenon. We can exemplify this process by invoking a "reductio ad absurdem" argument. If it were possible to show that vision was possible without the retina, this would exclude the retina as being "necessary" for the visual process. The demonstration that something is not necessary for something else to occur is a powerful and compelling kind of logic.

On the other hand, the retina can be shown to be *necessary* for vision by removing it and discovering that vision no longer occurs. It would be, however, far more difficult, in fact impossible, to demonstrate the *sufficiency* of the retina (remember this is an absurd *Gedanken* experiment) for vision, because removing the other portions of the visual system is an experimental procedure that would obviously destroy the organism being studied.

If one examines some of the visual experiments that I reviewed earlier, it becomes obvious that this is nearly the same logic that is applied there. That is, the attempt to prove that early vision (processes in the early regions of the visual pathway) can account for certain illusions is certainly based on what would be considered to be an erroneous kind of logic in statistics.

There is no way that the hypothesis that the medial temporal region accounts for the McCullough effect, for example, could be tested for sufficiency without the patently impossible ablation of other higher areas of the brain. I hope that this excursion into the impossible and the far-fetched makes clear how frail are some of the bridges constructed by this kind of neuroreductionism.

On the other hand, the demonstration by Roland and Guly'as (1994) that the lower cortical levels are not activated in some kinds of imagery experiments is more influential than the fact that in some other experiments they are. It is more powerful to reject a hypothesis by showing an exception than to accept one by showing an example.

Neuroreductionist Exclusion Experiments—
Some Special Cases

Although the *Gedanken* experiment that I have just described is unlikely to be carried out, it is possible to exclude some hypotheses on the basis of well-designed experiments. One such testable hypothesis emerged from studies in psychophysics and neuroanatomy. The conjecture was that the ocular dominance columns, discovered by Hubel and Wiesel (1965), are the functional loci of stereoscopic perception. This hypothesis was tested and ultimately rejected by Livingstone, Nori, Freeman, and Hubel (1995) in a logically sound and correct use of a very special anatomical situation. They used a squirrel monkey as their subject because this small primate does not have any identifiable ocular dominance columns. However, when tested for stereopsis, the monkey gave visually evoked brain potential responses that suggested that it was, in fact, able to discriminate depth. Thus, the hypothesis that ocular dominance columns were necessary for stereopsis could be rejected.

This analysis is an example of how a hypothesis can be rejected in a sound and logically straightforward way. It is analogous to removing the retina and determining that the specimen animal still could see. In this case, however, a curious anatomic anomaly provided the means of testing a system just as if the key region had been surgically ablated. The demonstration that a particular region was not necessary is convincing proof that the hypothetical association of it with a particular perceptual experience could not be correct.

This is a special case of disconfirmation or rejection of a hypothesis, however. The logic could not have been reversed to confirm an association between the anatomy and the perceptual results. There are several reasons for this lack of reversibility. One practical reason is that there are always many other regions that may be excited by the appropriate stimulus.

There is, of course, one remaining doubt. It is not entirely certain that the perceptual experience is actually reflected by the evoked potential measures used by Livingstone and her colleagues. This qualification notwithstanding, the experiment does illustrate an appropriate and useful comparison of neurophysiological and psychophysical findings.

There are a few other special anatomical situations on which some more or less robust neuroreductionist conclusions or exclusions can be based. The type of experiment to which I refer is often associated with the decussation of visual signals at the optic chiasm. An example of this approach is comprehensively discussed by Breitmeyer (1984), who showed how to use dichoptic (different stimuli to each eye) stimulation to determine if a phenomenon is the result of peripheral processes or must be attributed to more central interactions.

AN OVERVIEW

We have now reviewed a very small sample of the many recent attempts at bridge building between psychophysical and neurophysiological findings. I have attempted, by example, to illustrate some of the logical, theoretical, and empirical pitfalls that impede what is a very significant part of the activities of contemporary perceptual neuroscience from achieving its goals. Notwithstanding these difficulties, the impulse to proceed in a neuroreductionist direction is very powerful and recapitulates a long history of reductionist stirrings during the past 2,500 years of human history. From the time of humankind's earliest attempts to cope with its universe, naturalists, philosophers, and scientists of many different callings have tried to understand the relation between the mind and the body. Given the obviousness of the relationship to each individual at every moment and the traumatic disassociation of the two at the moment of death, this relation has been one of the driving forces of intellectual history. Clearly we are not talking about some minor technical point in the history or philosophy of science, but one of the major concerns of all of humanity. Whether it be the development of a new religion or the modeling of mental processes by whatever technology was available, this is an issue of paramount human importance.

In spite of these historical pressures, it is clear that many, if not most, researchers proposing neuroreductionist correlations are cautiously aware of some of the difficulties and problems that I have raised in earlier parts of this chapter. If it is not explicit, the general unease about the matter is highlighted by the prudent and circumspect language used in describing the implications of their work by even the most radical perceptual neuroreductionists. That there is a general awareness that the bridges being built are fragile indeed is strongly suggested by a tabulation of some of the phrases that have been used in making the hypothetical links, including:

- "Our data provide indirect support"
- "Are probably responsible"

- "Are consistent with"
- "Are not inconsistent with"
- "Are analogous to"
- "[Is] psychophysical evidence for a neural mechanism underlying"
- "It is possible that"
- "Our results indicate," "suggest," "imply"

What is missing from this list, of course, is a simple declarative monistic statement that A *is* B! The caution reflected by these phrases is evidence that, in spite of widespread support for and a strong urge to imply neuroreductionist conclusions, many of my colleagues share with me a hesitation, a concern, and some doubts about the limits of the neuroreductionist enterprise. I think the reason for this hesitation is a general sense of discomfort with the prospects for successful neuroreductionism as well as the usual scientific reticence. It reflects a sometimes vague and sometimes clear awareness that the process of relating neural to mental processes is a far more complicated process, technically and logically, than is evidenced in the typical experimental design or theoretical construction.

The scope of the problem with neuroreductionist efforts can be crystallized into a single quantitative comment. Whenever a perceptual phenomenon occurs, a huge number of neurons are activated by any stimulus, no matter how trivial that stimulus may be. Consider the most basic psychophysical detection experiment. A single quantum of visible light (Hecht, Shaler, & Pirenne, 1942; Sakitt, 1972) with an indivisibly small amount of energy is capable of producing a major perceptual and motor response ("Yes, I saw it"). Obviously, there has been a very wide dispersion and magnification of neural activity from the minute energy levels of the original stimulus. Equally obviously, a wide variety of neurons in many different places in the nervous system is responding with particular coded messages to the ultramicroscopic amount of energy in the stimulus. With all of this ongoing activity, the probability of finding something, somewhere, that correlates with the perceptual experience approaches unity. In fact, it is a little bit hard to imagine that it would not be possible to find almost anything in the multitude of responses that would be needed to flesh out even the least likely neuroreductionist hypothesis. This raises the question of false associations between percepts and neuronal responses, which is rarely, if ever, considered in the postulation of the "linking" theories, modules, and explanations. The matters of false positives, of tautologies, and of self-fulfilling prophesies are certainly not discussed enough.

To overcome the difficulty of a plethora of potential correlates and false associations, secondary criteria are often invoked. Is this the neuron with the lowest threshold? Is this the first identifiable neuron in the visual pathway that explicitly encodes the attribute of the percept under study? Is this the most economical or elegant explanation? Criteria like these, however, lead to other questions that also challenge the reductionist approach. What happens at other levels of the visual pathway? What are other responsive neurons doing even if they are not the ones with lowest threshold or the ones that first seem to explicitly track the stimuli? Finally, why should economy or simplicity be a criterion in a system that values redundancy and adaptability most highly? Lloyd Morgan's canon (the principle of parsimony) may simply not be appropriate in the cognitive neurosciences.

Obviously, too little thought has been given to the logic of the arguments supporting associations between perceptual phenomena and neurophysiological findings. Some day we may look back at this phase of our science with the same retrospective opinion now given to psychosurgery, phlogiston, or the many other kinds of well-intentioned, but ill-advised, theories of nature that have been subsequently rejected in more enlightened times.

To further illuminate the nature of the debate over the applicability of the neuroreductionist approach, in the following sections I consider a number of general questions that have arisen in the presentation of particular experimental details.

Is There Any Such Thing as Early Vision?

The research discussed so far in this chapter is bound together by a number of common underlying premises. One of the most important is the idea that there is some kind of "low-level" or "early" vision that is distinguishable from the attentive, cognitive, interpretative processes that are presumably carried out at higher levels. Although it is difficult to find a specific definition of early vision even in books and articles dedicated to the topic, the list of processes often included is suggestive of the breadth of the term. In one case, Papathomas, Chubb, Gorea, and Kowler (1995) did explicitly provide a list of "important low-level" visual processes: "binocular vision and stereopsis, the perception of movement, visual texture segregation, and attention and learning" (p. x). This is quite an amazing list if one reflects on it for a moment or two. The concept of "low-level attention" is in striking contrast to what many would consider to be the traditional view that assumes that attentive processes (especially) are the result of neural activities at relatively high cortical levels. However, as we have seen earlier, what are sometimes suggested to be low-level "attentive" effects are sometimes justified by the invention of centrifugal mechanisms that project down to modulate the "low-level" or "early" visual processes.

There is, I believe, a major misconception inherent in the entire discussion of low-level vision. This misconception exists because of a lack of clarification and consistency in discussions of the respective transmission and interpretation roles of the visual nervous system. The problem arises when coded activity in the periphery (broadly defined) transmitting information about the stimulus is confused with the high-level psychoneural equivalences where that transmitted neural activity "becomes" or "is" the mental event. I have already argued that the demonstration that the activity pattern of a neuron was associated with some aspect of a stimulus in the periphery should not be interpreted to mean that this is the site of the psychoneural equivalent. Alternatively, such a neural response might be far better identified as a candidate code (Uttal, 1973) that may or may not be conveying useful and, arguably, necessary input information to the higher centers where it becomes mental experience (see the following discussion). By no means should such a neural response be considered to be the locus of the site of the experience itself. The confusion of the transmission capabilities of the nervous system with the representation process where some further transformation of the signal creates the mental experience lies at the heart of what I believe is the fallacious "low-level" vision hypothesis.

It may be that "low-level" has meaning to some neuroscientists beyond its anatomical connotation. For example, Papathomas and his colleagues may have proposed such an inclusive list based on what they believe are relatively simple transformational processes that may occur any place in the brain. Their concept of low-level attention may be different from, for example, problem solving; and their concept of texture processing may connote a process that is somehow simpler than pattern recognition, as another example. In other words, "low-level" may mean *simple* as opposed to *peripheral*, and reflect a hierarchy of complexity rather than of anatomy. However, it is clear that this is not what low-level vision means to many others. In the examples that I have discussed earlier, low-level was clearly an anatomical concept and was specifically associated with such peripheral loci as V1 and V2.

The problem is also closely associated with the sign–code distinction that I raised some years ago (Uttal, 1965, 1967, 1969, 1973), but it is not quite identical. Although we have been discussing the transmission and representation functions, the sign–code distinction is between two possible roles of the transmitted signal. The sign–code distinction asserts that not all variations of neural activity in the ascending sensory pathways are actually decoded or used by the brain. Some dimensions of the signal may simply not be analyzable (or analyzed) by the higher level cortex where the mental process we call perception actually takes place. Signals that are not decoded (e.g., very small intervals) but that are measurable by an experimenter would be considered signs. They are covariant with some aspect of the stimulus, but they have no subsequent perceptual effect. A true code is a neural signal that actually produces some kind of a perceptual effect.

To determine whether a signal is a sign or a true information-bearing code, it is actually necessary to force the nervous signal (typically by external electrical stimulation) into the candidate pattern of activity and ask the ultimate final interpreter of the neural encoding—the human observer—if the variation in the signal can be discriminated from one not containing the variation. If it is not so discriminable, then although interesting and useful to the neurophysiologist in determining the properties of the receptor or some other peripheral portion of the pathway, the measured neural response fluctuation is merely a sign, unused by the higher levels of the brain, and without psychoneural significance. If it is perceptually discriminated, it is a true code signaling some aspect of the stimulus to the highest level interpreters. The term *candidate code* is reserved for any neural response that varies with some aspect of the stimulus, but that has not yet been determined to be either a sign or a code.

Pamela Smith and I (Uttal & Smith, 1967) carried out such an experiment. We determined that interpulse irregularity (i.e., the standard deviation of the intervals) of a train of electrical stimuli was discriminable even when the average interpulse interval was kept constant. Recent attempts to study this same problem from a purely neurophysiological point of view (Ferster & Spruston, 1995) by observing the irregularity of a naturally occurring spike train will always be challenged by the need for some criterion measure. There is, as yet, no "detector" equivalent to the human psychophysical response to evaluate whether interpulse irregularity is a sign or a code in the preparations they used.

There is no question that there are neurons tuned or selectively sensitive to certain highly specific spatial or temporal attributes of the visual stimulus at many levels of the nervous system. There is, equally well, no question that the signals ascending the visual pathway interact in ways that not only account for the specific sensitivities of these neurons, but also modify and modulate the message that is carried by these signals. The sources of these differential sensitivities range from the photochemical differences in the retinal receptors to the specific organizational details of the arrangements of networks of neurons in subsequent levels of the visual system. This level of physiological data and interpretation is incontestable; it represents a statement of raw neurophysiological observations. If one is using the term *low-level vision* to refer to the processing of afferent signals by the neurons and neural networks of the near periphery, then there is little to argue about.

Argument does arise, however, when perceptual phenomena are attributed to low-level mechanisms per se—that is, when we speak of low-level vision as if the activity of certain neurons in the peripheral pathway *is* the psychoneural equivalent of the perceptual phenomena. Although this may seem to many to be something of an overstatement of what is actually going on in contemporary theoretical circles, many authors do implicitly accept the notion that because some representation or coded form of some attribute or transformation of the signal is observable at some point in the ascending visual pathway, that point is the locus of the necessary and sufficient activity that is the equivalent of the experience.

What I have been suggesting in this chapter is that although the necessity (to transmit information) of relatively low levels of the visual pathway is certain, its sufficiency (to instantiate the perceptual experience) is highly unlikely. This is the crux of the misinterpretation of a considerable amount of thought about the problem of the relationship between neural activity and perceptual experience. When some of my colleagues attempt to link the perceptual experience with low-level processing, they are confusing the transmission and interpretation roles of two very different parts of the nervous system.

Especially disturbing to any implicit hypothesis concerning the role of early vision as a direct psychoneural equivalent of perception is the role played by attention or perceptual organization. The findings and data are abundant that processes that all would agree are among the most intricately encoded of our high-level cognitive processes (e.g., meaning) can modulate the effects of some otherwise simple stimuli. For example, the illusions produced by the master mime Marcelle Marceau can distort our perceptions of time and space in wonderful ways. The indications of "cognitive penetrability" are also ubiquitous in the psychophysical literature, from the apparent reversal of the Neckar cube (1832) to the estimation of the concavity or convexity of an image (Ramachandran, 1988). All such examples demonstrate that vision is not determined by the stimulus or simple algorithmic peripheral processes alone. It is only when the transmitted neural signals are processed and interpreted at some higher level that the message they carry becomes the psychoneural equivalent of a perceptual experience. From this point of view, the whole idea of early vision becomes questionable.

Indeed, it is not only the transformation of input signals to perceptual experience by cognitive (whatever that means neurophysiologically) processes that makes this point, but also the fact that even some of the most primitive aspects of visual perception are determined by their relationships with their surround in a way that may exceed by far the influence of the physical properties of the stimulus. For example, the hue of a given wavelength can be strongly influenced by its surround. The simultaneous color contrast phenomenon is a simple example of this sort of influence, as are the more extensive demonstrations of the "Mondrian" color effects reported by Land (1959a, 1959b, 1977). Similarly, as mentioned earlier, the lightness of an object is determined by its figural role in the stimulus scene—another high-level influence on the perceptual outcome of the attributes of the stimulus (Adelson, 1993; Gilchrist, 1977).

Ex post facto attempts to explain away "cognitive penetrability" by assuming that centrifugal activity modulates the peripheral response are unconvincing patches onto an otherwise failing theory. This does not mean that the idea that higher centers influence lower centers has to be rejected in its entirety. It is quite plausible to accept the suggestion that central activity can modulate or modify the sensitivity of peripheral structures. Afferent synapses are known to exist even on receptor neurons. What it does mean is that the modulated peripheral transmitted signal in the periphery is *not* the essential necessary and sufficient activity underlying the perceptual experience.

A cleaner and more parsimonious explanation (than the early vision suggestion) of the psychoneurally significant ensemble of neural processes underlying perception is that the ascending signals are merely transmitting the necessary sensory information to higher levels where the attentional or organizational factors are (a) intermixed with, (b) combined with, or (c) modulated to produce a pattern of neural network activity that is the real neural equivalent of the perceptual experience. It is at this level, and only at this level, that the critical and complex network events occur that can account for perceptual experience. According to this hypothesis, nothing equivalent to perception occurs peripherally.

I have already discussed a closely related point. That is, a neurophysiological recording that explicitly indicates for the first time in the ascending pathway some correlation with some property of the stimulus has no special theoretical or explanatory potency. The same message must have been encoded both earlier and later. The alternative—"early vision"—is a vestige of an earlier time when single-neuron encoding was supposed to have some special significance. Equally good codes can be conceived of, if not measured, instantiated in the population statistics of large networks of neurons at all levels of the nervous system.

What could have contributed to this misinterpretation of the role played by peripheral visual elements, as well as to the invention of the "low-level" vision hypothesis? It is hard to track the genesis of such ideas, but I have a suspicion that it may have had its origins in one of the classic controversies in cognitive psychology that I discuss more fully in chapter 4. For many years (see pp. 161–163 of chapter 4) there has been a dispute among cognitive psychologists over the nature of the representation of mental images. On the one side were those who said that images were stored in an pictorial or pictographic fashion. A perceived square was literally represented by a "square" arrangement of activity in the cortex. In other words, the shape of the representation was isomorphic to the shape of the original image. Proponents of the other side of the controversy argued that, on the contrary, the representation of any pattern was in a propositional form in which symbolic rather than isomorphic spatial codes were used. A square in this case might be represented by a set of construction rules, or something more akin to a linguistic structure.

Ignoring for the moment the possibility that this issue cannot be resolved, I only note that there has been vigorous support among many psychophysicists for the pictographic type of representation. The works of Shepard and Metzler (1971) and Kosslyn (1980, 1995) are among the most notable. Obviously the pictographic theories would be buttressed by the discovery of actual retinotopic or other forms of isomorphic neural patterns in the brain. Equally obviously, there was and remains little hope of finding such spatial congruences in the higher levels of the cortex, where the neural activity is so complex that it is unlikely to ever be examined in any manner that would expose spatial patterns that are isomorphic to the spatial stimuli. However, pictographic, isomorphic, and retinotopic representations are found in the lower levels, particularly in V1 and V2. It was a short jump, therefore, from a theoretical commitment to pictographic representation to the suggestion that the isomorphisms observed in the periphery were, in fact, the equivalents of the mental images.

Furthermore, it was all too easy to ignore two other salient ideas:

1. The isomorphic images observed in the more peripheral portions of the cerebral cortex may simply have been patterns of transmitted activity and not the psychoneural equivalents of the perceptual experiences.

2. Some attributes of images, such as greenness, cannot be encoded isomorphically.

The predilection for pictographic representations of cognitive processes such as perception and the presence of peripheral retinotopic representation may have conjoined to produce the erroneous conclusion that there was something called "low-level vision." The alternative hypothesis, that all of the neural activity that is important to representing images (or anything else) is to be found in the higher (and unobservably complex) levels of the nervous system, was simply ignored as many fragile comparisons were made between relatively peripheral (but observable) patterns of neural activity and perceptual experiences.

Logic such as this also led to such peculiar notions as the re-creation of isomorphic spatial representations in V1 or V2 when one imagined a scene. Obviously, there is no need for such an extraordinary suggestion if symbolic central representations are acceptable as a complete explanation of perceptual experience. In both cases, preexisting assumptions of pictographic representations led theorists both erroneously and implacably to demonstrably retinotopic, but irrelevant, regions and to far-fetched means of reconstructing imagined patterns in those regions.

The important point to be made here is that even though it is possible to decode the properties of the peripheral nervous system and see some similarities between these transmission codes and some perceptual experience, that should not be interpreted to mean that the psychoneural equivalent of the experience is localized there. The problem, as noted earlier, is that there is far too frequently a confusion of the transmission codes and the actual representation processes.

The Preattentive–Attentive Dichotomy

Closely related to the low-level (early) versus high-level vision terminology is the attentive–preattentive dichotomy. The general concepts denoted by the terms *preattentive* and *attentive* are easily definable in a psychological context. The term *preattentive* describes perceptual processes that occur automatically without effortful attention. Preattentive processes are often associated, correctly or incorrectly, with relatively simple, low-level neural mechanisms that operate in a bottom-up manner. The term *attentive* describes perceptual processes that are better explained as the function of very complex neural networks operating at relatively high levels of the nervous system. Attentive processes are not automatic; they require effortful attention and scrutiny.

The distinction between attentive and preattentive is exemplified in terms of certain search behaviors. In some situations, objects seem to "pop out" of a scene with very little mental effort. For example, a red object in a field of green objects can be located with very brief reaction times and little cognitive effort. This immediate response seems to be a result of visual mechanisms that effortlessly, automatically—in other words, preattentively—segregate the odd-colored item from the background. On the other hand, finding a particular target letter (e.g., a vowel in a field of consonants) requires that the searcher pay strict and serial attention to the material. Target letters do not "pop out." Instead, the list must be effortfully scrutinized nearly item by item to locate and identify it. It is for this reason that copyediting is such a difficult task and why misprints are found in even the best books.

It has been suggested that one factor that accounts for the errors in attentive search is that the configurational attributes of letters (the critical cue in their case) differ less than do the color attributes of a set of objects. As I say this, I appreciate that I have not defined the dimension along which "more" or "less" is measured. In any case, there appear to be major differences in the behavior involved in the two tasks. We know very little about the underlying processes and mechanisms, only that the superficial behavior is different. My guess, however, is that both attentive and preattentive cognitive processing of the kind discussed here is actually mediated by relatively high-level mechanisms.

The Top-Down/Bottom-Up Dichotomy

There is another direction from which some of the ideas underlying many neuroreductionist controversies can be examined. That is the difference in the basic paradigms of what has come to be known as the "bottom-up" and the "top-down" schools of thought. Adherents to "bottom-up" psychobiological philosophy prefer to think of many of the early, low-level, preattentive aspects of vision as reflecting the operation of deterministic systems reflecting the function of more or less fixed neural nets. Bottom-up reductionists look to the relatively well-ordered portions of the peripheral nervous system to explain, by means of computation-like and algorithmic-like mechanisms, a broad class of visual phenomena. Perceptual phenomena are attributed to the action of such specific neural mechanism as lateral inhibitory neural interactions or convergence.

Top-down—oriented perceptual scientists, on the other hand, prefer to emphasize the attentional, interpretive, cognitive, reconstructive, and organizational influences on perception. These processes, far less well defined than the bottom-up mechanism, are presumed to be the function of neural nets of such complexity that we are probably never going to be able to understand them in detail. Therefore, the molar language of psychology becomes the linguistic currency in their description.

The tendency in much of contemporary cognitive neuroscience to approach perceptual problems from a bottom-up point of view is extremely pervasive. It is not popular, nowadays, to challenge the "early vision" hypothesis. But psychologists of a more classic top-down persuasion do continue to assert that the symbolic aspects of a stimulus may be extremely influential in determining what we see. If one turns from the pages of a journal that has traditionally supported the bottom-up approach (e.g., *Vision Research*) to one that has emphasized the top-down approach (e.g., *Perception*), the transition from one scientific culture to the other becomes evident.

This clash of cultures, which I believe may be even more influential in determining one's choice of theoretical direction than one's empirical results, is obviously not likely to be resolved soon. There is a very large number of findings and results from both sides, and almost any plausible theory can find some support. The weight given to any particular set of data depends on things other than the data themselves. One does not have to delve very deeply into the literature to see that there are many reports showing that our perceptual experience is not rigidly defined by the stimulus or low-level mechanisms. On the other hand, there is a very impressive body of new findings that seem to show that critical events happening in the periphery do continue to have influence at what are presumably higher levels of the nervous system. Evidence for cognitive penetration is ubiquitous; however, so, too, are analogs of peripheral neural mechanisms that seem to mimic reported visual experiences.

Illusions as the Perceptual Fruit Fly

It is interesting that researchers who are seeking to characterize visual mechanisms as either low-level or high-level, as attentive or preattentive, or as early or late vision have turned so often to illusions as the medium for their experiments. Illusions are defined as discrepant perceptual responses to stimuli. Illusions, therefore, represent failures in veridicality of the visual system: An illusion occurs when the percept is not in agreement with the physical or geometrical attributes of the stimulus. Despite their reputations as "failures" of perceptual mechanisms, illusions do reflect the action of processes and operations that themselves may have some other very useful properties. Illusions distort physical reality in ways that help us to organize our visual worlds. For example, illusions of size and shape constancy help us to estimate the true shape or size of an object even when it is grossly distorted or magnified. Other illusions serve less obvious functions, but may simply be the inadvertent and concomitant result of meeting the needs of some other perceptual requirement.

Illusions tend to be very compelling. Sometimes they are even resistant to repeated demonstrations that they cannot be true representations of the stimulus scene. One has only to consider such a familiar illusion as the Muller–Lyer effect to appreciate how compelling is this perceptual error of figural length. Take a ruler, measure the respective lengths, convince yourself that the two lines are of equal length and then reexamine the stimulus. The illusion remains as strong as it was initially. In this case, there is little cognitive penetration.

Illusions of this sort are very useful just because of their stability. Therefore, they play the same role that the fruit fly did in biological studies of genetics—a stable, minimal model system that can be manipulated in many different ways to study the influence of a variety of independent variables and conditions on their perception. Recent favorite "fruit-fly" illusions for perceptual research have been the McCullough effect, the Neon spreading effect, the Mach band, and the Hermann grid.

Explanations for the existence, as well as the elicitation, of visual illusions has varied over the full range of possible explanatory theories. However, in spite of their apparent simplicity and their familiarity, illusions remain profound challenges to our explanatory powers, neuroreductionist or otherwise. These phenomena, superficially so simple, have been interpreted as the result of both low-level (Ginsberg, 1983) and high-level (Gregory, 1963;

Woodworth, 1938) neural mechanisms. Illusions occur in many types of visual situations. This is not the place for a full review of the topic of these violations of perceptual veridicality. The reader is referred elsewhere (Coren & Girgus, 1978; Gregory & Gombrich, 1973; Luckiesh, 1965; Robinson, 1972; Tolansky, 1964; Uttal, 1981a) for reviews of the phenomena themselves.

According to some perceptual scientists, all perceptual phenomena are illusory. This is the ultimate "top-down" approach. It asserts that all visual experiences are the results of reconstructive processes carried out at a very high level. Herman von Helmholtz (1821–1894) formulated the concept of "unconscious inference." Warren and Warren (1968) quoted him as saying:

> Now we have exactly the same case in our sense-perceptions. When those nervous mechanisms whose terminals lie on the right-hand portions of the retinas of the two eyes have been stimulated, our usual experience, repeated a million times all through life, has been that a luminous object was over there in front of us on our left. We had to lift the hand toward the left to hide the light or to grasp the luminous object; or we had to move toward the left to get closer to it. Thus, while in these cases no particular conscious conclusion may be present, yet the essential and original office of such a conclusion has been performed, and the result of it has been attained; simply, of course, by the unconscious processes of association of ideas going on in the dark background of our memory. Thus, too, its results are urged on our consciousness, so to speak, as if an external power had constrained us over which our will has no control.
>
> These inductive conclusions leading to the formation of our sense-perceptions certainly do lack the purifying and scrutinizing work of conscious thinking. Nevertheless, in my opinion, by their peculiar nature they may be classed as *conclusions*, inductive conclusions unconsciously formed. (p. 195)

Percepts, from this point of view, do not represent strict algorithmic transformations from the stimulus to the response, but rather are the decodings and interpretations of the meaning of heavily encoded and symbolic representations of the information impinging on receptors. Furthermore, they are heavily compromised or modified by the addition of "noise" (i.e., information, such as that stored in memory, that was not in the stimulus), from expectations, and from adaptive states, as well as from the many levels of neural transformation and processing they undergo as they pass up the afferent pathway.

It is not too much of a stretch of theory to assume then that all precepts are illusions in the sense that they are not directly determined by the stimulus and are, therefore, discrepant, illusory, or interpretive reconstructions of the stimulus scene. Indeed, according to this point of view, nothing is directly determined by the stimulus. Everything is so indirect and mediated by a series of transformations and interpretations that it is amazing that we are able to respond adaptively to events in our environment. If that is the case, then the idea that these perceptual "fruit flies" are really as simple as they may seem may be further from reality than many of us are willing to admit.

At an even deeper level of personal philosophy, such an interpretation leads us to a rather lonely and chilling thought. Perhaps we are all far more isolated from the external world than we had thought. Perhaps we (or whatever it is that corresponds to our self-awareness) are isolated sentiences at the end of a long series of codes and transformations. Perhaps our contact with the world is far more of an illusion itself than we would like to believe. A lonely thought, but a logical deduction from the idea of sensory codes and such concepts as cognitive reconstruction and unconscious inference.

Single Neurons and Population Statistics

Another dichotomous theme permeating much of the work that characterizes contemporary neuroreductionism is the tension between representation by single neurons, on the one hand, and by the population statistics of large arrays of neurons on the other. Despite the fact that the idea of population statistics has gained considerable currency, there is still plentiful theoretical attention paid to the idea that a single neuron can represent a complex idea or object—an observation clearly substantiated by the sampling of studies considered earlier in this chapter.

There is no doubt that the single-neuron theoretical orientation is driven by the technology of laboratory neurophysiological research. The tool, par excellence, for studying neurons is the microelectrode. But, however excellent, this device is not without its own shortcomings and constraining limitations. A microelectrode is sensitive only to the electrical signals that are localized to a single point in space over a period of time. Indeed, if properly placed, it may be sensitive only to the activity of a single neuron. Nevertheless, this highly specialized technology has profoundly affected the *zeitgeist* among neuroreductionists, one that is heavily directed toward the neuron *cum* neuron as the arbiter of perceptual experience. What I am suggesting is that the technology has forced the development of theory and explanation in a way that may be at odds with the biological reality of the nervous system.

This assertion that technology was and will remain prominent in defining our explanatory models does not deny that there may also be some real psychobiological forces driving the emphasis on single neurons in many of today's theories. Neurons do, for example, individually exhibit specific sensitivities to specific features of a stimulus. A rich history of demonstrations of selective spatiotemporal sensitivities of neurons, dating from the pioneering work of Hubel and Wiesel (1959) and Lettvin, Maturana, McCullough, and Pitts (1959), has also contributed to this emphasis. These data are not second-order theoretical interpretations; they are raw, first-order data and must be taken seriously.

Furthermore, no one can dispute the fact that the brain is made up of discrete anatomical units whose actions and interactions provide the ultimate foundation for mental phenomena. The controversy, therefore, must ultimately revolve around the emphasis that is placed on individual cellular *action* as opposed to population or network *interaction*.

Given the powerful impulse from the microelectrode technology and the resulting kinds of neurophysiological data that are obtained, it is understandable how individual neurons became the foundation of a great deal of theory when neuroreductionists attempted to link perceptual phenomena with the known properties of neurons. The phrase "Hubel and Wiesel" became almost a mystical incantation in the 1970s whenever perceptual psychophysicists tried to explain their findings in neurophysiological terms.

Perhaps the most extreme theoretical extension of the associationist and elementalist ideas implicit in a single-neuron theory of perception was postulated by Konorski. Konorski (1967) attempted to extend the neurophysiological observations of Hubel and Wiesel to explain much more complex psychological processes than simple spatiotemporal trigger sensitivity. He assumed that the visual system was organized into an extended hierarchy in which increasingly complex integration of the incoming information ultimately led to neurons of "cognitive complexity." Ultimately, these integrative processes culminated in a neuron (or small set of similar neurons) that was actually capable of what Konorski called "Gnostic" functions. Such Gnostic neurons, he further assumed, were actively formed by plastic neural mechanisms that are the biological equivalents of the molar process we call learning. The essential part of Konorski's theory was that all psychological processes, no matter how complex, can be understood in terms of the activity of single neurons that are conceptually identical in function and organization to the single neurons hypothesized to underlie feature sensitivity in the more peripheral portions of the visual system. They just had more complex activating triggers.

A more recent impetus to the development of single-neuron theories came from some startling work in which specific shapes and objects were found to activate what appeared to be neurons with extremely finely tuned sensitivities. For example, Gross, Rocha-Miranda, and Bender (1972) reported that there were neurons in the monkey's infero-temporal cortex that were specifically activated when it was shown its own hand. Similarly, Gross (1992) and Perrett, Heitanen, Oram, and Benson (1992) (among others) reported later that there were neurons in the temporal cortex that were specifically activated by "face" stimuli.

In all of these cases the specificity of the neural responses was so great that even slight modifications of the triggering stimulus greatly reduced the neuronal responsiveness. This is powerful stuff, indeed, if one is committed to a strong role for single neurons in the visual process.

Perhaps the best recent summary of this "neuron doctrine" can be found in an article by Barlow (1995). His argument for the priority of the individual neuron in the representation of a perceptual experience cannot be summed up in a few words, but a few key ideas presented in his summary help to understand some of the more important bases for the "neuron doctrine" as he saw it.

1. Neurons are much more pattern selective and reliable than was formerly believed (p. 430).
2. Neurons collect and combine information impinging on their synapses, generate a signal when a criterion is exceeded, and transmit this to other neurons in the brain (p. 431).

The interested reader will find that, to his credit and in spite of his radical single-neuron theoretical stance, Barlow himself raised many of the same problems and issues that I alluded to here and in my previous books to challenge the single-neuron doctrine. For the moment, however, some commentary on these two critical points may help to clarify my objections to the single-neuron doctrine of perceptual representation.

Let's deal first with the argument that neurons are "more pattern selective than previously believed." From a very general point of view, this is probably not sustainable as an argument for single-neuron representation. The characteristic nature of the response of virtually any neuron is that it is broadly tuned to variations in its trigger feature. From the absorption curves of the photoreceptors to the orientation tuning of cortical neurons, broadly tuned sensitivities are the rule, rather than narrowly tuned ones. No one, to my knowledge, has reported neuron tuning curves for any sensory dimension that comes close to the ultrafine tuning exhibited by the corresponding perceptual process. At this very basic level, therefore, one has to assume that fine perceptual discriminations must be mediated by the statistics of many neurons rather than by the fine tuning of individual ones.

There is another interpretation that can be given to Barlow's discussion. Perhaps he was referring to those recent reports that there seems to be very specific tuning for faces or hands in primate cortex. I believe, however, that these exciting, charming, and dramatic findings are among the most misleading set of scientific data presented in recent years.

Clarification of the real meaning of this kind of data has come from the laboratory of Tanaka (1993) in his implementation of what has to be considered a paradigmatic giant step forward in conceptualizing perceptual science. Like Gross and his colleagues and Perrett and his, Tanaka and his colleagues found inferotemporal neurons that seemed to have very specific sensitivities to such things as the head of a toy tiger. But, rather than calling this a "tiger head encoding neuron," Tanaka then proceeded to progressively simplify the stimulus. That is, he broke it down into progressively more abstract caricatures. In this manner he showed that the neuron was not specific to tiger heads per se. Instead, it had a general (and not very specific) sensitivity to geometrical stimuli that consisted of a white square (a head?) with a pair of black rectangles (ears?) superimposed on it. In other words, there was a generalized geometrical trigger for this neuron; the tiger's head simply satisfied these relatively abstract criteria better than any other tested stimulus form.

In another case, Tanaka found that a neuron that was presumed to be very sensitive to a human face was actually triggered by only a small part of the face—the lips. But, again, it was not that lips per se were important. Surprisingly, the side of a horizontal red pepper also included the real trigger for that neuron's activation—a red region broken into two lip-like parts.

Clearly, the method of progressively simplifying the images that Tanaka developed brings clarity to an otherwise badly misunderstood set of data. These neurons are not "tiger's head," "hand," or "face" sensitive neurons. They are just neurons that have a somewhat more complicated, but still broadly tuned, geometrical sensitivity to a particular stimulus pattern than do the classic simple, complex, and hypercomplex neurons discovered by Hubel and Wiesel. There is nothing extraordinarily startling about these neurons; they just represent a higher step in the hierarchical organization of spatiotemporal sensitivities now well known to exist at lower levels of the visual pathway. The mechanism accounting for this increased complexity is likely to be nothing other than the convergence of the lower level sensitivities on this higher level neuron. They are so general that the general organization attributes of complex stimuli can satisfy their trigger criteria. Whatever may happen later in the visual pathway, the suggestion that there are neurons specifically sensitive to faces in the inferotemporal cortex is seriously challenged by Tanaka's ingenious methodology.

What are we to make of this new understanding of the role of these inferotemporal neurons? I suggest that they must now be considered to be evidence for some kind of ensemble statistical representation rather than for the single-neuron doctrine that they were originally used to support.

Tanaka (1993) went on to present some additional findings that showed that the neurons in the inferotemporal cortex were arranged, again not surprisingly, in the form of columns. Vertical projections of the microelectrodes into the macaque monkey cortex in this region showed that the same sensitivities existed in most neurons in the column. This recapitulates findings in lower levels such as V1 and V2. But again the sensitivities were general and abstract and not specific to anything as specialized as a face, a hand, or even the classic grandmother or yellow Volkswagen. What allows us to recognize grandmother is, more likely, a statistical distribution of activity in an enormous number and variety of these generalized neurons. It almost has to be that way, given the basic fact that it is not a single neuron that responds to any given stimulus, but an enormous number of neurons scattered throughout the nervous system. This what we mean by an *ensemble response* in which the relative activity of many neurons defines a precise perceptual response.

That biological reality is now beginning to be exhibited in the form of exciting new neurophysiological data. Deadwyler and Hampson (1995) reviewed some of the new results that demonstrate how ensemble activity can be observed by appropriate statistical analysis of recordings from multiple electrode arrays. Using a well-defined learning task (matching to sample) they were able to demonstrate coherent spatiotemporal patterns of neural activity in hippocampal neurons. This coherent correlated activity was not observable in any single unit activity, even if that single neuron was one of the set that was simultaneously examined. Thus, the single-neuron activity, by itself, was not a meaningful code for the learning behavior exhibited in their preparation.

This brings up a general and very important issue. I contend that the interpretation of data from the neurophysiological laboratory is itself a theory-driven activity. The meaning of an experimental finding can and does vary from time to time. Data may be very reliable and yet may have a very different meaning at some later time. Indeed, as we have seen, the same data may be interpreted to support the opposite sides of the same controversy at different times in scientific history. In a field of inquiry as complex and multivariate as the one we are discussing here, it is absolutely necessary to separate the interpretation of a finding from the finding itself.

The Fourier Fallacy

The idea that distinct neuroanatomic channels exist in the nervous system and individually convey information about the specific spatial frequency components of a stimulus image is closely related to the neuron doctrine just discussed. It differs, however, in that the elements of this theoretical structure are often anatomically less well-defined entities than are the clearly demarcatable neurons. Spatial filter channel theories, however, are similar in attributing an analytic function to particular parts of the nervous system and thus are also highly localized, even microscopically localized, place theories.

Spatial frequency theories of this type are usually linked closely to the mathematics of the classic Fourier theorem. This mainstay of mathematical analysis asserted that any function that met certain conditions of continuity and superimposition could be analyzed into a set of sinusoidal functions of varying frequency and amplitude. Conversely, the theorem asserted that one could always find a subset of sinusoidal functions that could be added together to reproduce any waveform.

The use of sinusoids as the set of orthogonal functions that could be superimposed to produce other waveforms (or that would result from the application of the Fourier theorem) is not unique. Other orthogonal sets are now used, including Gabor functions (Gabor, 1946; A. B. Watson, 1987a, 1987b), Fourier descriptors (Cosgriff, 1960), wavelets (Daubechies, 1988; Mallat, 1989), and even sets of Gaussian curves (Poggio & Girossi, 1990). Although the computational details and the type of functions used in each of these analytical techniques differ, the general principle is the same—complex functions or signals can be separated into or created from the summation of a set of simpler functions. Mathematically this provides a powerful means of describing one- and two-dimensional signals, with the latter, of course, including visual images.

The mathematics of this kind of analysis is well developed and can unequivocally be used as a means of defining stimuli and analyzing results in psychophysical experiments. There is no question that it is a powerful descriptive tool in vision science. However, an important new addition beyond this descriptive use of Fourier analysis was introduced when it was suggested that the nervous system might be literally organized as a multichannel Fourier analytical system to account for two-dimensional pattern perception. This hypothesis assumed that the afferent nervous system consisted of a number of quasi-anatomic channels, each of which was selectively sensitive to a particular spatial frequency. This idea is opposed to the theory that one channel, differentially sensitive to the various spatial frequencies, underlay visual form perception. According to the channel model, form would be encoded by the relative amount of activity in the various channels, just as color was supposed to be encoded by the relative amount of activity among the three photochemically defined chromatic channels.

The application of Fourier theory to vision was originally suggested by Kabrisky (1966) as a mathematical model of the vision system. Later the idea was enhanced by some psychophysical results (selective adaptation of spatial frequency stimuli) obtained by Campbell and Robson (1968). Subsequently elaborated as a physiological theory by Blakemore and Campbell (1969), among many others, it has attracted an enormous amount of attention in the past three decades. Many attempts have been made to find physiological and anatomical correlates of the channels. Complete discussions of these topics can be found in De Valois and De Valois (1988) and in Graham (1989).

In spite of the extreme popularity of the Fourier approach, it is very important to note that the perceptual–neurophysiological Fourier theory goes far beyond the idea inherent in the mathematical analysis. There is no question, as I have noted, that Fourier analysis can be successfully be used to represent functions in some descriptive sense. But Kabrisky's (1966) and Blakemore and Campbell's (1969) original hypothesis goes far beyond the original analytic mathematics. In their case it is an anatomical and physiological proposition asserting the existence of a Fourier analyzing mechanism within the nervous system.

One overwhelming difficulty with the Fourier anatomical and physiological model is that the very generality of the mathematics (anything can, in theory, be represented by an appropriate set of orthogonal functions) means that it could hardly fail to work when describing a stimulus image, the response, or for that matter a set of physiological data. Therefore, it is imperative to distinguish between the mathematical analyzability of a function and the anatomical presence of a neural mechanism within the nervous system that actually implements that analysis to authenticate the neuroreductive theory. This is easier said than done.

It is also extremely interesting to note that the classic sinusoidal set of orthogonal functions used in the original Kabrisky and the Campbell and Robson models have gradually been replaced as new sets of more physiologically appropriate orthogonal components have been proposed. Nowadays, it is no longer a system of sinusoids that captures theoretical attention, but a system of Gabor patches or Fourier descriptors, each of which more closely resembles the receptive fields of retinal neurons than do the broad-area sinusoidal filters, that is invoked as the neurophysiological mechanism. Just as with the older technologies, the explanatory mechanism of choice seems to change with the availability of whatever new idea comes along.

There are other difficulties that have been raised about the Fourier theories over the years. Not unexpectedly, the empirical literature is mixed with regard to the applicability of the model. I could not begin to review all of the data that speak to this issue, and if I just selected those discrepant reports that support my counterargument, I would be applying the same kind of fallacious logic that I have criticized earlier.

There are, however, some key general arguments that can be made. In its earliest form, Fourier perceptual theory proposed spatial frequency channels that were not localized but, in accord with the mathematics, could be influenced by an appropriately tuned spatial frequency stimulating any point in the visual field. There is little evidence of a neural element with a field as broad as the entire retina. Nevertheless, the pure Fourier theory hypothesized an entire set of them with sensitivities peaking at many spatial frequencies. This posed a serious problem for the model. Later suggestions that a set of Gabor type filters (sinusoids localized by being convolved with a Gaussian function) partially overcame this difficulty, but raised another problem. The Gabor filters became very much like the Sinc function, a general-purpose curve-fitting device that can be used to model or analyze any image or function. Again, the proposed model was so powerful mathematically that it could represent anything and would always work, regardless of the actual anatomical reality.

A more serious criticism of the basic idea of Fourier analysis is that the components must be linear and superimpositionable. This means that one should be able to simply add up the values of the relevant components of the orthogonal set to arrive at the value of the composite function. However, it is well known that the visual system is nonlinear in many ways. Discrepancies and illusions, automatic gain controls, and other nonveridicalities are characteristic of spatial vision. All of these aberrations point to the strongly nonlinear nature of signal processing in vision. The basic incompatibility between the requirement for linearity in the model and the strong evidence for nonlinearity in the neuroscientific literature suggest that the model, although interesting and convenient for some purposes, is not well suited as a guide to understanding vision in terms of its most fundamental premises. Nevertheless, getting Fourier thinking out of the *zeitgeist* will be a formidable task.

Another difficulty with the Fourier model is a feature often forgotten by novices: The full mathematical development of the procedure not only requires that the power or energy in each putative channel be encoded, but also that the phase relations between the channels be preserved. Otherwise, two very different pictures could have the same power spectra and look alike, and yet be very different. "Channels" encoding the phase relations of the Fourier components of an image are still elusive in the neurophysiological literature.

The point is that the Fourier approach, and for that matter all other models that proposed real neural feature detectors or analyzers of any kind, was much too powerful and could mathematically model what did not physically exist. It was all too easy to use it imprudently. Just as with mathematics in general, it introduced superfluous meaning and descriptions that were misinterpreted as real neural mechanisms rather than as mathematical fictions. Like the single-neuron doctrine, the discrete spatial frequency channel hypothesis has probably outlived its usefulness.

For example, there exist instances in which the application of the Fourier model does not fully explain empirical phenomena in spite of some preliminary successes. My colleagues and I (Uttal, Baruch, & Allen, 1995a, 1995b, 1997) showed that the classic Harmon and Julesz (1972) spatial frequency explanation of the effect of cascaded degradations does not hold for all image sizes and tasks. Therefore, the Fourier approach fails to generalize to other than the specific and limited conditions under which the Harmon and Julesz data were originally collected.

In conclusion, while there is no argument that the Fourier mathematical tool will continue to be a powerful tool for describing and manipulating data and results, it is probably inadequate as a basis for a general theory of the anatomical and physiological mechanisms underlying a wide variety of visual phenomena.

Are "Neural" Theories Really Neural?

Another issue has concerned me for some years. Many theories that are presented as neural theories can, on closer examination, be seen to actually be something less than that. Many are actually nothing more than mathematical descriptions clothed in some neural terminology. To make this point clear, consider the phenomenon know as metacontrast. Just as the subjective contour and the McCullough effect are extremely popular perceptual "fruit flies" for the study of vision today, metacontrast served the same role as a vehicle for testing theories a couple of decades ago.

Metacontrast is a backward masking phenomenon in which flanking stimuli inhibit the perception of a preceding stimulus. The phenomenon was and is still of interest because of the paradoxical nature of the interaction. Events occurring as long as 80 msec after a stimulus could suppress that earlier stimulus. (A full discussion of the phenomenon can be found in Uttal, 1988.)

My interest in theories of the metacontrast phenomenon was stimulated by a trio of theoretical explanations that had been proposed to explain it. (For details see Breitmeyer & Ganz, 1976; Bridgeman, 1971; Weisstein, 1972; Weisstein, Ozog, & Szoc, 1975.) All were "neural" theories in terminology and by specific intent. Each was based on a particular neural mechanism such as lateral inhibitory interaction or channels of differing speed of conduction. The startling and annoying fact was that, in spite of their quite different neural assumptions, all three theories fit the data fairly well. All three predicted the wave of perceptual inhibition peaking at about the appropriate time and with the proper shape. A closer examination of the three models revealed another surprise—all three consisted of very similar mathematical formulations. Each proposed a function that involved manipulating two parameters; that is, each was a formula with two degrees of freedom!

It occurred to me that all three theories were what mathematicians call "duals of each other." That is, although their formulations were slightly different (as were the premises on which they were based), each of the three theories was formally equivalent to the other two. In spite of their vastly different neural assumptions, the essential formal parts of the three theories were identical. This suggested that the neural parts of the mathematical theory were nonessential for either the formularization or the fitted curves that resulted from evaluating the equations!

In fact, the neural assumptions could be stripped away completely from the mathematical assumptions without requiring changes in any of the theories. The neural assumptions were simply extra baggage that did not affect the predictability of the theories in any way. The key, and unifying factor, among the three theories was that all of them involved mathematical equations requiring only two degrees of freedom to control their course and replicate the shape of the relatively simple response curves that had been generated by the respective psychophysical experiments. The neural heuristics that served as the source of the equations with three degrees of freedom differed, but in fact the mathematical models could be derived one from the other.

This line of thought led to the further conclusion that none of these "neural" theories were neural at all. They were, in fact, curve-fitting efforts that successfully tracked the course of the response function with plausible yet interchangeable equations. The neural language and assumptions were completely separable from the essence of the theory and for all practical purposes irrelevant to them. The mathematics, however successful as descriptions of the functional form of the data, was totally neutral with regard to the underlying neural mechanisms, and thus, unrelated to the original neural premises. The authors of these three theories had each added a completely independent set of neural assumptions to their models, none of which was, in any way, uniquely linked to the mathematical descriptions. Nor, for that matter, were the neurophysiological assumptions relevant to the psychophysical data being modeled. The so-called neural assumptions were simply alternative ways to insert the respective pairs of parameters into the respective models.

Many other "neural theories" are of this same genre. They may invoke the language of neural interactions, but when closely inspected they also turn out to really be nothing more (nor less) than formal mathematical descriptions of the phenomena under consideration. The neural assumptions enter the discussion of the model in two ways. The first is as a visual aide. Visualization of the meaning of the mathematics can best be accomplished if the processes represented take on some kind of a graphic instantiation. When what is being modeled is certainly a brain process, why not use pictures of neurons as surrogates for the equations? However affirmative the answer to this rhetorical question, the actual biological neural mechanisms are not necessarily defined by the model.

Indeed, this has been acknowledged by many of the most active neural network modelers; there has been a trend in thinking about neural modeling in recent years to change the meaning of the constituent neuron-like objects used in their theories. Where originally they were considered to be individual neurons, now the fashion is to consider them as higher level functional units "with neuron-like properties."

The second way in which neurons can be utilized in neural models is as a symbol of the general heuristic relationship between the two sciences.

This is one way that neurophysiology has successfully contributed to current trends in modeling. This contribution is based on the transition of a general and completely valid idea—the parallel processing organization of the brain—from the biological sciences to the computational sciences. It seems likely that the awareness of the significance of parallel processing in the nervous system was a vital and important heuristic for parallel processing computers. The early work on the *Limulus* eye by such scientists as Hartline, Wagner, and Ratliff (1956) had an enormous impact on the way we think about image-processing systems long before adequate computer power was available to really test most of the generated ideas.

The success of the books by Rumelhart, McClelland, and their colleagues (1986a) and McClelland, Rumelhart, and their colleagues (1986) clearly illustrates that the idea of neural models had fallen on fertile ground originally tilled by Rosenblatt (1962) and Grossberg (1968), among many others.

As the years have gone by, both the theoretical models and the computational devices used by engineers have grown up and away from the neurophysiological data. One has only to pick up any one of the many computer vision journals (e.g., *Pattern Recognition*; *CVGIP: Graphical Models and Image Processing*; or *IEEE Transactions on Pattern Analysis and Machine Intelligence*) to read of models that perform visual functions but are not based on any immediate biological data, just engineering ingenuity and competence. One can then turn to journals that do purport to provide computational models of biological vision systems to see that the model has very often been developed far beyond the known biology. What is repeatedly encountered is a mathematical system that imitates the function or behavior of a biological system, but that is really as neutral about the visual neurophysiology as were the three "dual" models of metacontrast.

Are Neural Responses Stable Enough for Analysis?

Adding further uncertainty to how far we can go with neuroreductionist models of complex processes is a recent report by Arieli, Sterkin, Grinvald, and Aertsen (1996). This paper made the exceedingly relevant and important point that the response of any given brain region may not be the same under all conditions even if the stimulus is constant and the cognitive outcome is apparently the same from one trial to another. Using an optical imaging procedure rather than an electrophysiological one they observed wide variations in the shape of the electrical potentials driven by visual stimuli. This technique requires that a special voltage-sensitive dye be applied to the brain surface and the luminance measured by an array of photodiodes. In this manner a plot can be made of the spatially distributed electrical activity of the cortex.

The germane result of Arieli and his colleagues' work was the extreme variability of the cortical voltage responses to what appeared to be identical stimuli. However, they did observe that the particular pattern of neural activity could be rationalized if the nature of the ongoing activity prior to stimulation was taken into account. If the state of the ongoing activity was algebraically added to the activity induced by the stimulus, then the response could be predicted. The important point, however, was that the cumulative activity produced by the stimulus was essentially unpredictable and could be very different from trial to trial unless considered in the context of preceding activity.

This empirical tour de force is of considerable interest in the context of the present discussion because it highlights another major difficulty for any neuroreductionist enterprise. Not only is the electrophysiological response of the brain very complex, but it is also unstable. That is, the pattern of electrical responses observed on or in the brain may be very different even when the perceptual experience remains constant. Thus, there may be many equivalent patterns of neural activity that encode the same experience. Individual neurons may or may not be involved at any given time in what would be reported as identical percepts. Even worse than the variable role of the individual neuron is that the statistical distributions of the responses of very large numbers of cells may not be consistent from one trial to the next, even with what are likely to be identical perceptual experiences.

Arieli et al. (1996) worked with the cumulative evoked potential. Nevertheless, their work generally illustrates the dynamic nature of the coding schemes that are used by the nervous system. Their work raises a major additional obstacle to any hopes of decoding the brain activity associated with perceptual experience—it is a moving, as well as an enormously complicated, target.

SUMMARY

In this chapter, I have surveyed a number of ideas and findings that argue that contemporary neuroreductionism, although a seductive and intellectually exciting approach to the study of perceptual phenomena, is actually hindered by a substantial number of empirical, theoretical, and logical difficulties. In this final section, I want to summarize and list some of these difficulties, obstacles, problems, mind sets, and influences that have led to this overemphasis on neuroreductionism:

1. The confusion of peripheral transmission codes with the more central psychoneural equivalents.

2. A deification of isomorphic codes and messages even in light of the fact that some qualitative messages (e.g., the chromatic experience we call "greenness") cannot possibly be represented along the same dimensions as they are perceived.

3. The profound tendency to pick out, from the huge array of available neuronal responses, any one that happens to exhibit some kind of a functional similarity. This selective citation leads to a "How can you miss?" fallacy that can produce unlimited numbers of false positive associations. Thus, the tendency to select any data that match one's theoretical prejudgments can easily run amuck. Sometimes, refutation comes too late—very fragile neural data, subsequently to be contradicted, may have already become so widely accepted that their status can no longer easily be challenged.

4. The misunderstanding of the role of single neurons in a real world of ensemble population statistics. This misunderstanding is based on a historical tradition of and a continued affection for single-neuron representation theories. Such contemporary theories are driven by the prevailing microelectrode technology, a technology that produces a deep knowledge of single neurons, but very little data on the interactions of the vast networks of neurons that are the true psychoneural equivalents. All too much of our technological history forces us toward an elementalist, analytic, single-neuron tradition of thinking about neural processes. Biological reality, however, shouts the message: "It is the ensemble of neurons that is the basis of perception."

5. A lack of appreciation of the true nature of parallel processing and the population statistical basis of psychologically significant neural responses. This inattention to the role of population statistics is also a result of historical forces. We do not have the mathematical or the formal logical apparatus to deal synthetically with these complicated, distributed systems.

6. Overestimating the significance of the first time that the response of a neuron tracks the response of the perceived response.

7. Underestimating the significance of cognitive penetration on what may at first glance seem to be simple perceptual phenomena. The dependency of a visual illusion on some aspect of its meaning raises serious doubts about any peripheral or overly simplistic bottom-up explanation.

8. Reasoning by analogy. Assuming that because two analogous functions have isomorphic time courses or response shapes, they are also reductionist homologs of each other.

9. Inventing the implausible. Although one scientist's criteria for plausibility may be different from another's, some ideas (e.g., the reconstruction of a topographic map by centrifugal projections from an "imagined" visual scene) seem to rocket into a speculative space that is much further from biologically anchored reality than the inventors may appreciate. The phrase "going over the top" may be even more appropriate here than in the theater.

10. Attributing to the periphery that which is actually carried out in the central nervous system. Assuming that a neuron that responds to some attribute of a stimulus is the psychoneural equivalent of the perceptual responses generated by that stimulus.

11. A lack of appreciation of the fact that neural codes may be highly variable even for what seems to be perfectly stable perceptual experiences. The same percept may be produced by two or more very different patterns of neural activity depending on the previous state of the organism.

12. And, of course, the ultimate error—assuming that the problem of reducing perceptual phenomena to neural responses is tractable, in spite of the formal proofs that some problems are beyond any hope of realistic solution.

Finally, I want to I want to reemphasize several key ideas that are very likely to misinterpreted by readers of this critical review of neuroreductionism. First, the difficulties for neuroreductionism that I have considered here are epistemological issues. They are in no way intended to compromise the basic ontological premise that mind is nothing more or less than a process of the brain. Since I expect that many of my readers will infer that I think otherwise, this point cannot be repeated too often.

Second, I appreciate that every experiment and every theory that has been considered in this chapter may have been a necessary step in the historical quest for the next level of truth and understanding. Even those studies that will ultimately turn out to be dead ends or detours may have played an important role. Just as they were the natural evolutionary steps of earlier ideas, to not have gone through that phase might have cost our science something in the long run. Many of the empirical studies considered, whether psychophysical or neurophysiological, were, therefore, necessary steps in the development of this science. Nevertheless, our contemporary theories and insights must continue to evolve; they can only do so by avoiding some of the pitfalls that I just listed. I am simply arguing for a reinterpretation of what we can do in the future and what is the meaning of that which we have done in the past.

Third, by no means am I advocating a reduction in the neuroscience enterprise. The work done at all levels of the nervous system with many different technical approaches has been enormously productive. We know much more about the brain and its constituent parts than we did even a very few years ago. It is all of value, interesting, exciting, and, not the least, an elegant intellectual enterprise.

Fourth, in the same vein, perceptual research carried out at the psychophysical level is also of value and exciting. I am convinced that the future of perceptual science depends on some degree of rejection of the chimera of neuroreductionism. Otherwise, this effort will founder on the same inadequate theoretical rocks that doomed classic Gestalt psychology. However terribly seductive it may be, only by eschewing a false neuroreductionism will the study of molar mental processes reach its mature role in science.

4

THE CASE AGAINST
COGNITIVE REDUCTIONISM

So far in this book, I have argued two main points. The first was that all formal models, whether mathematical, computational, quasi-neural, or verbal, are neutral with regard to the inner workings of the brain–mind complex. By neutral, I mean that although both the mental and neural mechanisms can be functionally described by models, they cannot be reductively *explained* by them any more than can any other physical system. I argued that the reasons for this are fundamental and are not dependent on the current state or future possibilities of our technology.

The second main point was that, for many reasons, relations drawn between psychophysical data and neural mechanisms, although often quite imaginative and sometimes based on functional analogies, are almost always unconvincing and fanciful, if not downright wrong. The main reason for this conclusion was that psychophysical methods were prototypical input–output comparisons for which the "black box" constraint had to hold. Therefore, the top-down (from psychophysical findings to neurophysiological events) approach could never achieve its goals.

I also stressed the point that neurophysiological methods, even when they were successful in opening the "black box," could never, for equally compelling reasons, unravel the tangled web of interactions among the enormous number of neurons that make up our brains as well as our thoughts. The extreme levels of complexity that characterize realistic neural nets prohibit the bottom-up (from neurophysiological findings to mental events) approach from explaining psychological phenomena. The complexity of the brain, in the formal mathematical sense of the word, is far greater than most neuroreductionists seem willing to accept.

The reasons I presented for the limitations on integrating models, neurophysiological findings, and psychophysical data were sometimes general and sometimes special to each approach. Models were inhibited from reductive explanation of psychological observations, in particular, because of their fundamental descriptive nature. Descriptions of processes are, as a matter of principle, incapable of distinguishing between the innumerably large numbers of alternative underlying mechanisms that could produce the same externally observed course of action. Psychophysical data suffered from this same difficulty–there were too many possible alternative internal structures to characterize internal neural mechanisms definitively on the basis of molar behavior. An emerging generality should be clear by now: Any molar or behavioral approach, psychophysical or otherwise, must also be considered neutral and, in principle, incapable of distinguishing between the innumerable and computationally incalculable possible alternative internal neural structures and physiological processes.

The question to be discussed in this chapter is: Can we extrapolate logically from behavior to the components of an internal mental architecture? This is a different kind of reductionism. The elements are not the physically observable neural units of the brain and peripheral nervous system; rather, they are the functional components purported to be the cognitive process elements that collectively make up the mental world that can only be revealed by behavioral responses. I now consider the rationale behind the "hunt for the mental architecture" and its fundamental weaknesses.

The controversy revolving around this kind of cognitive reductionism is one of the great issues that has driven psychology's history for the last century. It is a conflict between psychologists who believe that behavior reflects mental stages in a strong enough way to permit us to access and determine the mental architecture, on the one hand, and those who believe that the mental architecture is inaccessible and, therefore, behavior itself is the only legitimate subject matter of psychology. The former approach asserts the reducibility of behavior to cognitive mechanisms and processes. The latter approach eschews that kind of cognitive reductive analysis.

The contest is between two schools of thought. One is traditionally called *behaviorism* in psychology or *operationalism* in other sciences. This point of view denies our ability to analyze the underlying mental components from the observed responses of an organism. The antithetical view, best known in its current instantiation as *cognitivism*, assumes that "hypothetical constructs" (MacCorquodale & Meehl, 1948) have validity as both theoretical and psychobiological elements of the mind. The dispute between these two philosophies of psychology concerns one of the most fundamental premises of our science and one that has repeatedly oscillated between the two traditions.

This controversy brings us face to face with the formidable task of evaluating the degree to which our externally communicated (interpersonal) behavior is related to our private (intrapersonal) mental responses, whatever and wherever they may be. This debate, of course, is no longer the same as the mind–brain problem–the brain is almost irrelevant once we agree that it is the mechanism for producing the mental processes of which we are aware and stimulating the effector transformations by means of which responses are generated. The issue now becomes: Can we determine what are the elemental cognitive processes and mechanisms that make up the units of our mental functioning by measuring behavior, in the same way that an automobile, for example, can be disassembled into its parts?

One of the forms of behavior that has been a major tool for psychologists in the past was introspection. This means of probing what is going on in the mind is really a mixture of two parts of the problem as I see it. The mental activity as people report their thoughts is as private and remote as any other mental process. The verbal responses themselves, on the other hand, differ in no substantial way from any other kind of response, verbal or motor. The problem with introspection has always been that it has been given a special role as a route into the mind when in fact it is not different from any other kind of motor response. The linkage between our thoughts and our responses about those thoughts is just as fragile as any other comparison of interpersonal and intrapersonal responses. In developing my new behaviorism, I join with the classic view that introspective reports are of little value for the kind of problems we discuss in this chapter. A more complete and detailed discussion of the limitations of this kind of behavioral measure can be found in Zuriff (1985). The reader should also look at Nisbett and Wilson's (1977) and Nisbett and Ross' (1980) studies of the lack of self-knowledge we have of our own mental processing to appreciate the gap between self-reports and actual mental activity.

I now strongly support the following corollary of the neutrality of models argument discussed in chapter 2 and of the anti-neuroreductionist arguments discussed in chapter 3. The thesis of this chapter is that this corollary holds, has held, and will always hold for psychological science. In brief: *However much we might wish them to be otherwise, behavioral measurements of any kind are universally incapable of saying anything definitive about the structure, nature, or arrangement of the cognitive processes that may emit, coexist with, underlie, represent, encode, image, account for, collectively make up, or "ARE"[1] our "minds."*

To the degree that one accepts this corollary, fundamental and serious problems arise concerning the representation of mental activity by cognitive

---

[1]The reader may choose his or her own preferred term here–the definition of the relation is wide open.

theories of any kind. Specifically, this corollary raises important issues concerning limits on the nature of explanation in psychology. One of the most important, of course, is the very existence of the hypothetical under- lying cognitive processes as anything more than manifestations of our ex- perimental techniques.

In earlier chapters I have been concerned with the relationship between models and behavior (in the form of psychophysical findings and observa- tions), models and neurophysiological mechanisms, and behavior and neurophysiological mechanisms. Now, another mysterious and only vaguely defined word has entered the discussion–the *mind* (the aggregate of our mental experiences)–and a new set of even more difficult-to-conceptualize logical problems emerges.

The introduction of the connotatively loaded term *mind* brings us to the very outermost fringes of our neuroscientific–psychological lexicon. Some of the mental terminology (e.g., consciousness, awareness, perception) is so vague and means so many different things to different people that great confusion is created even when reasonable people discuss relevant issues. Admittedly, some of these terms have been among the most elusive and difficult to define throughout the history of psychology. It should also not go unnoticed that there is even a considerable history of what amounts to the rejection of the whole terminology of mentalist words like "mind." The behaviorist tradition (Hull, 1943; Skinner, 1938; J. B. Watson, 1919, 1925) and their antecedents, the British empiricists (e.g., Locke, Hume, and Mill), the positivists (e.g., Comte), and the Vienna circle of logical positivists (e.g., Carnap, Schlick, and Wittgenstein) all sought to avoid the linguistic and philosophical difficulties that arise when these terms are injected into sci- entific discourse.

More recently, there has been an upswing of hope that neuroreduction- ism will come of age in the form of a new "eliminativist" tradition that also seeks to finesse the difficulties involved in an examination of mental proc- esses. Eliminativism, which may be classified as a latter-day positivism with a neurophysiological rather than a psychological perspective, clearly is hyperneuroreductionist in its goals. The eliminativist solution to the prob- lem of mind is simply to define the difficult mentalist words out of existence. It is assumed by them that we are close enough to a purely neural vocabu- lary to seriously consider eliminating use of the mental terminology alto- gether. Scientists and philosophers who seem committed to this approach (e.g., P. M. Churchland, 1979, 1981; P. S. Churchland, 1986; P. S. Churchland & Sejnowski, 1992; Crick, 1994) take an extremely optimistic view that the neuroreductionist revolution is already at hand and simply eschew the older mentalist terms. It is my feeling that this is much too optimistic a view and that the mentalist vocabulary will necessarily be with us for quite a while, if not forever. Psychology may have its problems, but it is not likely to become totally extinct in the foreseeable future as a result of being impaled by a microelectrode.

Indeed, there are few sciences that have disappeared as a result of reductionist progress. Even in this simplest of sciences, the expected reductionist revolution has not removed the need for molar physics. Terms such as *pressure* are still regularly used in spite of our appreciation of the basic role that the momenta of individual molecules play in the creation of the molar measure. The reasons for the continuation of the molar vocabulary are not related to any disagreement about the ultimate source of the forces on a tank of gas, but rather to the impracticality (as well as nonnecessity) of actually making the huge number of measurements and carrying out the bookkeeping that would be required to provide a fully reductionist account. The (ontological) reality of a large number of moving molecules as the root source of pressure is not challenged by the practical (epistemological) difficulty encountered should one attempt to sum their individual effects.

It seems certain that molar mental and behavioral vocabularies will also continue to be extensively used in psychological science. I intend to continue using (indeed, *must* continue to use) them in this chapter and in other parts of this book, in spite of the fact that they are sometimes confusing and always elusive of a universally accepted definition. It seems advisable, therefore, to provide a minilexicon of at least a few of the critical terms that will repeatedly appear in the subsequent discussion. Obviously, the whole vocabulary of psychological processes used in both public and scientific discourse is much, much larger; this list is but a sample of the full mentalist vocabulary. Equally obviously, my definitions will not satisfy all readers, but perhaps they will help to clarify some of the subsequent discussions and my use of them.

A MINILEXICON OF MENTAL TERMS

Mental terms are notoriously difficult to define. Any attempt to achieve a precise specification of their denotation, much less their connotation, ultimately becomes circular. In the final analysis mental definitions always seem to depend on a consensual agreement that one's own personal conscious experience is more or less like that of another. From a certain point of view, these basic mental terms may be more like the premises of a logical argument than the steps in its solution or, for that matter, the solution itself. Thus, when I use a word like *mind*, it has to be accepted as a consensually agreed "premise" of the discussion rather than as something that can independently be evaluated and delimited by other words. In fact, the very act of trying to define words like "mind" may bring some of the most difficult aspects of psychological inquiry to the fore better than any other kind of analysis.

Behavior. Behavior, as a whole, may be defined as the sum total of the interpersonally observable motor (including verbal) responses of the organism. A behavioral component is but one part of the total–one measurement, one observation, one report, or one rating. All measurements obtained in psychological experiments that use controlled stimulation and that acquire and measure some particular verbal or other motor response are behaviors. So, too, are the unstimulated emitted responses observed in instrumental conditioning experiments, in naturalistic field observations, or in the day-to-day interactions of people with each other or with other organisms and objects in their environment.

Psychological science can only measure behavior. Verbal reports of what is perceived, felt, or believed are behaviors, not that which is perceived, felt, or believed. The two may or may not be closely related, depending on the situation. The internal states are at best inferences drawn from behavior. However, great actors or pathological liars both constantly remind us that the internal mental states (including the parts of the introspective process that are purely intrapersonal) and the behaviors (including the parts of the introspective process that are interpersonal) may be completely independent of each other.

There are of course many other kinds of responses that are not usually called behavior that, nevertheless, may also be included in this rubric. For example, glandular responses, galvanic skin responses, and EEG, PET, and fMRI scans are sometimes difficult to distinguish from the motor responses we commonly call behavior. They may or may not be correlated with internal mental states, but they are not the mental states any more than is a verbalization or a muscle twitch. The near quackery practice of polygraphy remains intransigently resistant to most kinds of validity testing because of the lack of connection between these responses and the true intrapersonal privacy of a person's thoughts.

Sentience. Sentience is an older term that is not much used any more, but that denotes a general awareness of one's existence. It is a more broadly defined concept than the closely related term *consciousness* because it could include basic or undifferentiated awarenesses such as those that might characterize the "simpler minds" of species with less complicated brains than our own. Thus, a more or less undifferentiated sentience should be accepted as a primitive kind of mind that emerged first in the evolution of the brain. As more and more complex neural networks evolved, the degree of sentience presumably increased. Of course, no one knows at what evolutionary stage the most primitive forms of sentience emerged. Nor do we have a good idea of what would distinguish, or how we could distinguish between, the pre-sentient and the sentient, or, for that matter, how to measure different levels of sentience.

The main problem for anyone who tries to study sentience of any kind is to determine what it adds to the existence of the organism. Automata can at least be imagined that perform equally well in an adaptive sense, but do not require sentience of any kind. The problem of animal sentience is made terribly difficult by the fact that an automaton and an aware creature could be behaviorally indistinguishable.

The use (or nonuse) of language further complicates a comparative study of different levels of sentience. Our vocabulary is so profoundly dependent on a basic common understanding of what our kind of verbally mediated sentience is, that it is still not clear how we might communicate with an organism with a different kind. Certainly our experiences in trying to communicate with other mammals such as porpoises, sea lions, and even other primates have been fraught with controversy concerning the significance of what has been accomplished. The controversy over the existence or nonexistence of machine "intelligence" (for which no evidence of sentience has yet been observed) is just beginning and will probably permeate much of the same discussion of these issues in the future. I suspect it is equally unlikely to be resolved (as is the question of animal sentience or intelligence), even if computers become sufficiently complicated to exhibit animal or even human-like behavior. Precursors of this controversy can already be seen in the popular science fiction culture. For years writers have designed scenarios in which actively and adaptively behaving androids have their "sentience" questioned by human authorities.

Mind. Mind, by analogy to the definition of behavior, may be defined as the sum total of all intrapersonal brain responses of the organism of which the organism is aware and many of which it may not be aware. Intrapersonally private "mind," of course, bears a far more extensive connotative load to anyone who uses the term than does interpersonally observable behavior. Mind can also be considered to be the sum total of all of the perceptions, feelings, beliefs, desires, emotions, pains and pleasures, memories, attention, thoughts, decisions, hallucinations, and all other events that can affect behavior. The important distinction in my use of the word is that *mind* is not synonymous with *brain* in the way suggested by the eliminativist philosophy. Mind is a function of the material brain; the two words refer to very different, but tightly linked, concepts–one mechanism (brain) and one process (mind). A metaphor that I have used previously is that the mind is to the brain as rotation is to the wheel. Disembodied (i.e., dis-embrained) mind is as difficult to conceive of as rotation without a wheel.[2] The problems involved in even

---

[2]It may be difficult for me, but not everyone. Boyd (1980) raised such a possibility when he said: "It will follow that–even though mental states will always be physically realized in the actual world–there is no logical impossibility of their being non-physically realized in some other possible world" (p. 88).

defining this term are immense and have always been with mankind, and they are not likely to go away soon. Some would say that mind and brain refer to two such different kinds of entities that they require two different kinds of language. Dualists, of course, have long argued that these words are so different that they denote two different kinds of reality.

Consciousness or Awareness.   Attempts to define *awareness* or *consciousness* bring us to the limits of our lexicographic abilities. The use of these two words, as I have noted earlier, is something akin to the use of an irreducible premise or axiom in logic. If one checks a good dictionary, what one discovers is that the conscious and aware states are both defined in terms of the other. For example, conscious is often defined as–Having an awareness of one's environment and one's own existence, sensations, and thoughts. And then we are told–See Synonyms at aware. However, a common appreciation of the meaning of the word *conscious* is a fundamental foundation on which much of modern psychological discourse is based. Awareness, either of one's self or of one's environment, is the ultimate intrapersonal private experience. It is what characterizes our mind more than any other feature. That our own self-awareness exists is unquestioned; that another machine or organism is aware seems to be almost unconfirmable. Failed attempts to distinguish between a conscious human and a well-programmed computer by Turing's test have provided convincing evidence that the meaning of the word *conscious* is terribly elusive and difficult to define. Few synonyms even come close to approximating the meaning of *conscious* or *aware* (or *consciousness* and *awareness*), even though there is an abundance of words that are used in their place–including our old favorite, *mind*.

Nowhere is the difficulty of defining consciousness made more explicit than in Chalmers' (1995) attempt:

> When you look at the page, you are conscious of it, directly experiencing the images and words as part of your private mental life. You have vivid impressions of colored flowers and vibrant sky. At the same time you may be feeling some emotions and forming some thoughts. Together such experiences make up consciousness; the subjective, inner life of the mind. (p. 80)

Although poetic, this is hardly the stuff that empirical science can use to guide a research program. Unfortunately, I am not sure that any of us can do much better. How difficult in this context it would be to answer what Chalmers (1995) referred to as the hard problem of "how physical processes in the brain give rise to subjective experience" (p. 81).

Clearly, the words *consciousness* and *awareness* have a priori meanings unto themselves that arise out of our unique personal experiences. From our individual appreciation of our own awareness comes our ability to interact with others. The assumption is that if "I" am conscious, so too are "they" likely to be because of physical similarity, common and predictable behavior, and the behavioral expression of such processes as sympathy, empathy, and altruism, as well as greed, envy, and lust.

Another way to look at the meaning of these words is from the negative point of view. Our own consciousness is defined by its opposite–unconsciousness. Consciousness is that extra experience that accrues when we are not unconscious. Dictionaries typically add superfluous meaning to this axiomatic definition of consciousness or awareness, but almost all of the extras simply confuse this term with others (most notably, *soul*) that convey quite different meanings.

Cognition or Cognitive Processes.   In the past two or three decades there has been a major change in experimental psychology. It is not particularly defined by a change in technique, data, or theoretical position, although there have been changes and improvements in all of these aspects of the science. The change is that the science has now been renamed. *Experimental psychology* is now *cognitive science* or even *cognitive neuroscience*. The change in the name of the profession is not necessarily indicative of any fundamental change in the issues being studied or, for that matter, in the goals or aspirations of the science. It does, however, indicate another one of those sea changes that has both graced and cursed this profession since humans began to worry about these topics. The main shift in emphasis has been from a 1930–1960s nonreductive behaviorism to a contemporary cognitive reductionism that aspires to the elucidation of the structural architecture of the mind. Now I ask: Is this change appropriate?

To understand fully the change in experimental psychology in the past few decades, it is necessary to consider carefully what is meant by the word *cognitive*. One secondary factor that has been influential in renaming the field is an increasing appreciation that the study of mental functions was of broader interest than just to those who were identified as traditional psychologists. The term *cognitive science* currently includes practitioners of computer science, linguistics, neuroscience, and other fields that were not heavily represented in traditional experimental psychology for the simple reason that until recently these sciences did not exist. The phrase "did not exist" does not simply refer to the issue of the nomenclature of scientific fields themselves, but rather to the fact that the technologies, theories, and data of these sciences had, in some cases, not even been created until very recently. Now the necessary components and tools for these new approaches to understanding mental processes do exist and their practitioners have been confronted with some of the same challenges that traditional psychology has faced with its older technologies, theories, and data.

What, then, does *cognitive* mean today? There are several answers to this rhetorical question, but there is one common theme that seems to permeate most of the field. That theme is embodied in the conviction among cognitive scientists that there are isolatable processes going on in our thoughts (mind) that can be analyzed in the same way that chemical cycles can be broken apart into their constituent steps. More than its predecessors, modern cognitive psychology is seeking to determine the functional mental architecture of the mind. It is a patently reductionist approach of the same conceptual stripe as neuroreductionism. The main difference is that the components that are invoked are information-processing processes rather than neurons or neural centers. The basic premise of cognitive psychology (and of the cognitive sciences in general) is that the mind is made up of a set of more or less stable processing elements. Cognitive psychology of this kind often accepts the constraint that these processing elements cannot be understood in neurophysiological terms, but it attempts to reduce mental activities (revealed to us in the organism's behavior) to their constituent mental components.

The flow chart or block diagram, consisting of blocks, representing transformations or processes, and lines, representing the flow of information, has become a ubiquitous model of the mental architecture for cognitive psychologists. The consensus idea in this scientific approach is that cognition is made up of isolatable and independently measurable processes represented by the boxes.

The blocks in such a diagram, of course, are metaphors for the putatively isolatable cognitive processes. The problem is that these metaphors carry a very large conceptual and theoretical load themselves. As discussed later, the blocks are presumed to have certain properties (e.g., independence, seriality, stability) that beg the question of the nature of human thought rather than serving as potential answers to the nature of mind. By making the initial assumption that mental processes can be represented by this kind of model, psychologists may have prejudged the nature of our minds. The conceptual-theoretical tool that the block diagram model represents has, from one point of view, become the explanation rather than the means to an explanation. In many ways, the blocks in the diagram remind us of another, earlier attempt to organize human thoughts into separate "boxes"— the phrenological model of the previous century. The constraint on theory that is imposed by the block diagram model-*cum*-tool is comparable to the constraint on theory imposed by the microelectrode tool in the neuroreductionist domain.

In sum, the use of the word *cognitive* emphasizes the idea that separate thought processes or mental components, similar to the isolatable components of a machine or the steps in a computer program, reflect and model the functioning of the human mind. Perceptual and sensory components, decision processes, memory units, and error and noise sources are all postulated to function as the discrete parts of a system that integrates these and other components into a coherent mental experience and, ultimately, adaptive behavior.

That change in emphasis from "mind" as a singular, molar element to the concatenation of a number of interacting processes is one of the factors contributing to the name change from traditional "experimental psychology" to the new "cognitive science." This change also helps us to understand the current distinction between the modern word *cognition* and the classic one *mind*. Of course, this is by no means a totally novel idea. Elementalist-type thinking of this sort was an important part of several earlier psychological schools of thought, for example, Titchenerian structuralism. The ebb and flow of psychological thinking between these elementalist ideas and the more holistic psychologies such as the German Gestalt school has now brought us back, at least for this historical moment, to cognitive componentism.

To sum up this definition in this mentalist lexicon, *cognitive* is an adjective now used to characterize one very popular approach to the study of human thought processes. The cognitive approach typically presumes that mind is made up of independent and isolatable functional components that process information in a precisely defined manner. This type of theory of mental architecture is often instantiated in the form of a flow chart, examples of which are presented shortly.

Perception. Over the years, after frequent struggles with the task of defining the word *perception*, I have worked out a specific formal definition. I repeat it here without further comment, except to note that, like all the other definitions of terms I have included here, it cannot be totally satisfactory:

> Perception is the relatively immediate, intrapersonal, mental [experience] evoked as a partial, but not exclusive, result of impinging multidimensional stimuli, as modulated by the transforms imposed by the neural communication system, previous experience, and contextual reasonableness. Each percept is the conscious end product of both simple computational transformations and more complex constructionist interpretations. However, the underlying neural and symbolic processes are not part of the observer's awareness. (Uttal, 1981a, p. 14)

Readers will have to bear the circularity of this definition and its dependence on some of the other vaguely defined terms that make up the mental vocabulary. This definition, in spite of the many years of effort that have gone into sharpening it, illustrates how difficult it is to come to satisfactory definitions of mental words.

Imaginations, Images, Hallucinations, and Dreams. Having defined perception, however, it becomes easy, if equally circular, to define the intrinsically created experiences we call imaginations, hallucinations, or dreams.

Imagined images are the intrapersonal, mental response evoked by previous experience and contextual reasonableness. Each such experience is the conscious end product of complex constructionist interpretations, but is not triggered by external stimuli. Neither the internal triggering stimuli nor the underlying neural and symbolic processes are part of the observer's awareness, only the endogenously generated images themselves.

As a reminder, mirages are not imaginations or hallucinations; they are the veridical perceptual responses to aberrations in the physical stimuli. As such, they differ in no fundamental way from the perception of any other visual stimulus. Their lack of veridicality with the external physical reality is a result of the transformations carried out in the external physical world, not in the visual system of the observer.

Can an imagined scene be compelling? Of course it can. The human ability to imagine has been the source of enormous delight and much beauty. In chapter 3, I discussed a very challenging issue that has arisen in recent years: whether the neural responses to imagined and real stimuli are the same. Although this may remain an open question for some neuroscientists, it is not germane to the topic of this chapter, which is intended mainly as a consideration of the relationship between the behavioral and the mental domains.

Attention. In recent years, an extraordinary amount of research has been directed at the description of the cognitive process called attention. Curiously, a precise definition of the meaning of this oft-studied mental "stuff" is hard to find. Attention is usually defined in operational terms that depend on the amount of information that can be processed in some task, or the degree to which one stimulus rather than another is more salient at the moment. In other instances, attention is defined in terms of a subject's ability to select which alternative stimuli will be processed. Other psychologists suggest that attention is nothing more than the current contents of the "short-term memory"—whatever it is that is currently being remembered or, in some even vaguer sense, is present in consciousness at the moment.

None of these definitions satisfies. Rather, it seems that there is massive confusion between what might better be considered an experimental paradigm than a block in a putative cognitive architecture. Attention is defined mainly in terms of the steps used to measure it and the measures made of it. The intuitive feeling that there is some thing or some process inside each mind that is of limited capacity, that can be logically focused, or that even can be divided, has led to the probably fallacious notion that that "stuff" called attention has a kind of tangible reality. I would argue that it is a measurable characteristic of the mind, not a part of the mind. For example, attention is often described, rather than defined, as the allocation or even the control of mental resources. This description leads me to infer that it is incorrect to consider attention as a component, as an isolatable process, or as any kind of mental resource. Rather, it is a property of some other mental process or concatenation of processes. This is quite different from the notion of attention as the contents of working memory, an interpretation made popular by psychologists such as Baddeley (1992).

In other words, attention is not a thing; it is a descriptive measure—a behavior. This is so in spite of its repeated use as a noun. "How is attention allocated?" then becomes a meaningless question. There is no "amount of attention," only operational measures of amounts of information processed, or decisions made, or targets detected as determined in some experimental test. The attempt to measure "the amount of attention" allocated to one or another region of, for example a visual field, therefore, should be best thought of as a category error. One can measure the probability of detection in the various regions. However, to convert these probabilities into a substantial thing called attention is a questionable transformation. From this point of view, such a translation would be an example of erroneous cognitive reductionism—a measure has been made into a process.

Another way in which the word is often used is to distinguish between automatic and effortful mental processing. A substantial amount of visual processing seems to occur without any scrutinizing effort. For example, a red flower on a green background of foliage "pops out." Your eyes are drawn to the flower automatically—you do not have to search for it. Other processes, such as the search for a particular alphabetic character in a field of characters, requires that the observer exert mental effort to go from one character to the next until the target item is detected. The automatic versus effortful dichotomy is often used synonymously with the preattentive versus attentive alternatives that I discussed in chapter 3.

The clash between the semantic loading of attention as "contents," attention as "the process of allocation," or attentive as "effortful" makes it very difficult to provide a satisfactorily precise definition of the term as it is used in contemporary psychology. Obviously, the term *attention* is closely related to the terms *conscious* and *aware*. To pay attention to something is to be especially conscious or aware of it; to not attend to something is to be less aware of it. In this case, I am going to have to renege on my lexicographic responsibilities and simply suggest that this term be specifically defined, wherever used, in terms of the operations that have been used to measure it. The operational approach is particularly needed in this case. I argue later that this kind of operationalism may also require a revision in our thinking about many other areas of psychology.

Phenomena. The word *phenomenon* is clouded by so much excess meaning that it is important that I make clear exactly how I use it in this book. To me, a phenomenon is any percept, finding, report, observation, functional relationship, law, or other experiential or experimental descriptor of the interpersonal responses produced by stimulus scenes. Measurements of phenomena by means of experiments, demonstrations, surveys, observations, and even the much-criticized method of introspection constitute the empirical database of experimental psychology. They are the analogs of atoms, molecules, cells, organs, animals, and plants that make up the observational database of the other biological sciences. Certainly not all of them are valid indicators of psychological states, but all can serve as a means of describing something about mental activity.

Brain States. Finally, good monist that I am, I would like to add to this mini-lexicon another oft-used term–the *brain state*. The reason for introducing this term at this point is that all material monists are committed to the premise that mental states are nothing more nor less than the corresponding brain states. Thus, however differently it may (or may not) be measured, the term is connotatively identical to some of the terms just defined.

To me the brain state refers to the informationally significant arrangement of the logical components–the neurons–of this particular biological structure–the brain–at any particular moment. The chemical and metabolic details of the brain state are also of interest in their own right, but they are not germane to the informationally significant brain state in the way concerned here. Chemicals incontestably affect the brain, but that is not the proximal cause of the brain's mental activity. The proximal cause is the logical arrangement, which can in turn be affected by those chemical and metabolic states, but in a secondary way. The work of Arieli, Sterkin, Grinvald, and Aertsen (1996) described in chapter 3 is a compelling and recent argument for the huge impact of neural variability.

Brain states must be thought of multidimensionally. That is, they are not fixed in either time or space. They are dynamic, changing from moment to moment. These dynamic changes are also likely to be important codes of the accompanying mental experiences; they may occur over brief periods of time, over an extended period, or may even be fixed for a lifetime.

Brain states are, in principle, independently measurable without recourse to either overt behavior or introspective reports. The use of many new technological advances such as the PET scan, the fMRI, the EEG, even magnetic field measurements, and, last but not least, individual or arrays of microelectrodes allows us to observe signals from the brain. Many of the signals so recorded are of unknown relevance to mental actions, however.

Unfortunately, the particular brain state that seems most relevant to (i.e., is the *psychoneural equivalent* of) mental or cognitive processes is the pattern of organization of neurons in the great networks whose function is assumed to correspond with the mental activity to the point of identity. I say unfortunately because it is this level of network activity–the neuronal network–that seems beyond measurement because of its complexity and distribution. Nevertheless, for every aspect of mind, there must be an equivalent brain state. This is a restatement of the fundamental materialist monist premise I have put forward several times previously in this book.

Different patterns of network organization, therefore, are assumed, but cannot be proven to be, the same as different mental states. That is, a neural state is the physical instantiation of the set of processes that results in the self-aware mental entity that is the essential "me" to each of us. The organization of the neuronal network, therefore, should be considered to be the "proper level of inquiry" if one is interested in analyzing mental processes at the physiological level. Alas, however "proper," it is–for the several reasons discussed in chapters 2 and 3–unobservable!

WHAT IS COGNITIVE REDUCTIONISM?

With these definitions in hand, we can now go about the main business of this chapter. My goal is to examine critically a sample portion of the psychological literature that purports to analyze the molar behavior of an organism into its component underlying mental parts. Before proceeding, I want to remind my readers that the papers and books that I have chosen to target for this critique are among the most prominent in their respective fields. I hope that the targets of my criticism will also appreciate that the very fact that I have chosen to discuss their work is intended as a compliment, no matter how severe the theoretical disagreement.

The cognitive reductionist approach, which has been such an important part of the new experimental psychology, is analogous to the neuroreductionist approach discussed earlier. Cognitive reductionism shares a basic premise with neuroreductionism–that molar mental events can be analyzed into their components. Cognitive psychology presupposes that behavior can be reduced to procedural or process components, just as neuroreductionism asserts that behavior can be reduced to its neural components and processes. In other words, just as the neurophysiologists and neuroanatomists are attempting to determine the anatomical and physiological architecture of the nervous system, cognitive psychologists are trying to determine the functional architecture of the mind.

My argument in this chapter is that this premise is as invalid in the cognitive context as it was in the neural context. The blocks and arrows of the typical cognitive block diagram are as logically and empirically unsustainable as are the hypothesized neurons or neural networks. Neurons at least have a tangibility that is independent of the theories in which they are used. This advantage is not shared with the mental process component analysis. In the cognitive domain, the blocks have no independent existence—they are purely theoretical hypothetical constructs. Nevertheless, they are not without their own impact on psychological theory. There is a strong feedback from the mere enunciation of the existence of a component or block mode of existence that can spuriously reinforce itself. Along with that specific self-reinforcement, it must also be acknowledged that one's a priori approach can have a profound effect on theory in general. As demonstrated later, the expression of the component's existence comes complete with certain assumptions that are all too often reified in the later steps of the theoretical development.

It should not go unmentioned that in the last few years some cognitive psychologists have increasingly tended to identify some functional blocks of their hypothetical mental architecture with specific anatomic regions in the brain. In light of the fact that most cognitive functions are so poorly defined, the future of this effort is problematical. In chapter 3, I alluded to the work of Van Orden and his colleagues in this context. It is important to reiterate the very important message sent by Van Orden and Papp (in press) in particular. Brain imaging procedures that attempt to link "pieces of the mind" with "parts of the brain" are confounded by one especially frail premise (among others). This premise is that the cognitive components under study actually exist as isolatable entities. As discussed later, some of us do not believe this to be valid, and this weakness invalidates many of the conclusions drawn from brain imaging studies that purport to localize these mythical components.

It is important as we proceed through the following discussion that a distinction also be made between the application of mathematics to describe such processes and the diagram of components and connections, itself, as a cognitive reductionist tool. Mathematical formulations, as I have repeatedly asserted, can properly be used to describe the course of events observed in behavioral experiments. Mathematics of all kinds, from the lowliest algebra to the most elevated forms of analysis, carry out their descriptive functions in a powerful and useful, albeit nonreductive, manner. Differential equations, for example, can suggest and represent such properties as the rate of a process, its change in rate, or, less frequently, its change in change in rate.

I hope that by this point it is understood that such a mathematical representation can, indeed must, be accomplished without any consideration of the nature of the specific mechanics of the underlying system. The mathematical formulation can describe certain integrated properties of the many functional transforms that can occur within a closed system (e.g., the lag or bandpass of the entire system). However, these transforms must always be dealt with as collective and cumulative measures. As I noted many times previously, a mathematical description based only on input–output relations is fundamentally incapable of saying anything about the detailed nature of the internal mechanisms or separating the unified processes into their components. Unfortunately, these admonitions are ignored in control system models of the human system.

To make this point clear in the present instance, let's take as an example the overall lag of a mechanical system: the time between an input and the elicited output. The mathematics describing the behavior of the system can compare the input and output of the entire system and determine that there is a temporal discrepancy between them. The mathematics describing the overall function of the system is totally incapable, however, of breaking the cause of this lag down into its components. The observed system lag may have been caused by one element in the system, by a serial cascade of shorter delays, or even in some way by the collective action of an array of both parallel and serial mechanisms. Indeed, there are infinite combinations of delay components that could account for the total system delay. This was the message of the Moore (1956) theorem, a profound intellectual invention to which I referred previously.

I now argue that the central premise of cognitive psychology, that the underlying process can be disassembled into its components by experimental techniques, is equally incapable of achieving its stated goal. Just as mathematics cannot analyze an internal mechanism, so too is the cognitive approach prevented, in fundamental principle, from achieving its goal. This is obviously going to be a controversial (if not contentious) statement, but in the remainder of this chapter I attempt to spell out my reasons for believing that this assertion is actually a reasonable and appropriate one.

Specifically, I suggest that the blocks in the block diagram have only an illusory tangibility. First, let's be sure what the argument is about. The blocks in the classical cognitive model have an implicit meaning; they are intended to represent the basic and presumably independent components of mental activity. They are assumed to be invariant (to a degree that is in conflict with other interpretations of the adaptive nature of mental processes), responding in a fixed manner in a fixed period of time as each is invoked. They are assumed to change only minimally regardless of where they are placed in the model and therefore to be, in the main, unaffected by what happens before or after they execute. In other words, the very assertion of this type of model comes with a heavy baggage of assumptions and preconditions.

This may be criticized as too strong an interpretation of the mental architecture approach, but without this assumption of the quasi-independence of the blocks, the whole theoretical framework of this kind of reductive cognitive psychology collapses. If a block is not almost independent, but varies depending on how it is used, than none of the methods described later in this chapter makes any sense. The entire edifice of cognitive reductionism depends on the time taken, for example, to encode a stimulus being roughly the same from one experimental condition to another. On the other hand, if this and other functional elements are labile and vary from condition to condition, then it would become impossible to support the logic of any of the subtractive or additive methods that are about to be discussed.

To make my argument more specific, let us now consider a few exemplary cognitive models that purport to carry out a successful search for the mental architecture. Examples of these models are scattered throughout the contemporary psychological literature, including most current textbooks. I have chosen but a few of the more notable and influential ones to consider. But the argument (and more seriously, the same incapacitating and restricting assumptions) are obviously transferable to others that share the same approach.

Perhaps the simplest and most familiar block diagram representation or model of cognitive processes is the hierarchy of memories that has been postulated to be present in human thought processes. A very large amount of research (e.g., Atkinson & Shiffrin, 1968; Shiffrin & Atkinson, 1969) has been done on memory processes that has led to the generalized model shown in Fig. 4.1. The traditional hierarchy of memory systems is purported to be composed of a number of different kinds of memories with different functional properties. The model depicts the very briefly enduring, but large-capacity *short-term sensory store*, the relatively small-capacity and intermediate-duration *short-term memory*, and the very-large capacity, long-duration *long-term memory*. The lines on this map represent postulated flows of information, for example, from the short-duration sensory store to the short-term memory. Other lines indicate suggested processes for renewing or registering the memorized information, how information may be lost or distorted, or how it may be moved back and forth in the hierarchy between the lower level transient memories and the higher level permanent memories.

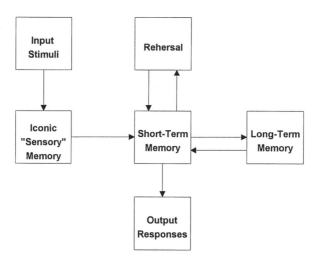

FIG. 4.1. A simplified block diagram model of the memory systems that are believed by many to be present in human cognition.

Implicit in this model are several very important assumptions. One, of course, is most fundamental, that there exists a hierarchy of isolatable and distinguishable memory systems. Information is assumed to move from the sensory store to the short-term to the long-term memory. Each memory type has its own properties and each is assumed, furthermore, to be more or less independent of the others. The components are also purported to be truly separate and distinct in some real biological-structural or psychological-functional sense. That is, the components are assumed not to be artifacts of the methods used to measure them or of the theoretician's conceptualization of the structure. Whatever experiments are used to explore these components, it is argued that the true nature of the components will emerge.

However, a little reflection suggests that it would be very difficult to isolate these memorial processes completely from each other in any experimental design. The measurement of the sensory store requires the intervention of the short-term memory to assay the properties of the sensory store. Similarly, evaluations of long-term memory cannot be made without in some way bringing the recalled information into short-term memory. Indeed, it is hard to imagine that it would be possible to evaluate the sensory store without involving recognition processes that must be based on the very-long-term storage of the forms to be recognized and reported.

A more complicated model of the cognitive system is shown in Fig. 4.2. Here we see additional blocks being added to the basic memory system: decision and recognition processes, response selectors, and schema and planning components. Lines are added that indicate incoming information other than the triggering external stimulus that can alter the arousal level

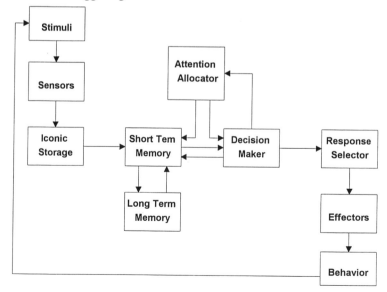

FIG. 4.2. A more complex block diagram model of human cognition.

including the level of vigilance, or the general set or state of the cognitizing organism. Some lines may indicate something about how attention is allocated or what is selected for attention. Other lines may stand for the encoding processes by which information is transformed from one representation to another. Additional boxes may suggest that there are limits on the information-processing capability of the organism or indicate how the organism adjusts the criterion levels on which decisions are based. Other boxes may represent the source of perceptual errors, illusions, or other kinds of non-veridicalities. The possibilities are endless and the maps that have been published over the years innumerable.

There are, however, serious general problems with the internal component analysis or mental architecture approach epitomized in these diagrams. In the following sections of this chapter I consider several of these problems. First, I briefly discuss some of the general difficulties involved in this kind of "cognitive" block diagram theorizing. Second, I consider some special examples from the recent cognitive literature to demonstrate how these general principles may or may not apply to these examples.

The argument I intend to make here is straightforward—no cognitive research paradigm is capable of truly isolating any component of the entire mental system. Even the simplified flow of information shown in Fig. 4.2, for example, illustrates how interconnected are all of the processes of the mind. This fact is obscured by the very nature of the block diagram type theory. In a very fundamental sense, these are not molar theories; they are elementalist, component-type theories that assume fixed functions embodied in the forms of demarcatable blocks. This approach seems to be more of an intellectual artifice that helps cognitive scientists to organize experiments than a precise specification of the psychobiological nature of the cognitive system. From one point of view the initial choice of the block diagram, and all of its attendant conceptual baggage, begs the most important questions of the organization of perceptual and other cognitive processes.

Now that I have set out the thesis of this chapter, let's look at some of the general difficulties faced by searchers for the mental architecture.

SOME GENERAL DIFFICULTIES WITH THE "COGNITIVE" APPROACH

Models Are Abstractions—Life Is More Complicated

One great problem with the block diagram as a theoretical tool is that, like all other models and maps, it can only be an abstraction of reality–a point treated more extensively in chapter 2. There is, however, something even more profoundly wrong with this type of chart (and the theoretical perspective it epitomizes) that becomes clear if the nature of thought is considered without preconceptions. The "flow of information" in real life is conceptual, associative, and dependent on the meaning of the information itself. It is not simply a matter of a passive flow of coded information from block to block along well-defined pathways between units with precise functions. The basic logic of the mind is fundamentally different from that suggested by the block diagram–a tool that has its origins and utility in the description of relatively simple engineering or business systems.

Indeed, if one actually analyzes any real cognitive process, as opposed to the oversimplified theoretical description instantiated by a block diagram, it quickly becomes clear that the model is not only incomplete, but may be completely misleading in terms of the context in which it places our theories. For example, it is unlikely that information flows in a simple linear manner from one discrete block to another as depicted in a typical cognitive model. Perhaps a better characterization of the real complexity of a thought process is the one shown in Fig. 4.3. This diagram, prepared by Scragg (1975), more realistically reflects the logical and, perhaps, "illogical" (but "meaningful") flow of development of a thought. Obviously, this is both a much more complicated and a much more realistic depiction of a cognitive system than the traditional diagram shown in Fig. 4.2. Even more germane to the present discussion is not that it is quantitatively more complex, but rather that it is a qualitatively different conceptualization of the nature of the way the mind deals with ideas. Information is guided from one meaningful process to another by virtue of its semantic content in a disordered, indirect, and associative manner, rather than in neat flows from one functionally fixed block to another. In other words, perhaps the components in the block diagram should, at the very least, be thought of as dynamic rather than fixed, and varying from one mental act to another. It just may be that the misconception inherent in the block diagram develops because cognitive scientists tend to think more mechanically of information than symbolically of meaning.

The more realistic model of Fig. 4.3 is organized very differently from a traditional block diagram such as the one shown in Fig. 4.2. The flow is not a passive one of certain precisely defined patterns from processing block to processing block in a manner independent of the content of the message. Rather, it is from ideas and concepts to other ideas and concepts. The process most likely depends more on the semantic content of the message than on the syntax of the neural or other language used. Notwithstanding the convenience of the block and line model, most cognitive psychologists would admit that we have very little idea about how this flow of meaning among ideas is handled by the computational circuitry of the brain or the equally little-known logic of human thought. We simply do not know what the rules of logic are that govern mental processing. Many of us suspect, though, that they are very different from the kinds of functions described by the blocks of a conventional cognitive block diagram theory.

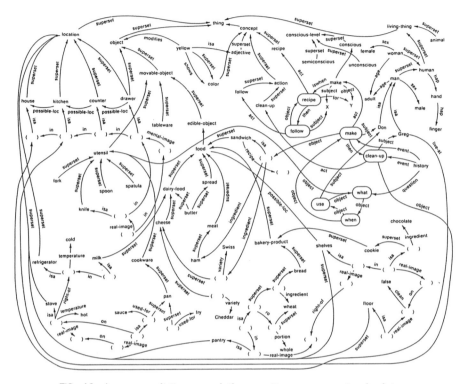

FIG. 4.3. A more realistic map of the cognitive processes involved in answering simple questions such as, what ingredients do you need to make a cake, and what would you get dirty? This sort of map is rarely encountered these days as cognitive psychologists seek to achieve reduction by oversimplification. From *Explorations in Cognition* by Norman and Rumelhart © 1975 by W. H. Freeman and Company. Reproduced with permission.

Cognitive Models Assume a Structural Rigidity That Is Not Justified

As noted, the block diagram or cognitive architecture approach to understanding the organization of the mind is based on certain key, but questionable, assumptions. For the approach to have any chance of succeeding, it must be assumed that the component blocks must be more, rather than less, independent of each other. This is another way of saying that the blocks can be inserted or removed from the process with only minimal effects on other blocks.

A corollary of this assumption is that each individual block is more or less fixed in how long it takes to carry out its function. Thus by adding or subtracting the time taken to carry out various combinations of the components, we should be able to tell how the mental system is organized, by means of the differences that are measured in such dependent variables as reaction times. As shown later, assumptions like this are highly fragile. In particular, see the discussion of the very important work of Pachella (1974) later in this chapter. They assume a rigidity of mental processing, rather than a flexibility and adaptability, that hardly seems to hold for simple cognitive processes and even less so for more complex processes.

Blocks Are Methods, Not Psychological Entities

As I just noted, the block diagram-*cum*-cognitive architectural model is primarily based on the assumption that each block represents an independent and more or less fixed mental process. As demonstrated later, a considerable amount of evidence indicates that the blocks are not stable in this way. What, then, are the blocks? Do they have any reality? How did they achieve such a major influence on our thinking? The answer to these questions is that the blocks are really manifestations of the kind of research paradigms that we have designed and used. They are not realistic statements of the components of human thought processes; rather, they are an expression of our experimental methods! I do not believe that they represent the arrangement or logic of the biological mind–brain; they represent attributes of the experimental paradigms used to study memory, not those of the memory itself. To put it baldly, they are in disturbingly large part artifactual!

In the absence of any real knowledge or, for that matter, any conceivable strategy for using the input–output method to define the components of the internal mental architecture (as well as internal neural mechanisms), cognitive scientists have developed a set of theories, in fact an entire science, of the mind that is actually only portraying the methods used to study thought, not thought itself. We study sensory memory by measuring the number of items that can be briefly recalled after a single presentation when a mask follows the stimulus; we study intermediate-term memory by asking subjects to recall information as a function of time with or without rehearsal; we study long-term memory by asking how a memory changes over longer periods of time; in other words, we study the many manifestations of mental activity by designing paradigms and methods that themselves have become reified as our theories.

Thus, given some new paradigm, a new type of "memory" is very likely to be discovered. This is already evident in the emergence of new kinds of memory every so often in the cognitive literature. Such terms as *episodic* and *semantic*, *declarative* and *procedural*, and *explicit* and *implicit* have appeared in recent years as new experimental protocols have been designed. We also have already seen how this is the case in the Ishai and Sagi (1995) report described in chapter 3. A completely new form of memory with a 5-min lifetime was postulated as the result of the application of a new method. This is unfortunate for all of these examples; the goal of any science should be to determine the physical, biological, or psychological realities, not to study the effects of our research methodology.

Of course, one can raise a question concerning how tightly bound the empirical outcomes of these theory-driving methods are to the true mental processes. It may be argued that perhaps our methods are driven by the nature of the underlying processes, that we are actually determining more about the biopsychological reality of the system than I have allowed so far in this discussion. To a certain degree this must be true—people do remember things. However, there should be some solid base of repeatable observations and phenomena, as well as some continuity in the developing theoretical structure, regardless of the methodology and from one situation to another. To the contrary, we are sometimes hard pressed to find persistent theoretical elements and even to locate long-lasting data in the field of cognitive psychology. In an earlier book (Uttal, 1988), I made a serious attempt to do so for the "higher levels" of visual processing. Unfortunately, I discovered very little, even in the way of the most basic data regarding the higher level of perception, that was first discovered, later substantiated, and then persisted uncontested in the perceptual literature. The actual measurements, as well as their theoretical interpretations, reported by one group of investigators were almost always contradicted by some subsequent study. Rejection, rather than replication, was the rule in this phase of the study of human thought. Repeatable and general laws were few and far between.

Why has even the most basic data of visual cognition become so transient? I suspect that one reason is that most cognitive experiments deal with very small fractional parts of the total complex of events involved in even the simplest thought. In order to carry out an experiment, we must control all "irrelevant variables" and measure "the" dependent ones. This isolation of components often leads to an emphasis on the examination of mechanisms and subprocesses that themselves may be trivial or irrelevant to the process being studied. Furthermore, most mental processes are much more likely than not to be extremely adaptive. Responses and strategies can change drastically between what may seem to be only slightly different experimental contexts. This chameleon-like property of mental processes is not a defect, but a manifestation of the best qualities of human adaptability and intelligence. Thus, we should expect that the "blocks" in the flow charts are not fixed and invariant; rather, they should be constantly changing, not only their extent or duration, but also their quality.

I cannot complete this section without noting that there is another reason why the block diagram has become so prevalent as a theoretical tool. That reason is that the block diagram is the archetype of scientific and engineering thinking in our time. Engineers have the luxury of dealing with relatively simple systems, which can be opened, and for which the components can be empirically separated and are generally stable. Successes in that domain have stimulated the application of engineering methods, techniques, and concepts to the cognitive domain, in which they simply may not apply.

The block diagram is also the tool of choice when one is planning to program another kind of information-processing engine–the modern digital computer. As has been usual throughout the long history of philosophical and scientific concern with the nature of the mind, we are now at another point (recall the hydraulic, pneumatic, telephonic, and computer models) at which the contemporary technology may have been uncritically adopted as the foundation premise of theories of how the mind operates.

Is the Question of the Internal Representation a Resolvable Issue?

The question of whether the internal structure of a mental system–the mental architecture–can be resolved is and has been a matter of considerable theoretical controversy for many years. The reader is directed to Kosslyn's (1995) book for a complete review of the issue, with the understanding that Kosslyn is a strong proponent of the resolvability of the question. The argument reached the boiling point with the advent of modern cognitive psychology in the 1970s. The debate raged about two extreme possibilities for the representation of mental images: (a) images represented by isomorphic (pictorial) patterns of activity and (b) images represented by symbolic or propositional codes, perhaps like language, but also possibly in the form of symbols of which we know nothing except that they were equivalent in some way to the percepts.

The question posed here is not a simple one. Its answer may be different at different levels of the nervous system. There is little question that much visual information is represented in a topologically constant manner in the retina and also at the earliest levels of the visual pathways. There, the nature of the representation is clearly pictorial in the manner described earlier. But the main concern is with the regions of the brain that account for our cognitive activity. It is there that retinotopic plans are almost certainly lost, and it is there that the issue of resolvability becomes much more contentious. Brain scans of various kinds give a kind of illusory understanding of what is going on. The PET or fMRI scans, for example, operate at a level that is, at best, able to specify what part of the brain is using more or less sugar or oxygen at any given moment than other areas. It is, however, insensitive to the details of the interneuronal information processing that could help to answer the question of the resolvability of the representation issue.

J. R. Anderson (1978) was one of the first to suggest that the matter of internal representation was not resolvable with behavioral methods. Anderson's main antagonist in this debate of resolvability was Pylyshyn (1979), who asserted that the issue is capable of adjudication, that it can be resolved one way or another. Specifically, Pylyshyn supported a propositional explanation for the representation of images.

A substantial amount of support for the pictorial representation of percepts came from work on mental rotation, particularly that reported by Shepard and Metzler (1971) and Shepard and Cooper (1982). Their general finding was that the amount of time it took to determine whether two projective drawings were of the same object was a linear function of the angular difference in their orientation. Their subjects, therefore, took an amount of time that was functionally related to the time it would have taken to physically rotate the two depicted objects into the same orientation. Shepard and his colleagues interpreted this finding to mean that the objects were literally represented in the brain in a way that was spatially isomorphic to the stimuli—in other words, in the form of a pictorial rather than a propositional representation. Indeed, the term *mental rotation* suggests a process that is literally a pictorial, isomorphic, three-dimensional manipulation of the perceived three-dimensional object. It does not imply a response to a two-dimensional projective drawing that had been presented as a stimulus. Shepard and Metzler's "angles of rotation" are angles in this three-dimensional space, not in the picture plane.

At the simplest conceptual level, as discussed in chapter 2, this interpretation must be flawed. It is an extrapolation from psychophysical data to the underlying mechanisms, contrary to Moore's theorem. The question of the resolvability of internal representations is primary in this case and has been finessed. The commitment to a pictorial answer ignores the simple fact that an excellent internal propositional system and an excellent internal pictorial system could both produce the same psychophysical outcome!

We can go beyond this epistemological point, however, because there are some empirical data that challenge the specific proposition put forward by Shepard and his colleagues. Niall (1997) rejected this interpretation in a very complete review of the entire problem of mental rotation. He carried out a series of experiments that discriminated between rotation in the picture plane and rotation in depth. The total angular difference between two images was the independent variable; the time taken to determine whether two figures are the same or different was the dependent variable. Niall showed by his experiments that the mean response time can vary substantially even though the total angular difference (depth rotation plus plane rotation) is held constant. The constant angular difference in space is accomplished by varying the depth rotation of the images in tandem. He interpreted these results as a challenge to the Shepard and Metzler mental rotation hypothesis, and therefore to the notion of a pictorially isomorphic mental representation. The account Niall offered in its place was a geometric theory of invariants in which the properties of the object that do not change are more important than the overall geometry of the object. For example, the differences between two objects in the perspective drawings in the plane may be sufficient to distinguish them as "same or different" even in the absence of any knowledge of their three-dimensional properties.

Niall's disassociation of some parts of the mental rotation process from others means that the entire three-dimensional shape of the discriminated objects is no longer key and that an isomorphic representation in the form of Shepard and Metzler's mental rotation is unnecessary. Indeed, no three-dimensional rotation at all is required to describe the data. Niall provides a perfectly good alternative explanation that does not involve mental rotation of such objects. From this point of view, the concept of any kind of an isomorphic spatial representation becomes irrelevant and unnecessary, as well as inconclusive. Niall's experiments delinking rotation in depth from rotation in the plane also delink the behavioral reports from a specific cognitive process, mental rotation, which then becomes a cognitive process or component that may or may not exist beyond its role in the theory.

Another situation in which this debate on representation has become embodied is in the lively discussions between Ratcliff and Hacker (1982) on the one hand and Proctor and Rao (1981) on the other. The issue in this case was whether reaction-time differences between positive and negative responses are satisfactory criteria for distinguishing between alternative models of matching tasks. The specific question that divided these two groups was whether reaction times were associated with processing times in some simple and direct manner. It was argued by Proctor and Rao that such an association, if well founded, would allow a cognitive-reductionist model of the underlying processes to be developed.

Ratcliff and Hacker, on the other hand, argued that reaction-time measures are indeterminate with regard to the duration of the underlying processes. They argued in favor of a nonreductive model more like Ratcliff's (1981) descriptive statistics, which did not employ precise deterministic descriptions of the properties of the underlying mechanisms. I believe that Ratcliff and his colleagues argued a specific case of the more general antireductionist hypothesis that I have presented here. They, too, seemed to believe that the detailed structure of the underlying mental architecture is not discernible using input–output methods. Of course, this is the key issue in the debate over the suitability of cognitive reductionism. A negative answer to the question of the resolvability of internal representation would be equivalent to the stand that I have taken here. Ratcliff's statistical model is a descriptive and behavioral approach that is quite compatible with my own thinking.

SOME CONTEMPORARY APPROACHES

Studies That Purport to Assay the Underlying Cognitive Processes Directly

Serial and Parallel Processing—A False Dichotomy[3]

A major problem with much of cognitive reductionism is that its practitioners often set up false controversies, based on extreme and unrealistic dichotomies, as straw men on which to exercise their particular theories. One of the most obvious examples of such a pseudo-controversy is the attempt to distinguish between two possible internal arrangements of human search and recognition behavior—serial and parallel processing.

The history of the serial versus parallel processing problem has been studied by J. T. Townsend (1974) for over 25 years. Perhaps more than anyone else, he has been centrally involved in the study and critical analysis of this problem (e.g., Townsend, 1969, 1971, 1972, 1974; Townsend & Thomas, 1994). Townsend (1974) notes that the problem is of ancient lineage, having been discussed in the time of Plato and Aristotle. He goes on to note that the first scientists to be actively interested in the problem were not psychologists but astronomers interested in the differences in the variable reaction times when measuring transits of an object across a cross hair in a telescope.

Townsend (1974) was among the first to suggest that there have been major difficulties attacking the serial versus parallel problem from its very inception. The main argument for the difficulty, if not the intractability, of the problem is the same as Moore's (1956)—the general problem faced when confronted when trying to analyze a closed system. In Townsend's (1974) words

> The difficulties arise, of course, when we wish to make inferences about the inner workings of the system for some reason but cannot actually inspect these, because it is too difficult or because society frowns on indiscriminate slicing into certain black boxes of interest to psychology. Then it may be that a model, hypothesized to describe these workings and employed to predict input-output behavior of the system, may be similar or even identical to a model that began by picturing the system in a drastically different way. That the models may be equivalent does not mean that the systems they refer to are equivalent, but only that they may act in an equivalent manner, when we can observe what happens at the input (stimulus) and output (response) stages. (p. 139)

---

[3]Some of this section on serial and parallel processing has been adapted from my earlier book *On Seeing Forms* (Uttal, 1988).

This language, of course, is but another way of expressing the inherent limits of any cognitive reductive approach and the need for the constraints embodied in a behaviorist approach to the study of mental processes.

Townsend goes on in this same article and elsewhere (Townsend, 1972) to describe how serial and parallel models may mimic each other in a way that makes it difficult, if not impossible, to discriminate between serial and parallel processes. The point he is making is that two models that are apparently different from each other may actually be identical, that is, mathematical duals of each other. He gives examples of both parallel models that mimic serial behavior and serial models that mimic parallel behavior.

The problem is extremely difficult, of this there is no question. Townsend and Ashby (1983) suggest some methods that may work in special cases and under only certain conditions. In many cases these conditions do not obtain and a general solution remains elusive. Nevertheless, almost three decades later, as I discuss later in this chapter, Townsend (Townsend & Thomas, 1994) was still wrestling with the serial versus parallel problem and concerned about the plausibility of ever solving it.

I would go even further and suggest that the question of whether some process is serial or parallel is, in fact, a "bad question." It preassumes an extreme dichotomous nature of the underlying cognitive processes when they are more likely to be far more flexible and incorporate both types of processes.

I argue in this section that the processes involved in the typical search experiment are not so simple nor so extremely defined as may be suggested by an either/or controversy between serial and parallel underlying processes. I take this position despite the fact that in large part most contemporary psychologists believe that these questions are legitimate and can be attacked empirically. For example, there is a near consensus supporting the conjecture that for the nonphysical, semantic type of search material, a serial sequence of selectively and individually attentive judgments must be made. The problem is that the behavior measured may be an answer to some question other than the one with which it is usually associated.

Let us consider the search paradigm first. One approach to resolving the serial–parallel issue concerns whether a serial search is exhaustive (i.e., even though the search may be serial, are all items in a searched list evaluated before a decision is made?) or self-terminating (i.e., does the search process stop when the target item is located?). Although it might seem very inefficient to continue a search once the target is located, there is, in fact, some evidence that exhaustive searching may occur in some situations. Sample evidence supporting parallel processing would be of the form of response times that do not vary as a function of the position of the target item in lists of constant length.

Another set of questions revolves around the matter of whether or not the items in the ensemble interact with each other. It seems clear that the interaction of an item with its semantic neighbors is likely to be much more complex (because they share common meanings) than in the simple sense of a spatial inhibition mediated by, say, interaction among neural receptors. Even though this latter type of interaction is popular in the passive models of low-level visual processes, it is obviously a very different kind of "interaction" from that occurring in semantic systems. Interactions among semantic categories and classes are of enormous complexity, involving mechanisms at the highest cognitive levels. How, for example, can we possibly explain a visual search for a word that was the name of a member of the cat family whose outcome is affected by nontarget words that are the names of invertebrates? Nevertheless, this result is typical of observed search behavior. Experiments of this kind explore the impact of a kind of conceptual clustering, as opposed to simple geometrical propinquity, on recognition in the search paradigm. Some older theories of cognition based on list-processing computer languages attempted to simulate propinquity in meaning by adjacency in lists, but this was obviously an artifice that could only roughly approximate the conceptual association accomplished in the human cognitive system.

Another important issue in visual search experiments concerns the impact of the degree of familiarity of a word on its recognizability. It is presumed that more familiar words are more likely to be recognized than less familiar words. Indeed, targets made up of strings of letters that are not words do seem to be harder to locate than those that do make up words. Here again, the complexity of the human thought process vastly exceeds the ability of any model to do more than describe these functions.

Another closely related question concerns whether or not the information about the category to which the items in the search array belong must be determined prior to their recognition. If prior categorization is required, this would imply that some kind of a cognitive evaluation of the items occurred prior to full-blown recognition. Such an outcome would be strong evidence that the search-and-recognition process for items differing only in semantic content is actually carried out in a series of stages.

Let us consider the current status of the answers to some of these issues as a means of understanding another reason why ontological cognitive reductionism of any kind is likely to remain elusive. I begin with a discussion of the basic serial–parallel controversy itself.

Search behavior has long been considered to be a powerful assay tool for studying the serial versus parallel problem. The problem was brought back to scientific attention when Sternberg (1966, 1967) published two relatively brief but extremely influential articles in the journals *Science* and *Perception and Psychophysics*. Sternberg reasoned that if a search process of the kind we have described took place in serial order, the larger the number of items in a limited set of alphabetic characters, the longer would be the reaction time to search through that set. If, on the other hand, the search process occurred in parallel, then the length of the list should not materially affect the reaction time. To carry out this experiment in a way that was free of many of the difficulties that exceptionally long lists would entail, Sternberg exposed relatively short lists of alphabetic characters to the observer in a tachistoscope. After the list was presented and, presumably, stored by the observer in some kind of short-term memory (the specific nature of which is not material at this point) a single probe character was presented. The observer's task was to specify whether or not the particular alphabetic character was in the list originally presented.

The results of Sternberg's experiment seemed very clear-cut. The reaction times measured were strong linear functions of the number of items in the list that had been presented to the observer and committed to short-term memory. The search process seemed, therefore, to be best characterized as being serial; it could also be characterized as being self-terminating because the process was completed when the target item was identified. Reaction times were strong functions of where the item was positioned in the memorized list. That is, if the item occurred early in the list, then the reaction times were short; if later, they were longer.

Many others have followed in Sternberg's footsteps and provided similar kinds of data supporting the contention that the search for a single target alphabetic character is a self-terminating, serial process in which each character takes about 30 to 35 msec to process. However, others have argued that there is evidence that similar search processes are, quite to the contrary, carried out in parallel. The arguments for parallel processing are somewhat less direct and compelling, even given the apparent inadequacies of any experiments of this kind. Most deal with "pop-out" effects dependent on the basic physical nature of the stimulus rather than its meaning. Thus, once again, we see how two sides of a controversy often depend on the experimental conditions more than the psychobiology. It is truly the case that, all too often, arguments erupt between sides that have literally not made empirical or theoretical contact.

One modestly strong argument against the existence of either pure serial or parallel processing is to be found in the observation that categorical and contextual effects, of the kind I mentioned earlier, are exhibited in the results of search experiments. If any interaction (as evidenced by the modulation of reaction times as a result of the relations between the semantic content of the items in the list) occurs between the items in a search, then it must be inferred that the examination of each item in the list is not entirely independent of the nature of the other items. This argument goes on to assert that such an interaction is tantamount to some partial parallel interaction, if not a patently parallel processing solution of all parts of the problem. "Interaction" of this sort is an initial indication of the failure of the dichotomous premise on which much of this work is based. To the degree that reaction times can be varied by changing the nature of the stimulus material, the notion of a fixed system, either parallel or serial, becomes disputable.

Further attempts have been made to improve upon the Sternberg method. For example, Taylor (1976) developed a method that used the interactions rather than the failures of interactions as the criterion events. Nevertheless, the problem still remains difficult and perhaps even intractable. Taylor, for example, referring to the possibility of determining how long the steps in a reaction time experiment take, concludes by noting that:

> It is clear from the results of the preceding section that it is not feasible, given the methods currently available, to make direct measurements of stage times. For this reason it is virtually impossible to evaluate the suitability of a model to a particular stage in isolation of the effects of the other stages. (p. 183)

And, conversely, comparing serial and parallel processing models and noting that they make the same predictions, he says: "The fact that two models of stage time are using different processing schemes does not necessarily mean that their predictions will differ" (p. 185).

Another set of somewhat stronger arguments for distinguishing between parallel and serial search processes has come from the work of Shiffrin and Schneider (1977; Schneider & Shiffrin, 1977). The experimental design they used differed from the Sternberg paradigm in several ways. The critical difference, however, between the two experimental procedures lay in the fact that the observer in Shiffrin and Schneider's studies was required to search for any one of several different targets rather than for only one single target letter. The argument is that if the observer has to compare each item in the nontarget list with only one target, it should take less time than if he has to make the comparison for all of the possibilities of the alternative targets serially. Indeed, this is what seemed to happen initially to their untrained observers: The response time to specify the presence of a target varied linearly, as in the Sternberg experiment, but in this case as a function of the number of possible target items. Serial processing was thus initially supported for this kind of experiment.

Shiffrin and Schneider's subsequent results, however, indicated that something quite different was occurring later when the observers were well trained: As long as the multiple target items and the nontarget items in the ensemble were always used in the same way (i.e., the target items were either all letters or all numerals and the nontarget items were always chosen from the other category—a condition referred to as *homogeneous*), there was little difference in the search times required for the observer to report whether or not any of the target items were present as a function of the number of possible alternative targets. There was only a slight degradation in the performance (i.e., elongated reaction times) of the well-trained observers when they were asked to look for six as opposed to one target letter. This result suggested the possibility of the conversion of a serial to a parallel process with experience.

In the context of our present discussion, these results were presented by Shiffrin and Schneider as a proof of the existence of parallel processing under certain conditions of stimuli and experience. Whether it was called "automatic" processing (as some researchers more interested in memory than perception are likely to do) or "parallel" processing (as students of perception are likely to do), the absence of a prolongation of response times with increasing difficulty of the task suggests that some mental processes may be occurring simultaneously. On the other hand, if the items of the same category could be used as both target or distractor (nontarget) items (a condition referred to as *heterogeneous*), then there was always nearly a linear increase in search times.

However, there is an argument that may refute the line of logic suggesting that observers in this experiment were converting from a serial to a parallel process or vice versa with experience when the experiment went from a homogeneous to a heterogeneous type. It was also possible that the observers were not learning how to carry out a fixed set of underlying processes in parallel, but had actually changed the nature of the task in some fundamental way. That is, as observers become well practiced, there was no assurance that they had not changed the task from a letter-by-letter comparison to a multiple simultaneous comparison late in training. Perhaps all of the letters become a single kind of stimulus for a higher level of information encoding that subsequently required only a single comparison ("letter" or not) to be made where many were required previously.

The enormous adaptability of the human observer evidenced in these experiments makes arguments for cognitive theories based on comparisons of reaction times difficult, if not impossible, to test rigorously. The major dichotomous premise of the serial–parallel argument simply may no longer be valid: In a world of such variability and adaptability, it becomes difficult to provide a compelling argument for one side or the other of the controversy. Indeed, when viewed from this point of view the whole question of a dichotomous kind of information processing within the human cognitive system becomes highly questionable. If the process is so dependent on experimental conditions or the subject's experience, is there anything fundamental about the process itself? Are we exploring a fundamental aspect of human perception or are we simply assaying the effects of the design of our experimental probes?

Shiffrin and Schneider's (1977) experiment is, therefore, likely to be tapping much more complicated perceptual processes than it may seem at first. From one point of view, the sometimes-parallel results (no change in response time as a function of the number of target items) and the sometimes-serial results (a linear increase in response times with an increase in the number of target items) may be considered to be only the endpoints of a continuum describing the behavior of observers when they are presented with tasks of varying levels of difficulty and at various stages of learning. When the task is relatively simple, then faster and less computationally demanding processes can be executed in what seems to be a parallel manner. The simplest condition of all exists when the stimuli are so distinctly different in some raw physical manner (color, shape, size, statistical structure, etc.) and the processing is so fast that the target "pops out" in a virtually automatic and preattentive way (Julesz, 1981, 1983; Triesman & Patterson, 1984), thus reflecting a patently parallel discrimination rather than serial search or recognition processes.

There are other alternatives that can simulate parallel processing, such as the substitution of one process for another that I mentioned earlier. More difficult tasks may not be so easily restructured in new forms and may require more extensive, attentive effort. As the computational and analytic complexities increase, the observer must concentrate on a more narrowly defined portion of the task at hand. As the observer concentrates and slows down, the underlying processes may simply be becoming more difficult and must increasingly be carried out in sequence; they thus appear to the experimenter in the guise that we have come to call "serial."

This line of thought adds further support to the contention that the serial and parallel controversy may be based on a false dichotomy. Rather, it may be that some kind of psychobiological reality exists in which there is a more or less constant amount of "mental processing capacity" (if I may use this phrase without being challenged to define it too precisely) that can be allocated either to single difficult tasks or to multiple easy tasks. This is exactly the theoretical theme proposed by the late Marilyn Shaw and her colleagues. Shaw (1978), like Townsend, proposed a model that emphasized that in addition to some limit on the amount of information that could be stored in the various memories of the observer, there was also a limit on the amount of processing capacity available. Depending on the nature and difficulty of the tasks with which the observer was confronted, various numbers of processes could be simultaneously executed.

In her work, Shaw joined with other colleagues (Harris, Shaw, & Altom, 1985; Harris, Shaw, & Bates, 1979) to expand this allocation-of-limited-store-of-attentive-energy theory in ways that are extremely germane to the present discussion. Although I do not take the "limited store" idea too literally, Shaw and her colleagues made an important contribution in adding to the argument that the serial–parallel dichotomy hypothesis itself must be much too rigid to explain anything. The original model (Shaw, 1978) was expanded in these two papers from one purely dependent on limited capacity to one that stressed the overlapping of various subprocesses in the visual-search tasks with which we are now concerned. The term *overlapping*, the essential idea in the Shaw et al. theory, is presented by them as an alternative hypothesis to an extreme serial-versus-parallel dichotomy. This new version of their theory proposes the existence of a "scanning" mechanism that, under certain conditions, is able to process more than one item at a time. The process is sequential in terms of its information acquisition, but can operate on several items simultaneously. Thus, there is an overlap of the processing of items that entered previously but that have not yet been completely processed, and those that enter later.

Accepting a fundamental measurement from the work of Sperling (1960), that it takes about 10 msec to process a single character, Shaw and her colleagues proposed that the scanning mechanism stepped along from alphabetic character to alphabetic character, sequentially entering a new item into the processing mechanism at this rate. However, the essentially new aspect of their model is the proposal that the processing need not be completed for any character in the 10-msec acquisition period. If the processing takes longer than that quantal period of time, several items may simultaneously be processed. The processing of several items thus overlaps in time; by one definition this is a partially parallel system. Of course, from another point of view, it is also a serial system, in that the items are accessed in serial order. In point of fact, it is neither a serial nor a parallel system in the extreme dichotomous sense, but an overlapping one that can simulate either at its extremes. Most important to the present discussion is that the processing system also behaves quite differently from either a serial or parallel one in intermediate conditions.

The amount of service that an item receives by the processing mechanism is a function of several factors, according to Shaw and her colleagues. First, it is a function of the number of items in the processor at any given time. Second, it depends to a different degree on the number of items that entered the processor before the item being processed and the number of items that entered the processor after the item currently being processed. There is also a minimum amount of time within which any character can be processed, a value that for quite separate reasons the authors assumed was about 40 msec. But for lists with multiple items the factors mentioned here may prolong this processing time. Obviously–and this is the essence of the Shaw et al. theory–if the minimum processing time for each item is 40 msec and the access time for each item is 10 msec, the processing of items must overlap.

The overlap theory is empirically quite effective in modeling a wide variety of data. In the last paper in this series (Harris et al., 1985), the authors noted that most of the previous experimental attempts to distinguish between serial and parallel processes produced inconclusive results—results that completely reflected neither serial nor parallel mechanisms. The very inconclusive nature of the data forthcoming from so many of these experiments is itself compelling evidence that something intermediate between the two may actually be occurring and that the serial/parallel dichotomy of the extremes is probably an inappropriate model of the actual mechanisms.

It must be remembered that neither Shaw's overlap model nor any other mathematical formulation can establish beyond doubt anything specific about the nature of the underlying mechanisms. What these models do accomplish is to raise serious questions about the extreme serial–parallel hypothesis. Shaw's findings and her model do, however, serve as existence proofs that something intermediate between the two extreme alternatives can and probably does exist. As such, the serial–parallel question is transformed from one of great and enthusiastic absoluteness, involving an unrealistic dichotomy, into a more reasonable and realistic description of an adaptive, flexible, and creative cognitive system of great power. As I have already noted, virtually everyone who has approached this problem has confronted the true difficulty of what at first may have seemed to be a straightforward question.

The eventual resolution of extreme dichotomy controversies, such as the parallel–serial argument, in the form of some sort of an intermediate compromise represents a step forward in our science. Not only does it represent a maturation of thinking about thinking, but it also allows psychology to rise to the level already achieved by many other sciences. An intermediate compromise is typical of the eventual outcome of rigid dichotomous arguments in any science. Perhaps the best known analogy is from physics—the wave-and-quantum issue that divided physicists for so many years and proved to be equally inappropriate there. This issue has now been resolved there in favor of the dual nature of matter–energy. There are other significant and important historical examples of the power of such theoretical compromises. Another is the heredity–environment or nature–nurture debate that ravished good sense in both psychology and biology until it came to be appreciated that neither could fully explain the richness and variety of adult behavior. In the same way, the serial–parallel controversy was brought closer to some kind of sensible resolution by the overlap theory proposed by Shaw and her colleagues. The overlap theory is beset by the same epistemological problems as any other, of course. Nevertheless, its adaptability and variability makes it a closer approximation as a description of what may actually be executed in the cognitive system.

The strong evidence that some kind of overlapping must occur in the visual search task that has been provided by Shaw and her colleagues, and the formal demonstration by Jordan (1986), and Townsend (1969, 1974, 1983), among others, of the fact that parallel mechanisms can imitate serial behavior if it is slow enough (and vice versa; if the serial process is fast enough, apparently parallel system behavior emerges from the operation of a single, but very fast, serial mechanism), raise additional questions about the strong form of the serial-parallel premise. Confounding the difficulty of distinguishing between a serial and a parallel mechanism is the "black-box problem" alluded to earlier in this chapter in different words.

Even Townsend, who is perhaps the most sophisticated student of the serial versus parallel problem, still has reservations about its tractability. Townsend, working with such colleagues as R. Schweickert and F. G. Ashby, has been searching for empirical tests that might or might not be useful in discriminating the internal architecture of the mind. In a recent article Townsend and Thomas (1994) reviewed some of the main issues and described how the dependencies that exist in serial and parallel systems can affect the interactions measured in factorial experiments. Townsend and Thomas precisely defined the basic terms used in this discussion. In particular, the Townsend and Thomas paper spelled out, in a formal mathematical manner, what is meant by serial and parallel and what is meant by the kinds of "influence" that experimental parameters can exert on serial and parallel systems, respectively. The dense mathematical arguments of Townsend and Thomas' paper need not be replicated here. However, they do come to some conclusions that suggest that even these proponents of experimental analyses as a tool to determine underlying mental architecture are not yet fully convinced that the quest is achievable. In particular, they ask of the analyses they carried out in this paper:

> Can these results be fruitfully employed to help identify underlying architectures? In general, dependencies can clearly obfuscate that architecture by allowing a structure of one type to mimic the factorial contrast of another. However, single factor reversal and contrast changes can, at least theoretically, aid in detecting the presence of dependencies. (p. 30)

And later:

> It is too early to tell if these new features of processing can actually be effective in architecture identification in experimental tasks and model testing in general. One direction to go may be to construct experimental tasks that encourage strong negative dependencies and therefore possible reversals. Another is to perform factorial experiments over wide ranges of the factor levels to look for contrast change. (p. 31)

My interest in presenting these quotations is not to recruit Townsend to my critique of cognitive reductionism. My guess is that he would probably come down on the side of those who believe that this is a valid enterprise. Rather, I wish only to point out that even a very strong proponent of the approach is well aware of the treacherous grounds on which much less sophisticated cognitive reductionists have built their models. His analysis of the problem led Townsend to the very cautious statements I have just quoted. I am particularly interested in his warning about dependencies because, as discussed next, this is a crucial assumption of many of the methods that have been proposed to analyze other cognitive processes underlying variations in human reaction times, a topic to which I now turn.

Addition and Subtraction of Reaction Times

During the past century, even before the evolution of experimental psychology into cognitive psychology, there was an effort to determine the "mental architecture" by manipulating reaction times. Reaction time is generally defined as the time between the stimulus and the beginning of a response. A fundamental assumption of this kind of research is that reaction-time measurements are assumed to closely track the time it takes for the mental processing of input information. It is generally assumed, and indeed has been empirically established, that the greater the amount of information in the stimulus and the more decisions that have to be made, the longer the time taken to process the information and, thus, the longer the reaction time. In general, this relation between informational complexity and reaction times is referred to as the Hick–Hyman Law (Hick, 1952; Hyman, 1953). Many other factors, however, also influence the measured reaction time, and these can be found in any elementary text on human cognition.

The use of reaction times as indicators of the underlying mental architecture, as shown later, is based on several critical and what some of us now believe are totally unsubstantiated simplifying assumptions. Some of these assumptions are dealt with explicitly, but many are often hidden in the discussion cryptically or implicitly. For example, another very important assumption in the modern effort to determine the architecture of the mind is that reaction times are composed of a number of isolatable subcomponents. For what appear in retrospect to be relatively arbitrary reasons, the total reaction time is often broken up into the simple reaction time (the minimum time required to respond to an expected single stimulus), the time required for the identification of the stimulus when there are multiple stimuli, and the time required for the selection of the response when there are several response options. This analysis depends on very restricted experimental conditions and, therefore, highly constrained notions of what constitutes a reaction time experiment. In this analysis, the stimuli are assumed to be highly discrete physical entities with little semantic content—a light comes on or not. Similarly, responses are assumed to be discrete motor responses. Obviously, experiments of this kind are carried out in a highly limited domain that grossly underestimates the true complexity of human reaction processes to more complicated stimulus and response situations.

Another equally basic, fundamental, and terribly flawed assumption is usually introduced into analyses of reaction time data. Indeed, it is this assumption on which the entire philosophy that the architectural structure of mental processes can be assayed by judicious reaction times experiments is based. That additional assumption is that the components of the reaction time are, themselves, more fixed, stable, and rigid than not. That is, it is presumed that the components are independent of each other as well as independent of the ways in which they are organized into more complex systems. This independence refers not only to the immutability of the component itself, but also to the fact that its removal or addition will not alter the function of the other components of the reaction time system.

Furthermore, from one task or one experimental situation to another, each component is assumed to be inelastic; that is, it will take the same amount of time to carry out its function in one role as in any other. Implicit in this assumption is the idea that each component is the same "thing" in one cognitive information-processing system as in any other.

Another assumption almost always involved in this type of component analysis of reaction times is that of seriality. Seriality means that the components of the reaction time are not only independent of each other but are organized in a tail-to-head version like the links in a chain. Link 2 can occur, according to this assumption, only after link 1 completes its function. Although it is never made explicit, many experimental attempts to determine the underlying nature of the mental architecture implicitly assume that the several steps are not overlapping. As we have seen, Shaw's analyses and findings strongly contradict this assumption.

Pachella (1974) was among the first to challenge this entire edifice of reaction time analysis. He pointed out additional assumptions and criticized both the subtraction method and the additive factors methods (both of which are next described in detail) in terms of these and related logical frailties. As a general criticism, Pachella noted that the very existence of the reaction-time components is questionable. I discuss his and other criticisms of each of these research methodologies in the next sections after introducing the basic ideas inherent in each of these theoretical approaches.

Donders' Subtraction Method. A classic reaction time method that has attracted a great deal of attention for almost a century, and continues to be a ubiquitous component of any elementary textbook, is Donders' (1868/1969) subtraction method. This approach is based on the drastically simplified concept of the nature of the cognitive processing—the idea that the time taken to react to a stimulus is the linear sum of the time taken by each of the three constituent mental processes described previously. Given the assumption of the linear addition of the component times, it was an easy step to the idea that these times could be subtracted from each other to determine the times taken by each. Donders (1868/1969) designed the following three prototype experimental paradigms to test his ideas:

1. The A reaction: This procedure measures the basic physiological response, including the minimum time taken for the stimulus information to be acquired by the nervous system plus the minimum time taken to respond. In this case, it was assumed that there was only a minimal need for any "cognitive" processing to take place. The stimulus was a single, well-expected event and there was only one possible response. The single stimulus was assumed to be almost directly linked to the single response. This situation defined what has come to be called Donder's A reaction—the simple reaction time.

2. The B reaction: Donders also realized that there were situations in which the stimulus could only be one of several possible alternatives and similarly that there might be more than one possible response. Therefore, he designed a procedure in which the salient stimulus had to be identified (a component cognitive process) before an appropriate one of several possible responses could be selected (another component cognitive process). Furthermore, both processes had to be carried out independently and in sequence. Donders defined this situation—multiple possible stimuli and multiple possible responses—as the B reaction. We now refer to this task as the choice reaction time experimental design. The B reaction, therefore, was supposed to take place over an interval made up of three parts: (a) the simple reaction time establishing a minimum time, (b) the time required for identification of the stimulus, and (c) the time required to decide which response was appropriate.

3. The C reaction: Donders also proposed that there was an intermediate form of reaction-time paradigm in which the subject was presented with one of several alternative stimuli but had only one possible response. The appropriate response was released only when the particular one of several potential stimuli occurred. Otherwise no response was to be made to any other stimulus. This "go–no go" type experiment defined Donders' C reaction.

Donders proposed that the length of time required for any of the three component processes (i.e., simple reaction time, stimulus identification time, and response selection time) to run its course was sufficiently constant (although dependent on the difficulty of the task) to be measured by carrying out appropriate combination experiments. The simple reaction time, of course, was measured simply by performing the A reaction time experiment. By subtracting the simple reaction time A from the C reaction time (which required time to determine which stimulus had occurred, but no time to choose a response), the time required for the stimulus identification process could be determined. Similarly, by subtracting the C reaction time from the

B choice reaction time, Donders proposed that the difference would be a measure of the response selection time.

Although there is now considerable skepticism about the exactness and stability of such measurements, Donders' subtraction method is still taught as the prototype of an approach in which reaction times can be used to measure proposed internal processes and mechanisms. There are many difficulties with this approach, however. Although some processes may take longer than others, the probability of a nonserial internal mechanism, or one that violates any of the assumptions that I described earlier in this section, is much too high to permit such a simplistic model to be accepted uncritically. The virtual certainty that cognitive processes are elastic and adaptive must be contrasted against the simplified idealization of a serial system of rigidly and fixed processing components that is implicit in the assumptions. Shaw showed us that the serial–parallel pseudo-controversy could best be resolved by assuming that there was considerable overlap in the constituent processes. It is equally necessary to appreciate that the components of Donders' reaction-time prototypes need not be independent of the task in the way that would justify the use of this simple arithmetic analysis.

Pachella (1974), in his very important but generally overlooked article, listed several specific criticisms that can be directed at the subtractive method. More important, however, is the general idea implicit in his comments that such an approach will never permit a reconstruction of the mental architecture of even such relatively simple processes as those underlying reaction times. In his words:

> First, the Subtraction Method begs one of the most fundamental questions underlying information processing research, namely, the description of the mental events involved in an experimental task. The starting point for the application of the method is a relatively sophisticated one: In order to construct a comparison task, one must already know the sequence of events that transpire between stimulus and response. Such sophisticated knowledge is rarely available. Rather, it is more often the case that the structure of mental events is presented with only logical or intuitive (as opposed to empirical) justification. (p. 47)

I would go even further: The definition of the "sequence of events" (*events* being equivalent to the term *components* that I used earlier) is not and cannot be empirically justified by any series of experiments. Of course, in a nutshell this is the thesis of this entire chapter. The a priori invoked events or components are intuitive, albeit ingenious, inventions, but without empirical substance. No empirical means is available to the psychologist to identify one plausible event or component as the salient one from among all of the other possible ones. The hypothetical mental events, like so many other suggestions of internal structure, are actually defined more by the nature of the experimental procedure than they are forced by the psycho-biological facts of the mind–brain.

Pachella (1974) then raised another important point concerning the independence of the events or components from each other. As I noted earlier, this is a necessary assumption of all reaction-time manipulation research of the subtraction type. He stated:

> A second general criticism of the Subtraction Method concerns the comparability of the experimental and comparison tasks, or as Sternberg (1969b) has called it, the assumption of pure insertion. This refers to the assumption that it is possible to delete (or insert) completely mental events from an information processing task without changing the nature of the other constituent mental operations. (p. 48)

This comment attacks the fundamental assumption of the independence of the processes, but also speaks to their additivity, stability, and, in fact, their very existence as anything other than artifacts of the experimental procedure.

A related source of difficulty with Donders' subtractive technique is the very great variability of reaction times in realistic situations. Reaction times are not stable in most practical situations. Nor is it at all certain that they are in the experimental laboratory, as the subtraction method requires. Olson, Cleveland, Fancher, Kostyniuk, and Schneider (1984) showed that the response time to "unexpected intrusions" when one is driving a car is enormously varied, ranging from 0.8 sec to 1.8 sec in comparable situations. The enormous variability of the total reaction time in such cases also argues against the stability of the hypothetical components or mental events even under well-controlled laboratory conditions. The necessity for pooling data from many different subjects to achieve some stable picture of what is going on may also obscure this very significant fact.

Alternatively, this variability and wide-ranging individual differences suggest a much greater degree of flexibility and adaptability on the part of the hypothetical logical information-processing mechanisms of the cognitive system than would be required for the subtraction method to work. The fact that individual measurements vary so much raises the possibility that the numbers forthcoming from a Donders subtraction type experiment may reflect the pooling or averaging process rather than the stability of the components themselves. Either interpretation of the meaning of individual differences and experimental variability raises serious questions for the subtractive method.

Sternberg's Additive Factors Method. Sternberg's (1969a, 1969b, 1975) additive factors method was also developed to determine the nature and processing time of the components of the mental architecture. The additive factors method was designed to overcome some of the difficulties of the Donders subtractive method. It also manipulates reaction times, but not simply by subtracting them from each other. Instead, it depends on the degree of statistical interaction between or additivity of two or more variables.

The basic idea in the additive factors method is that a pair of independent variables will interact statistically if they are acting on the same cognitive component. On the other hand, their effects will simply add if they are acting on separate components. By carrying out a large number of pairings of a reasonable number of independent variables, it is proposed that the true nature of the cognitive components can be identified.

The logic behind the Sternberg additive factors method was also based on certain assumptions that are difficult to support, for reasons similar to those discussed in the section on the Donders subtractive method. For example, the seriality assumption (that there exists a string of components that sequentially execute well demarcated functions) is also an essential foundation premise of this model. As in the subtractive method, the collective time taken for each of the components to execute their individual function constituted and determined the entire externally measured reaction time. The Sternberg additive method, like the Donders subtractive technique, also assumed a stability of the various components from one experimental design to another. Indeed, this is the essence of Sternberg's concept of "pure insertion."

Unlike the subtractive method, however, there was no need in the additive factors method for a set of component functions to be specified in advance. In this regard, the approach resolved one of the basic criticisms of the Donders subtractive method–begging the question by predefining the components. The hope implicit in the additive factors method was that it offered a means to define the various components or blocks empirically as an outcome of the experiments, rather than as a precursor to them.

Although the additive factors method did not require an a priori statement of the nature of the components, it did require that the experimenter make an initial choice of the various independent variable parameters or stimulus factors that would be used to influence the overall reaction time. These factors included such independent variables as the discriminability of the stimulus, whether or not a mask was present, the nature of the response, the size of the stimulus set, stimulus–response compatibility, response complexity, and the number of alternative responses. This prior selection of the parameters of the experiment is a perfectly acceptable procedure because the selection of each one was determined by previous experimental experiences. A suggested parameter could be placed on the list of influential parameters if it was already known to produce some effect on the dependent variable.

The additive factors technique is an expensive procedure in the sense that a large number of experiments must be carried out to bring it to fruition.

In a typical experiment two of the chosen parameters were simultaneously manipulated, typically at two different values of each. This sparse sampling of independent variable values could lead to difficulties in some cases. However, the desired information is just the answer to a simple yes–no or binary type of question: Do the two variables interact or do they add? Thus, in this case, where many experiments must be carried out to compare all possible combinations of potentially relevant variables, the sparseness of the data is itself not an overwhelming problem.

The results of individual additive factors experiments, therefore, are often presented as plots that look like Fig. 4.4, panels A and B. The distinction between these two diagrams is the degree of statistical interaction between the two parameters, for example, as would be measured using an analysis of variance statistic. Interaction, in this context, implies that the two parameters affect each other in such a way that the difference in or relative values of the measured reaction times are dependent on the values of the independent parameter. The fact that the two curves in Fig. 4.4A are parallel (i.e., the *difference* between the two scores does not change as the two parameters are varied) indicates that there is no interaction–their effects simply add. From this kind of noninteractive data, additive factors theorists would draw the conclusion that these two factors exist independently of

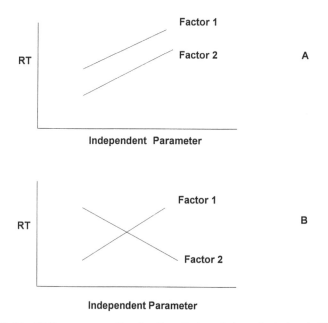

FIG. 4.4. (A) Two response time functions that are independent of each. (B) Two response time functions that interact. Refer to the text to appreciate that this is both an unrealistic and a nondiagnostic outcome of most psychophysical experiments.

each other, and therefore do not affect the same component of the mental architecture. Figure 4.4B, however, presents a different kind of result. The lines are not parallel; they cross, implying that the two factors do interact statistically. This is interpreted to mean that the two factors are affecting the same component of the mental architecture.

Additive factor theoreticians argue that if one carries out a sufficiently extensive program of research involving many of these two parameter experiments, a pattern will emerge that can be used to define the specific components (to the exclusion of other possible ones) that make up this part of the cognitive architecture. They assert that the need to define these components a priori has been averted. The factors can be named whatever one wishes, but their existence as relatively independent units is based on an empirical foundation and reflects psychobiological reality rather than experimental methodology. A substantial body of information was developed over the years that led many investigators to believe that they had actually identified specific components that could be designated by such arbitrary names as stimulus encoding, recognition, response selection, and response execution as a result of the pattern of additive and interactive relationships among the independent variables that affected the reaction time.

Clearly, the additive factors approach is, like the subtractive approach, based on some critical assumptions that seem to many to actually represent oversimplifications of what is intrinsically a much more complicated cognitive system. In his insightful article, Pachella (1974) also criticized this technique as well as the subtractive technique. Among the most salient of the doubts that he raised are:

1. The underlying mental architecture is simply not as rigid and stable as it would have to be to justify the approach. Pachella said, "The manipulation of factor levels may cause a fundamental change in the processing sequence as may happen with the deletion of an entire stage with the Subtraction Method" (1974, p. 57). It should be pointed out that this would make interaction effects more likely. Therefore, any purely "additive" effects that were observed would have more credibility than otherwise.

2. It is sometimes difficult to determine whether the data is strictly additive or strictly interactive. Pachella went on to say, "The data needed in order to demonstrate true additivity [parallel lines] requires a precision that few reaction time experiments obtain" (p. 57). In other words, additive curves are rarely perfectly parallel; the criterion is statistical insignificance of the differences, and therefore with small samples there always remains a doubt about the true independence of the effect.

3. The basic assumption of the additive factors method–two parameters that affect a different component will produce additive effects on reaction times, whereas two that affect the same component will interact–may be

flawed. This was just too much of a simplifying assumption for Pachella, who then suggested, "In situations where stages have some independent definition, it is perfectly conceivable that the two factors might affect a single stage in an additive manner or they might affect different stages and interact" (p. 58).

In addition, Pachella also pointed out that there is nothing in the experimental data that speaks to the problem of the order of the components. It is still a more or less arbitrary matter how the system is pieced together, just as what one names the purported blocks is a judgmental matter.

The two greatest difficulties with both the Donders subtraction method and Sternberg's additive factors method are well expressed by Pachella's criticisms. I now place them in the context of other general assertions made earlier. First, using behavioral data of this kind to define the internal mental architecture violates the very fundamental "black box" theorem. Input–output methods simply are not sufficient, in principle, to prove the necessity and sufficiency of any unique arrangement of possible internal components. There are too many degrees of freedom and too many alternative arrangements remaining to permit us to do anything more than reject a few of the most implausible architectures. I noted earlier how this important idea received rigorous mathematical support in the work of Moore (1956), but I would like to quote Pachella one more time to show that this grand constraining principle also permeates experimental psychology, albeit in a considerably less visible manner:

> Thus, a model of processing in which the stages are defined by an Additive Factors analysis may not be identifiably different from an alternative model *based on a different definition of stage* in which the properties of the stages do not lead to the simple patterns described above. They may just be two different conceptualizations of the structure underlying some body of data. (Pachella, 1974, p. 58; italics added)

Throughout this book we have seen many instances in which this idea has been expressed in different words but with the same meaning.

Second, the entire attempt to develop a mental architecture is based on the highly unlikely hypothesis that the architecture is functionally fixed and stable over wide ranges of experimental conditions even in the unlikely case that they are anatomically fixed. This fundamental simplifying assumption, so basic to both the Donders and Sternberg methods, as well as any other similarly founded approach (such as that of Taylor, 1976), is so out of context with the rest of our appreciation of human mental adaptability and flexibility that it seems to disqualify this particular method, in particular, and the search for a mental architecture by means of psychophysical experiments, in general.

The limitations of reaction times as a means of uncovering the mental architecture have been appreciated, even by those who have used them as dependent variables in their own studies. For example, in a very important book, Posner (1978) defined an experimental paradigm that has now come to be considered a much more compelling use of reaction times than either the subtraction or addition methods.

The key result of this part of Posner's research program was the outcome that substantial differences in the way matches were made depended on the nature of the criterion that was used to justify the match. That is, the experimenter may ask the observer to compare two letters on the basis of a purely physical match (e.g., two uppercase B's must be reported to be the "same" according to this criterion, but an uppercase B and a lowercase b must be reported to be different); on the basis of a name match (e.g., an uppercase B would be reported to be the "same" as a lowercase b according to this criterion); or, finally, on the basis of some more elaborate rule such as whether or not the two letters were both vowels (e.g., an uppercase E and a lowercase u must be reported to be the "same" if the observer followed this rule). In general, reaction times increased as one went from one level of stimulus complexity to higher ones. But the effects were always complex and not adequately explained by additive factors concepts.

Posner's results are interesting, but I find even more relevance in the present context in his explicit discussion of the assumptions that both motivated and underlay his work. In many ways, they support the arguments that I have made in this book. For example, when discussing the fact that many previous psychophysical experiments had shown that there is a summation of the time required to process repeated events, a fact often used to support a serial organization of cognitive processes, he noted: "It is not appropriate to conclude from such results that the human is always limited to one event at a time or that stages never overlap" (Posner, 1978, p. 218).

Concerning his own work, Posner asserted that he was not trying to make a "detailed experimental analysis of any task," but rather to determine the effect of some aspect of the experimental design on some psychological process (e.g., alertness) by using the task as a probe. The use of such data to describe the rules of mental transformation without attempting to define internal mechanism is entirely acceptable to behaviorists.

Vigilance

Another cognitive process that has been of great interest and intense research examination, especially in an applied setting, is vigilance. Vigilance experiments are mainly designed to measure the ability of an observer to maintain a high level of detection performance over long periods. In general, as time goes by in a repetitive task, the ability of the observer to perform that task declines. The term *vigilance* is obviously closely related to the term *attention*. Indeed, vigilance has been often defined as the "ability to sustain attention" or, even more simply, "sustained attention" itself (Parasuraman, 1986). It also has been defined as "a neural or physiological state of readiness" or, equally simply, as "arousal." These latter terms have been used especially by the more physiologically oriented of our colleagues.

The phrases "ability to sustain attention" and "physiological state" initially suggest that a new component, or ability, of the mental architecture has been identified. The suggestion is that this "ability" can vary in amount and that the amount can be measured. However, when a more detailed definition of vigilance is pursued, it is interesting to note that it is not usually dealt with as a property or amount of some component of the mental architecture. Rather, the level of vigilance is defined in terms of the operations with which it is measured. For example, Davies and Parasuraman (1982) defined the level of vigilance as nothing more than the "overall level of detection performance."

In this context, vigilance should more properly be thought of as an operationally defined dependent variable rather than as a component of the mental architecture. It is a score, not an ability, a mechanism, or even a process. Like any physiological or psychophysical indicator of activity, it is a measure of some process or structure, but it is not that process or structure. It is highly unlikely that a "vigilance center" would or could be found in the nervous system in spite of the fact that some center could be (and has been) found that could regulate the overall arousal of the organism. The classic idea of the reticular activating system (RAS) is of this genre, but that does not mean that the RAS is a vigilance center. Vigilance scores are simply measures of the functioning of this part of the brain in concert with what must be a large number of others. Indeed, it is now becoming clear that the vigilance measure is not even attributable to a single process, but actually represents a composite measure of several different mental activities.

The composite nature of "vigilance" becomes clear when it is analyzed using a signal detection theory (SDT). Swets (1977) reviewed the literature in which SDT was used to measure declining performance in detection tasks. The advantage of this approach in analyzing vigilance is that it separates the influence on performance into two kinds, the sensitivity of the organism (d') and the decision criterion level (β). Earlier research with high target probabilities typically showed the entire performance decrement might be attributable to a decline in β; there appeared to be very little reduction in the sensitivity of the observer as measured by d'. Swets (1977) also described how this conclusion was overturned by subsequent studies that showed that, in a richer variety of environments than military watch activities, both d' and β varied as vigilance scores changed. How much each contributed to the decline in detection scores depended on the frequency with which targets appeared and the task, as well as the sensory modality being studied.

Although these results are interesting, the most important fact about the SDT analysis is that it clearly shows that vigilance is not a single entity, property, mechanism, process, or behavior. Rather, since both the inferred payoff matrix underlying β and whatever fatigue factors influence d' can affect the outcome, the experimental paradigm we call vigilance must obviously be the sum of at least two and probably many different psychological processes.

The important conclusion is that just because a single measure of some complex cognitive function has been developed on the basis of what may even seem to be a clean-cut experimental design, it is not necessary that that measure reflects the operation of an equally singular mental mechanism. That is, of course, a reiteration of the argument that I have been making that the behavior, no matter how well quantified by some well-behaved numerical psychophysical measure, is not and cannot be used as an argument that some particular underlying mental mechanism is at work. On the contrary, even the simplest experimental design must assay the effects of a complex of underlying mental activities that may be completely hidden in the observed phenomena.

Psychophysical Data Suggest Strong Interattribute Interaction

In an important paper, Stoner and Albright (1993) made the case that individual attributes of visual perception cannot be studied in isolation from each other with psychophysical techniques. They pointed out that the strong interactions that occur between the various components or attributes of a visual scene make it difficult to study any one of them in functional isolation from any of the others. For example, they reviewed the literature and showed that motion perception is dependent on how the image is segmented. Because the perceptual process is studied as a unitary whole with psychophysical methodologies, they suggested that it may be that the dream of studying the components in isolation is only that–a dream. This argument is analogous to the one being made in this chapter–namely, that reduction to cognitive components is not feasible.

This does not mean that the components may not exist in the nervous system or that the neurophysiological coding of the separate pathways cannot be examined. In that case, isolation is possible because neurophysiological methods are inherently analytic. The problem in this case is that the recombination process requires a synthetic approach, and that is as far beyond the ability of the neurophysiological methodology as analysis is beyond psychophysics.

SUMMARY

Finally, let us sum up by listing some of the assumptions necessary for cognitive reductionism that have arisen in the course of this discussion. The main issue remains: Can human mentation be reduced to a set of components in a mental architecture, stable enough from situation to situation to be considered as an explanatory theory of perception in particular and cognition in general? An affirmative answer to this general question would require that many of the following assumptions (depending on which are invoked in any given theory) be accepted.

1. The assumption of seriality and/or parallelicity. The blocks are processed in either a serial or a parallel order but with no overlap or time sharing.
2. The assumption of summation. The time taken to process each block can be added to that of all others to estimate the total time for a task to be completed.
3. The assumption of functional rigidity or "pure insertion." Blocks can be inserted or removed by adjusting the nature of the task without any effect on the execution time of any other block.
4. The assumption of independence. The execution time of any block is independent of how it is used in tasks of equivalent difficulty.
5. The assumption of additivity versus interaction as a criterion for distinguishing between "same" or "different" blocks in an additive factors approach.
6. The assumption of precision. Reaction time and other processing-dependent variables can be measured accurately enough to distinguish between alternative models.
7. The assumption of replication. There is a sufficiently substantial body of replicated and confirmed data concerning cognitive information processing on which to base specific models.
8. The assumption of the transparent black box. It is possible by input–output (stimulus-response) techniques to determine the nature of the internal mental architecture.

In my judgment, none of these assumptions can be validated, verified, or even tested, and they are all, therefore, likely to be insupportable. Therefore, I conclude this chapter with a very strong and, I am sure, unpopular statement: *The entire effort to reduce mental functions to some kind of an underlying architecture of cognitive components is wasted!*

This does not mean that all studies of human cognitive function are also pointless. The descriptions of how we think provide a valuable and powerful means of understanding human mentation. We can suggest laws of molar behavior even though the component processes, if they exist as isolatable entities, may be hidden. However, when reduction, rather than description, becomes the goal, fantastic speculation replaces verifiable science.

5

TOWARD A NEW BEHAVIORISM—
A SUMMARY AND SOME CONCLUSIONS[1]

In the previous three chapters of this book, I criticized a number of the contemporary paradigms of perceptual science. I argued for the acceptance of three major principles governing the use of models, neuroreductionism, and the search for a cognitive architecture, respectively.

1. Models can be, at best, descriptions of the course of a process and can never achieve the much stronger role of ontologically reductive explanations.

2. Neuroreductionism is far more difficult and far less well accomplished than many of my colleagues believe. Given the problems of complexity, chaos, and other well-accepted physical science principles, it is unlikely that a neuronal network explanation of other than a few peripheral processes will be achieved.

3. Despite the often stated goals of contemporary cognitive psychology, behavioral (stimulus-response, input–output) analyses are incapable of identifying the components of an internal mental architecture. The methods available are not suitable and, in any event, the task of identifying internal structure with behavioral techniques is impossible in principle. The entire approach is based on an interlocking nest of invalid assumptions.

---

[1]This chapter is an adaptation of material originally presented as an essay (Uttal, 1993) in the book *Foundations of Perceptual Theory*, edited by Sergio Masin of the University of Padua, Italy. This book was published by North-Holland Publishers of Amsterdam. The adaptation presented here is included through the courtesy of the publisher.

The tone of much of the material that I have been discussing may seem to some to be overly pessimistic, but I do not believe this to be the case. However close my critique is to some "unpleasant truth," it is also an opportunity for reevaluation, and perhaps even for change in the goals and strategies of perceptual science. From this point of view, my entire effort in this book must be considered to be an optimistic expression that some progressive evolution of our overall scientific perspective may be achievable. To meet this responsibility, I must now take a different tack and suggest what can be done to overcome some of the difficulties and challenges that my critique has identified.

This chapter, therefore, is intended to offer suggestions about where we should go and what we should do in response to the previously described difficulties. It is an unabashed call for a basic revision in the paradigm of contemporary perceptual science. Here I consider the implications of the previous chapters for what perceptual science can and should do in the future.

As I begin this task, I must acknowledge that many of the things that I have written about in previous chapters and discuss in the present one are matters of taste and judgment rather than rigor. Perceptual science is not yet at the point where many of the arguments that have been presented can be resolved beyond refutation. Empirical evidence in this field is almost always fragile and ambiguous. Individual scientists have different thresholds for accepting both classic and novel ideas. Theoretical premises sometimes lead inexorably to particular ways of viewing data, ideas, theories, and explanations. And, of course, we all have our hopes and dreams that understanding will be achieved in our particular domain.

As much as I have tried to provide adequate definitions in previous chapters, I know full well that my use of some of the key words is not the same as that of some of my colleagues. Nevertheless, it may be that lexicographic agreement is more central to resolving controversies than anything else in this field. In this context it is disturbing to realize that there is no science in which the basic vocabulary is so difficult to define and agreement is so elusive as ours.

I also understand that many, if not most, of my colleagues will disagree with the behaviorist approach I will now champion. To some it is an old-fashioned idea that has had its time and has been superseded by the many technical achievements of the past few decades. I sincerely believe, however, that much of the progress that has been made in reductionist explanations of visual processes is illusory and will in the long run be rejected and replaced with new ideas. The problem is that the quest that has been undertaken is far more complex and difficult than has hitherto been appreciated. Whether it will prove to be as fundamentally intractable as it seems to be to some of us is for the future to say.

To predict the future, we have to know something about the past. I have written before (Uttal, 1981a, and the preface of this book) about the swing of a theoretical pendulum in psychology that has oscillated between recent emphases on elementalist psychobiological reductionism and inferential speculation about underlying cognitive mechanisms, on the one hand, and earlier positivistic views captured under the rubric of molar behaviorism, on the other. To support this argument further, the past and present states of the foundation epistemological premises of perceptual science must now be briefly explored.

During the last century, psychological theories have alternated between the two poles I have just briefly characterized. The nonreductionist, behaviorist tradition eschewed both neural and cognitive reductionism, particularly introspective reports. One way to appreciate what behaviorism means and what it does not is to note that it assumes that, although we can measure the transforms and the *effects* of the operations or processes that are executed by both kinds of transformations—the cognitive ones and the neural ones—the operations, processes, and mechanisms themselves are invisible to both the scientist and the individual experiencing them.

However, contrary to conventional wisdom, most behaviorists accept the private neural and mental mechanisms to be as real as the behavioral responses that are interpersonally communicable. Jokes about the use of the word *mind* that were popular a few decades ago grossly misinterpreted serious behaviorist doctrine. A radical behaviorism—like its sister epistemologies, logical positivism and logical empiricism—asserts that the only data useful to the student of the mind are the observable responses of an organism. To invent hypothetical constructs (e.g., thoughts, motives, images, feelings, desires, perceptions, etc.) implied to the behaviorist violation of laws of mathematics or principles of parsimony and created conflicts of "data languages." However, there is a more moderate version of behaviorism possible in which mental responses are considered to be real and cognitive processes are carried out, but that also limits our findings, conclusions, and theories to that which can be observed. The fact that mind happens to be private does not mean that it does not exist. The acceptance of this point of view can be an important bridge between modern cognitive psychology and the behaviorist tradition of an older experimental psychology.

In the preceding paragraphs, I have given a very brief introduction to what behaviorism means to me. This capsule description of a complex school of thought is totally incapable of conveying the full richness of all of the issues that characterized historical behaviorism. A capsule statement like this, however, is not intended to be a comprehensive review of all of the issues that have confronted this facet of the psychological sciences. My interests and the topics covered in this book are mainly concerned with the separable issue of reductionism. Those who would like a fuller treatment of behaviorism are directed to the very thoughtful volumes by Zuriff (1985), Rachlin (1994), or Staddon (1993), as well as the classic works of Hull (1943), J. B. Watson (1925), and Skinner (1953, 1963). The more patient of my readers may wait for the successor volume to this one.

As we have seen throughout this book, the currently dominant, nonbehaviorist approaches to perceptual psychology—formal modeling, reductive cognitivism, and neuroreductionism—all assume, on the other hand, that behavioral responses can reveal the underlying mechanisms. These mechanisms may be either neurophysiological structures presumed to account directly for the generation of the observed behaviors, or cognitive components that participate in transforming information, and thus in selecting or shaping behaviors. Even more fundamental to these reductive approaches is the idea that, in principle, observed behavior can be a window into mental processes. Nonbehaviorist science is based on the hope that our research will ultimately permit us to infer unique internal explanatory mechanisms, given enough experiments and "converging" experimental evidence.

It must be emphasized that there seems to be no essential disagreement between moderate versions of either behaviorism or these reductionisms with regard to the reality of mental processes or the relevance of neurophysiological mechanisms; they differ only with regard to their attitudes toward the accessibility of underlying mechanism through input–output (i.e., behavioral, stimulus-response, psychophysical) experiments. The pioneering behaviorist B. F. Skinner (1963) said:

> An adequate science of behavior must consider events taking place within the skin of the organism, not as physiological mediators of behavior, but as part of behavior itself. (p. 951)
> The relation between an analysis of behavior as such and physiology is no problem. Each of these sciences has instruments and methods appropriate to part of a behavioral episode. There are inevitable gaps in a behavioral account. (p. 782)

Clearly Skinner rejected neither the physiological basis of behavior nor the monist point of view. It is only the validity of introspective reports, the vagueness and lack of uniqueness of hypothetical constructs, or any presumption of the observability of the intervening (internal) events that he and other behaviorists questioned as they eschewed the questionable reductionism of mental constructs and physiological mechanisms from behavioral data.

Other criticisms of Skinner's behaviorism (e.g., that it was not theoretical) seem quaint in light of many of the theoretical constructions that Skinner himself used in his written work. Another important modern behaviorist, P. R. Killeen (1988), clarified the falsity of this criticism when he emphasized both Skinner's deep theoretical intuition and his repeated use of concepts such as the "reflex reserve" as models of the forces that drive behavior. Killeen pointed out that Skinner (1953) did not deny the existence of inner states, but rather placed them in another scientific context: "The objection to inner states is not that they do not exist, but that they are not relevant in a functional analysis" (Killeen, 1988, p. 35). Skinner, therefore, was simply designating mental and physiological mechanisms as irrelevant to the study of behavior, not denying their reality. In this light it is clear that the essence of Skinnerian behaviorism was that theories should be formulated in the concepts, terms, and logical units (i.e., the language) from the same level whence came the empirical observations. The influence of his logical positivist, operationalist philosophical heritage is apparent when viewed from this point.

It is also important to appreciate that not all behaviorists rejected reductionism. The father of modern American behaviorism as we know it, J. B. Watson, was clearly a materialist and a reductionist. Watson's (1925) text of behaviorism is replete with physiological information and explanations. It is clear that he was, in fundamental principle, a reductionist, not just to physiological entities (brain centers and neurons) but to the physical elements (atoms and molecules) themselves. Physiology was merely an intermediate step interspersed between the ultimate source (physical forces) of the behavior. If one keeps the two issues—materialist monism and reductionism, one reality and one strategy—separate, one can accept the former while rejecting the latter. It is, in other words, possible to have materialism without reductionism. This is the conceptual key to the new behaviorism I am proposing here. The task is to keep our metaphysics and our epistemology separate.

Similarly, modeling was not rejected by behaviorists. A strong proponent of behaviorism, yet one also quite clearly and very heavily committed to theoretical elaboration, was C. L. Hull (1943). Hull proposed the development of a "hypothetical-deductive" system that was construed in the language of a single level—the observable molar behavior of the organism. The conceptual methodology of his system is indistinguishable, in principle, from the approaches of formal mathematics, statistics, or computational modeling popular today. Forces such as "drive" appear throughout his system as evidence that his behaviorism did not entirely reject inner states. Hull, therefore, was not denying the essential physiological basis of behavior or even the influence of mental states. They were, in fact, a critical part of his hypothetical-deductive system. The issues that must be kept separate in this case are, can we build models, and what can our models do and what can they not do?

What the behaviorists essentially championed was an emphasis on empirical data collection of the physically and interpersonally communicable (as opposed to constructs that were inferred rather than measured) and, with the exception of Hull, descriptive theory (as opposed to some kinds of falsely reductive pseudo-physiology.) They argued against reductive theories, not theories in general, and against fallacious attempts to measure those responses that were, in fact, intrapersonally private or too complex to be unraveled. Their argument was not against mental or neurophysiological reality, but against false bridge building between behavior and imperfectly measured (or, even worse, unmeasured) internal states and mechanisms. Needless to say, I feel that this point of view was closer to the "correct" one than the cognitive or neuroreductive approaches I have criticized in earlier chapters.

However, this tactical difference between behaviorism and reductionism in either its physical, neurophysiological, or cognitive forms is not a small matter. The crux of conflict between these two points of view over the accessibility of mental and physiological processes by behavioral experiments is the major intellectual focus of a persistent controversy in experimental psychology. It may even be the key to understanding the history of our science. The oscillation between these two points of view has been continuous during the first century of our science. The underlying mental and neural processes have been respectable objects of psychological inquiry or not during this century, depending on which point of view was currently in favor.

Currently we are at a peak of interest in neural and cognitive reductionism. A major theme of this currently popular approach is that behavioral responses directly implicate specific neural or cognitive mechanisms. As I have shown, fantastic and insupportable claims are routinely being made. Having now demonstrated that there are more or less formal and logical proofs that neural or cognitive reduction is not feasible, it is appropriate to reconsider what behaviorism is and whether or not we should return to this currently unpopular approach to the study of psychology.

These two traditions—positivistic behaviorism, on the one hand, and reductionist psychobiology and cognitivism, on the other—had their origins in 18th century empiricism and 17th century rationalism, respectively. Each school of thought has been subsequently influenced by positive intellectual developments in other cognate sciences (evolutionary theory, neurobiology, logical positivism, computer science, etc.). However, each also responded negatively in reaction to what were perceived to be the inadequacies of the other.

The current high level of support for reductive explanations has been further enhanced by successes in the artificial intelligence field in simulating or analogizing behavioral processes. It must be recognized, on the contrary, that the many applied computer vision and artificial intelligence (AI) models of human form perception, however useful they may be and however well they mimic the properties of human vision, are not valid ontological explanations or theories of human vision. At best, they are functional descriptions or analogs. Indeed, it can be argued that some models (such as "expert systems" and "list-processing" languages) are a complete surrender of the hope that we can really model human mental processes. These table-lookup operations clearly do not model the way human associative thinking works, but merely simulate the behavior by logic and mechanisms that are beyond any doubt entirely different from those used in human cognition. It is essential that the relationship between imitation by an analogy and reduction to homologous mechanisms be clarified and understood. Although we can admire and respect the practical and useful accomplishments of this field of engineering application and development (i.e., AI), we must rid ourselves of any misconception that such engineering tools are more likely than any other model to be valid theories of human perception.

Like many other forms of psychology, perceptual science has profited enormously by representing itself as a reductive science. As I discussed in chapter 1, the assurance of our profession to our supporters, patrons, and to society at large has been that we are not just a descriptive science, but a reductively explanatory one. The implicit promise has been, at one time or another, the production of either neural or cognitive process reductionist explanations. This terribly ambitious pledge of our profession has thus been that sooner or later we will be able to answer questions of the underlying localization, mechanism, function, and processes of psychological experiences in terms of neural and cognitive mechanisms. Theory in perceptual psychology, although rarely fulfilling the promise, is presented as reductive and explanatory in the sense that the underlying neural or cognitive mechanisms are being assayed, if not exposed, by psychophysical or other behavioral tests. Reductionism also has the appearance of progress. The model of physics, a science moving ever deeper into ever more microscopic fundamentals of reality, set the stage for psychology in particular and the neurosciences in general. Progress was identified with reductionism without regard for the constraints and barriers that might prevent achieving that goal. The contrary view, that the goal of internal structure analysis is actually unobtainable and thus irrelevant, is unpopular, and, in a certain sense, antiprogressive. Yet it is at the heart of the new behaviorist point of view proposed here.

In earlier chapters, I reviewed some of the mathematical, physical, and logical arguments that contend that psychological (i.e., stimulus response, input–output, etc.) methods are, in principle (except in some extraordinary cases where additional macro-anatomical evidence is available), incapable of resolving disputes between alternative theories of internal structure or mechanism. The arguments that I used to support this conclusion are exclusively formal. That is, they did not depend on any equivocation concerning the lack of existence of mental processes, or any philosophical speculation about reductionism. Rather, they are the direct conclusions of mathematical and physical principles that have emerged in recent years, but that have been all but ignored by psychologists and other behavioral scientists. I interpret these conclusions to mean that a strong case can be made that there are provable, formal difficulties in principle in linking the descriptions of behavior to the inferred mechanisms. I believe the case is strong even if my argument would not satisfy a rigorous mathematician. As seen in chapter 2, they come from combinatorial mathematics, the theory of chaos, physical principles such as the Second Law of Thermodynamics, generally accepted engineering limits on black box experiments, theorems from automata theory, and Goedel's incompleteness theorem. The conclusions drawn are also based on a consideration of the fundamental nature of mathematics as a method of analogy and description rather than of homology and structural analysis.

The point is that, even without introducing much less well-defined ideas such as the nature of consciousness, awareness, mental experiences, or any of the other conundrums that have historically driven so much human fancy as well as serious thought, it is possible to argue reasonably, if not to prove, that any attempt to develop a reductionist psychology based on behavioral measures is doomed to failure. The disappointment is that so many members of our community uncritically refuse to acknowledge the same constraints and limits on our complex and multivariate science that have been accepted in comparable situations by students of much less complex problem areas.

Perceptual psychologists deal with processes that are conceptually closer to the neural mechanisms than some of the higher level cognitive processes. Yet, even at this arguably simpler perceptual level, it seems clear that the association of neural network architecture and function is an overwhelmingly difficult task, if not an impossible one. Only in a few specific situations can definitive statements be made of sensory mechanisms. Anatomical facts, such as our dichoptic viewing system or the crossover of visual signals at the optic chiasm, are among rare situations where behavioral tests can make conclusive statements about the locus of the transformations. Accepting this difficulty, given the relative orderliness of the stimulus material, the relative simplicity of the sensory nervous system, and the more or less direct isomorphism between structure and representation in the perceptual domain, it seems even less likely that higher level cognitive influences on perception should be candidates for the kinds of reductive explanations that are often implicitly and sometimes explicitly promised by contemporary cognitivists.

Of course, any discussion of an issue such as the present one that opens by expressing the caveat that observed behavior or mental response may be indisputably related, yet still be causally ambiguous, with regard to neural mechanism (or vice versa) immediately runs the danger of being labeled as some kind of a crypto- or neodualism. It is essential for me to reassert that the conclusions I draw and the recommendations I present in this chapter are not based on any kind of a dualism, either explicit or cryptic. Quite to the contrary, as stated several times earlier in this book, the conceptual foundations of my approach to perceptual science are based on a highly monistic ontology: Mental events are the real actions of some kind of a physical (i.e., neural) substrate. The dichotomy between an ontological monism and an epistemological dualism has been referred to as theory dualism by Churchland and Sejnowski (1989). I suppose this means that my approach can be classified as such a theory dualism.

An emphasis on the formal mathematical arguments against neuroreductionism as an obtainable goal is not a denial of the materialistic basis of mental processes. It is comparable to the computer scientist's consideration of the *computability* of an algorithm or *solvability* of a problem. It is not equivalent to saying that the problem cannot be expressed in words, numbers, or other symbols or that the complex situation cannot exist. After all, we exist and think and, assuming the validity of the materialistic monistic fundamental principle, neurons in the aggregate can and do produce all of the wonders of thought. It is, however, an expression of the difficulty and probable practical impossibility of carrying out an analysis of the complex situation. In other words, along with the other theory dualists, I assert that a monist ontology can coexist with a dualist epistemology within the rubric of a respectable scientific enterprise. The goal of the remainder of this chapter is to explain why such a neobehavioral, nonreductionist approach is the most defensible position scientifically, and why perceptual science should take this direction in the future.

SOME THINGS TO DO

Toward a New Taxonomy

Experimental psychology in general, and perceptual science in particular, relatively new sciences that have developed mainly within the last century, have neglected one of the most important tasks of any science—the organization and classification of their respective databases. It is almost as if this science had been fixed at some pre-Linnean level of thought. Rather than organizing our discoveries into a coherent taxonomic system, modern perceptual scientists seem to behave like a huge disorganized mass of hyperempirical data collectors, rather than observers–organizers–interpreters. Only in the rarest instances have they sought out the common features of the phenomena in the enormous number of results and findings reported over the course of the last century. Rather, perceptual science is usually taught and studied as a mélange of microuniverses, each of which seems unconnected to any other. This leads to great difficulty in replication of findings, so much so that the very database of our science is often questionable.

Many instructive models of ideal taxonomies are available to us from the other sciences. Linneus pioneered taxonomy for biology. Mendelleev's periodic table played the same critical role for chemistry and ultimately led to another taxonomy, that proposed by Gell-Mann (1964), consisting of such categories as hadrons, leptons, and photons. The important thing is that in each of these cases it was not simply a matter of creating a pretty picture from a chaotic jumble, but rather of providing some pattern, form, or organization of the data of a science that had enormous theoretical implications for all subsequent work. The Linnean system was a necessary precursor not only for biological theories of evolution, but ultimately for all other biological studies. The periodic table led directly to the atomic theory of matter and ultimately to what we now believe to be the ultimate in our search for the basic particles of nature—the quarks.

The two questions that we should ask are: Why did traditional experimental psychology not follow this same reasonable course, and what might have been if it had? The former question is possible to answer by noting that the dimensions of psychology are so much more numerous and the interactions so much more complex that any potential order might be obscure to the latent taxonomist. But this is no excuse, because even beset by this complexity, it should have been possible to divide the field of experimental psychology into subsets that should have been more amenable to some kind of systemization than the field currently is. Why it was not, like the other sciences, so organized, however, still remains a mystery to me.

The existence of this mystery is confirmed by others. Rakover (1986), in a spirited defense of behaviorism and a rejection of the suggestion that it is "trivial," reminds us of an extraordinary fact that was compiled by White (1985). White surveyed seven of what he perceived to be the most important books in experimental psychology and found that 3,200 references were cited collectively in all of them. However, "only nineteen publications were mentioned in all seven books" (p. 117). This is reminiscent of a recent *New York Times* front-page article. Ten distinguished psychologists were surveyed and asked to list the 10 most important new ideas in psychology. The 10 lists did not overlap! No item was found to be present in any two of the lists.

The second question is also very difficult to answer in specific detail, but it does seem certain that a greater taxonomic effort might have paid off with substantial insight into the fundamental principles of perceptual psychology as opposed to the grab bag of isolated phenomena that fills the literature in this field. Psychology has classically been a set of explorations into "little science"—situation-specific theories, isolated experimental results, and cute but cryptic phenomenal demonstrations—rather than a science graced by a unified set of principles or grand unifying theory. The result of this internal fractionation has been to make theories transitory. It has led to a conceptual isolation among scientists in this field and seriously inhibited our effort to produce universal accounts of perceptual function. This is not surprising: If one does not know how one's work is related to that of one's colleagues, how can one be expected to see the commonalities? It has only been in recent years that a few efforts toward unification have been made (e.g., Newell, 1990; Uttal, 1981a), and clearly both of these examples were as incomplete as were any other efforts of this kind. In fact, neither of these two efforts overlaps with the subject matter of the other. A universal perspective of cognitive and perceptual science, therefore, is still elusive.

A major obstacle to the generation of a valid taxonomy of perceptual science should also be noted. Very often, we discover that what seem to be similar paradigms actually assay very different processes (e.g., see the comments on this problem in the work of Cheal & Lyon, 1992). Small changes in experimental design may produce vast differences in results as we cross over from assaying one process to another without appreciating the discontinuity. Two quite different experimental paradigms, on the other hand, may actually have been probing the same perceptual process. The figure completion studies of Ericksen and Collins (1967) are certainly tapping into the same fundamental visual processes as are the masking studies I carried out some time ago (Uttal, 1971b). The exact values for persistence measured in each of these studies may differ slightly, but that is a matter of experimental procedure and design criteria rather than a real biological difference.

The difficulty of producing a useful taxonomy generated by the complexity of the subject matter notwithstanding, I am convinced that progress can be made. There is always the hope that from such a taxonomic effort might come essential integrating concepts that will lead to a breakthrough in psychology of the same import as the ones that occurred in biology, chemistry, and physics. Of course, there can be no guarantees.

A Continuation of Empirical Research

If taxonomy has been insufficiently emphasized, there is no question that the search for new perceptual phenomena has not. From the days of Grosseteste, through the teaching of Bacon, to the *méthode* of Descartes; from Weber's mystic psychophysics, to Wundt's Leipzig laboratory; through the many schools of psychology, rationalist and empiricist, to today's modern conceptualization of cognitive science, empirical research has been the sine qua non of all sciences including psychology and its predecessors. There is no question that testing nature in a controlled manner is the unique defining attribute of any science and must continue to be the heart of scientific psychology.

However, this does not mean that there may not be some changes re-quired in the nature of the experimental paradigms of perceptual science. In the past, the classic type of experimental perceptual research was the psychophysical experiment in which a single stimulus dimension (S) is manipulated and a single behavioral response dimension (R) measured. Formally, this can be represented as:

$$\mathbf{R} = f(\mathbf{S}) \tag{1}$$

All other dimensions of the stimulus were "controlled" to the maximum extent possible. This is the embodiment of the advice given to us by Des-cartes in proposing his *méthode* concerning the isolation and separation of variables. However, if there is anything certain in perceptual science, it is our appreciation that organisms do not really function in this manner. As useful and as simplifying as the analytic *méthode* is, it must now be appre-ciated that such an elemental, analytical approach often obscures the fact that organisms perceive on the basis of multiple cues, dimensions, and attributes of both the stimulus and the internal state. It is the interaction among and combinations of these different properties, not a mechanical and automatic response to a single dimension or attribute, that accounts not just for the richness and variety of organic behavior, but also for the ex-traordinary fact that we can perceive at all.

A more accurate formularization of the true biological relationship be-tween responses and stimuli should look something like this:

$$\mathbf{R} = f(\mathbf{S}_1, \mathbf{S}_2, \mathbf{S}_3, \ldots, \mathbf{S}_n, \mathbf{S}_1\mathbf{S}_2, \mathbf{S}_1\mathbf{S}_3, \mathbf{S}_2\mathbf{S}_3, \ldots,$$
$$\mathbf{S}_n\mathbf{S}_m, \mathbf{S}_n\mathbf{S}_m\mathbf{S}_o, \ldots, \mathbf{Mem}, \mathbf{Set}, \text{etc.}) \tag{2}$$

where $\mathbf{S}_n$ tabulates the various attributes of the stimulus, $\mathbf{S}_n\mathbf{S}_m\mathbf{S}_o \ldots$ suggest the interaction of multiple attributes, **Mem** denotes the collective memories and experiences of the organism, **Set** denotes its current state, and **etc.** denotes a host of other variables that may influence the response. For example, it is becoming increasingly evident that no single attribute can be decoded sufficiently well to produce a complete, multidimensional visual experience; all perceptual experiences must be based on interactions of multiple attributes of the stimulus. The emergence of perceptual "quality," in particular, seems to require comparisons of different dimensions or at-tributes of the stimulus. (See my discussion of this matter in chapter 11 of Uttal, 1981a). The question remains: Given this complexity, is the situation, however real, possible of solution using the conventional analytic techniques of experimental psychology? Or, to the contrary, must new, more global approaches be developed?

In the past, the empirical quest has been continuous and energetic. This is as it should be. Ideas must be tested in experiments. We must gain knowledge, not by authority or speculation, but by test and observation. An enormously sophisticated methodology has grown up in experimental psychology that is dedicated to the fulfillment of this very important premise. The prototypical scientist is an experimenter, and this emphasis must continue. The archival journal, containing empirical articles reported in a firmly prescribed and highly stylized format, is the most distinguished and prestigious outlet for one's "scientific" activities. For many, science *is* nothing but controlled observation or experimentation; everything else is viewed as being not quite respectable. (This may be another hint why taxonomic efforts have been held in such low repute.)

From one perspective, this is as it should be. Speculation without experimentation would be sterile armchair philosophy, and a data-free taxonomic effort would be pointless. However, there are some substantial changes to the contemporary experimental strategy that are necessary as our science matures and we begin to understand that it is most likely that the interaction and arrangement of the elements are more important than their nature.

Obviously, there is still ample necessity to control extraneous and irrelevant variables. However, there is also a potential richness of thought and depth of understanding in considering any perceptual phenomenon to have multidimensional, rather than unidimensional, determinants. Instead of computing correlation coefficients between a single independent variable and a single dependent variable, efforts should be made to make all contemporary experimental designs multicorrelational. Rather than plotting a two-dimensional graph of obtained data, we should take advantage of modern data visualization techniques to display the joint effects of two, three, four, or even more stimulus dimensions on a behavioral response. To do so would help us to characterize and describe the behavior of perceiving organisms more realistically and more thoroughly than was ever possible with a simple one-to-one relation between a single stimulus variable and a single response variable. That older approach produced a compelling intellectual force itself that led us to emphasize a low-level, automatic, elementalist approach to perception that seems now wildly out of date.

In a related vein, our previous approach to psychological experimentation has been that of analysis. That is, in accord with Descartes' admonition, we have striven to take the complex stimulus apart and present it as someone might dissect a frog and then measure the properties of the individual parts with consideration of their relationship to the whole organism. A formidable challenge awaits us, however, as perceptual science evolves toward a new synthetic epistemology. Admittedly, this approach is currently limited because the global arrangement of the parts is itself an important aspect that is ignored when we uncritically follow Descartes' *méthode*. For example, as we discover how the various attributes of a visual stimulus interactively affect a perceptual experience, is it not possible that we will also be able to suggest how the various attributes might be combined so that a full perceptual experience could be regenerated from the ensemble of individual attributes? This is the essence of the *binding* problem. Such an approach would have many potential practical outcomes. It would be possible to design efficient communication links that passed only the necessary information to a display, for example. Even more important, however, is the potential for stimulating us to achieve new insights into the rich complexity of human perception in ways that may not even be imagined a priori. This inability to predict the impact of future experiments is hardly unique to experimental psychology. No science can anticipate what the outcome, practical or theoretical, will be a of a fact undiscovered, a place unexplored, or an idea untested.

A New Role for Theory

The role of theory must also change as perceptual science matures. The naive view that a theory can delve more deeply into the inner workings of some system than the data on which the theory is based must be abandoned. It seems imperative that we accept the fact that all theoretical syntheses are at best descriptive and at worst untestable. All that really can be said is that the model and the reality exhibit a fit sufficiently close so that one can be accepted as a description or analog of the other. The overly optimistic expectation that we can obtain otherwise unobtainable knowledge by the use of "convergent operations" is probably more fantasy than reality. Theories based on input–output analyses alone always will permit an infinity of possible mechanisms and require infinite and therefore unobtainably large numbers of experiments to resolve even simple questions of internal structure. Once again, I call attention to Moore's (1956) very important paper.

In this light, theories of mental processes, however they may have been intended to be reductive, should come to be considered more akin to summaries and organizations of knowledge than new knowledge generating media. Formal theories of the mathematical or computational kind can be extremely powerful, of course, in their ability to predict the course of events in some system. Such formal theories also have the power to suggest ways in which a certain system may not function by highlighting the impossibility of a particular sequence of events. Theories *cum* process summaries also have the power to describe clearly the transformations that can occur even if they cannot distinguish among the many possible mechanisms that might account for those transformations. Most of all, theories are summarizing and organizing tools that help us to clarify the cumulative impact of findings from a variety of experiments. It is especially frustrating, therefore, to observe how microscopic most theories of perception are. Virtually all of the so-called theories of perceptual phenomena describe the function of but a single phenomenon (e.g., an illusion, depth from disparity, color appearance, etc.). How much more exciting it would be if global theories of vision as a whole were more prevalent. My group has worked on such a global model and recently published two accounts of our efforts in Uttal, Bradshaw, Dayanand, Lovell, Shepherd, Kakarala, Skifsted, and Tupper (1992) and Uttal, Kakarala, Dayanand, Shepherd, Kalki, Lunskis, and Liu (1998), respectively.

However powerful theories may be, these capabilities do not support the wistful hope that theories are potentially reductive. What theories do well is allow our imaginations to go beyond the data in the same way that metaphors and heuristics stimulate speculation. But they cannot be either definitive or ontologically reductive. At some basic level all theories must be inductive rather than deductive, and descriptive rather than explanatory. The ability to predict subsequent performance steps by mathematical derivations may suggest a reductive role that is actually illusory.

Given these strengths and constraints, what then is the primary role of an inductive, summarizing theory? The answer to this question is simple: Theory is the raison d'être of science! It is the supreme goal of all scientific research. It is the ultimately sought contribution and the objective toward which all empirical work should be aimed. Theories are general, inclusive, and comprehensive statements of our understanding of the nature of the world we inhabit—as we know it at the moment. They are the goal of science, not the adjuncts of highly contrived experiments. It is the global view that justifies the entire scientific enterprise, not the particular phenomenon. This is why illusions have played such an important role in perceptual science, not because they are amusing parlor demonstrations. In themselves they are not very important, but they do provide a vehicle that takes us to the more general understanding of the nature of perception just because of their nonveridicality. Theories, notwithstanding their central importance, come and go. Our understanding is a dynamic thing that evolves from one experiment to the next. This is as it should be; otherwise the quest built in to the scientific enterprise would be pointless.

Surprisingly, understanding has not always been a primary goal of all science. In fact, older forms of the behaviorism that I champion here have sometimes eschewed that quest. Smith (1992) presented a very clear argument that Skinner, at least the early Skinner, was more interested in the prediction and control of behavior than understanding it. Skinner was, as Smith pointed out, profoundly influenced by Francis Bacon's pragmatic (as well as experimental) approach to science. Words, of course, are only words, but Smith made it clear that there are two possible meanings to the word *understanding*. He noted that two "ideal-types of science" exist: "The contemplative ideal which seeks to understand the natural world and its causes and the technological ideal, originating with Bacon, which seeks means of controlling, making, and remaking the world" (p. 216). Skinner (again, this may be only the early Skinnerian ideology) was suggesting that understanding is not necessary if one can successfully control a system. The main point, he felt, was to control behavior, and it really is only an unnecessary luxury to require, beyond that, understanding. In the case of the human mind–brain, of course, it is questionable whether that "luxury" is actually obtainable even if one makes a commitment to seek it. Certainly this question must have influenced Skinner, as well as the other behaviorists and logical positivists.

As for my personal point of view, I think that understanding beyond control has always been and will remain the main goal. Control is nice, but it is more of an economic or ecological convenience than a criterion satisfying the deepest of human intellectual urges. Even more important, I believe it is possible to achieve understanding in the context of a nonreductionist behaviorism. Finally, understanding, in the best possible scientific sense, is synonymous with integrative theory, regardless of the epistemological foundations and constraints of that theory.

It is also important to appreciate the relationships between experiments and understanding (or theory). Experiments are merely controlled probes or assays that help us toward general understanding. We conduct experiments to provide the grist for the theoretical mill; we do not concoct theories simply to provide a framework for a set of data. The essential idea, in this case, is that the theory is the primary goal; the collection of data is secondary! "Barefooted" empiricism, devoid of synthetic summary, is a sterile and empty endeavor, an affront to the real goals of science. Mere data collection, without reason or possible extrapolation, is waste incarnate. Taxonomies can help by collecting, organizing, and cataloging, but even that role is secondary. The ultimate role of science is to summarize and, by doing so, surpass the accumulated data by stimulating general statements of understanding—in other words, to formulate transcendent theories. A theory is, at its most fundamental level, a statement of the universals for the domain of ideas with which it deals. The domain need not be all-inclusive; it may itself be a microuniverse of limited extent. Nevertheless, any theory of even a restricted domain should strive for the most comprehensive statement of the nature of that domain as its ideal goal.

Thus, the role of the theoretical must never be minimized or ignored if the science is to be of the first quality. Science cannot survive without the confrontations with nature we call experiments, of course, but it is a truism that no particular experiment is essential. Should any particular experiment not be carried out, the loss would not be great. Almost certainly, another exemplar of the same general point would subsequently become available. If no summary is created of a body of individually nonessential experiments, however, the loss is profound because the goal of general understanding would not be achieved.

Theories come in many guises. Traditionally, experimental psychology crafted its theories out of the raw material of data summarized by descriptive statistics. Null hypotheses were generated and then tested to see if statistical differences could be detected that would allow their rejection. If the null hypothesis could be rejected the hypothesis was tentatively accepted. Such hypotheses-driven theories had a tendency to be highly circumscribed and limited to a very restricted domain of inquiry—sometimes to only an experiment or two.

In recent years, theories and models of many different and more general kinds have evolved. Structural models have been developed that associate the behavioral and presumed mental functions with the operations of other devices. Computer programs serve as models of perceptual (as well as more complex cognitive) processes and neuroanatomical mechanisms. "Flow chart" models of the underlying mental architecture are regularly invoked to simulate or describe cognitive processes, as we have seen in chapter 4. Mathematical models that differ greatly from the statistical ones of the past have been developed that are particularly relevant to the modeling of perceptual phenomena. Analogies drawn between mental and physical systems, a strategy that has a long history, are updated as each new technology or mathematical system emerges. Most recently, some of our colleagues have utilized concepts of chaos (e.g., Skarda & Freeman, 1987; Townsend, 1990) as models of brain and mind systems; others use the language of quantum mechanics (Bennett, Hoffman, & Prakash, 1989); and still others find that the metaphor of waves describes a wide variety of psychophysical judgments (Link, 1992).

Whatever the theoretical approach, it is clear that there has been a gradual evolution over the years from micromodels to more expansive, but still domain-limited, macromodels. Although there is great diversity in the exact mechanics invoked, most interesting steps forward have tended to be more inclusive than was typical only a few years ago. Whatever the scope, whatever the domain, the important thing is that human progress in acquiring knowledge and wisdom and solving problems depends mainly on our theoretical achievements. The rest (i.e., the solutions to the practical problems that face us) follows automatically once basic understanding is in place.

The main point with which I wish to conclude this section is that a commitment to the ideal of theoretical understanding can best be achieved within a nonreductionist and behaviorist tradition that culminates in a maximally inclusive description.

Physiological Research

In previous chapters of this book and elsewhere (Uttal, 1988), I have repeatedly spoken of the limits of input–output (stimulus-response) approaches definitively defining any underlying mechanisms. I have argued that the neurophysiological approach (in which the "black box" of the brain is physically opened) is itself constrained by limits of numerousness; chaotic, apparently random, organization; and thermodynamic principles. In this context, it is important to remember that none of the arguments I have presented should be misconstrued to imply that I am suggesting any kind of a moratorium or delay in the pursuit of neurophysiological knowledge.

The arguments for this pursuit are strong and sufficient in their own right for many reasons. First, studies that attack the chemical, biophysical, or adaptive nature of neurons, on the one hand, or information communication, integrative interactions, or even the localization of function in the large centers of the nervous system, on the other, are sufficiently fascinating, useful, and elegant to justify these lines of research fully. Neurophysiology, neuroanatomy, and neurochemistry do not have to support the goals of psychological science to justify themselves: They are substantial sciences with their own agenda and their own significant research goals.

With regard to their relationship to psychological issues, however, the role of the neurosciences is more controversial than many workers in this field may accept. I have contended that in principle behavioral data cannot be validly reduced to physiological mechanisms, and that physiological data, for reasons of equally fundamental nature, cannot be synthesized to global psychological phenomena. This is the crux of the argument that there are significant barriers that exist between the neural and the psychological research agenda.

How, then, do we deal with the enormous amount of neuroscientific research that purports to be directly relevant to psychological issues? My answer to this rhetorical question is that much of the biochemical, anatomical, and physiological research *is* relevant, but only in a practical, applied, utilitarian manner. It is, however, essentially theoretically agnostic in the context of the mind–brain perplexity. Much of this enormous body of useful and fascinating research offers very little to us in understanding the relationship between brain and mind. Some neuroscientific data is too microscopic, aimed only at the physics or chemistry of the neuronal components or even the subcellular components of these wonderful cells. Some, on the other hand, is too macroscopic, only elucidating the relationship between huge chunks of the brain and behavior—the localization problem. The key issue, to reiterate an essential point, is: What is the proper level of analysis if understanding the physiological basis of mental processes is the goal? Studies of individual neurons, their parts, and their synaptic machinery are research carried out at too fine a level. Studies of the massive effects of a drug, of electroencephalographic signals, or of the localization of mental functions with state-of-the-art brain imaging systems, although interesting, are attacking the problem at too gross a level to answer this question.

For example, let us consider neurochemistry and explain what I mean by the assertion that much of neuroscience is "atheoretical." Although all of us can look with pride and a sense of relief at the enormous therapeutic progress that has been made with psychoactive drugs, it seems to me that this serious social need has been fulfilled with little or no theoretical significance for the mind–brain issue, other than simply reaffirming that brain states are intimately related to mental states and that chemicals can systematically affect mental states by altering brain states. We know that the introduction of these drugs into the nervous system may affect some of the great transmitter systems or even specific regions of the brain, inhibiting or exciting synaptic conductivity in a general way. Furthermore, we may know in detail the biochemistry of how these drugs act to reduce or enhance the synaptic process either at the individual presynaptic release site or at the postsynaptic receptor site.

However, neither the macroscopic activity of whole systems nor the microscopic activity of individual neurons or synapses speaks at the "proper" level at which mental processes are encoded in neuronal mechanisms. That proper level must be expressed in terms of the details of the spatial and temporal organization of the neural network. In fact, we do not know how membrane conductivity changes produced by drugs actually affect the ultracomplex and unknown web of neural interactions that is the essential (as opposed to the irrelevant) psychoneural basis of mental processes.

As useful and interesting as it is in its own right and as psychologically active as these wonderful drugs may be, neurochemistry finesses the proper form of the essential mind–brain question: How does neuronal organization (not chemistry) produce mind? Thus, although this valuable science profoundly influences and may even improve the quality of human existence, the development and use of these drugs is only a more or less successful empirical attack on the very real and tragic problem of mental aberrations. Unfortunately, this essentially empirical science does not bring any depth of understanding to the actual and specific details of how the modified activity of the neural net produces the changes in interpersonally observable behavior and intrapersonally private peace of mind. The science of psychotropic drugs provides the illusion of understanding without actually contributing to answering the great question of how brains encode mind. Of course, not all of my colleagues agree with this point, but the deeper the discussion, the more likely is agreement on major principles to emerge.

Remember that the key question is: What are the details of the psychoneurally equivalent neural network? Some other approaches ask questions that are very interesting, but are irrelevant to this key question. The illusion that we know more than we do arises from the fact that these techniques all measure some thing happening in the brain. These measurements may even be correlated with some mental or behavioral event. Unfortunately, correlation is not tantamount to identity. These other approaches to studying brain–mind relationships seem to be nothing more than "displacement activities" in the words of the ethologists—busywork that is done in order to avoid the more immediately relevant activities. At the risk of offending some very active scientists, I would include in these displacement activities the new techniques for examining chemical functions or anatomical structures inside the head, such as PET and fMRI imaging procedures. All of these techniques may be of some utility (within the limits expressed by Van Orden & Papp, in press), but they have minimum theoretical significance for the key psychobiological question of neural net interactions.

Similarly, all compound electrical potentials (e.g., evoked brain potentials and electroencephalograms), even though they come from the brain, obscure the details of the essential neuronal network action by their very integrated nature. They may have great utility for solving some problems— they may help in localizing areas where critical functions or lesions may occur, and they may help to estimate the speed of information transmission from peripheral to central nervous structures. But they are not suitable for analysis of the neuronal net any more than the spectacular pictures produced by the exciting new noninvasive techniques for examining brain structure and localization of function. They provide illusions of progress toward understanding brain–mind relations, but in the context of the essential question of psychoneural equivalence, they answer the wrong question.

The future of neurochemical, neuroanatomical, and neurophysiological research, I repeat, is not in question. Research should and will continue in these fields because of their intrinsic significance and the probability of potentially important contributions in achieving their own practical and theoretical goals. On the other hand, it does seem appropriate to reinterpret what such techniques mean, what they can do successfully, and what they are forever prohibited from accomplishing.

Toward a New Mathematics

Mathematics is a powerful tool; indeed, it is so powerful that "it can model truth and drivel with equal felicity" (Cutting, 1986, p. xi). However, as I hope my readers appreciate by now, mathematics is fundamentally neutral with regard to underlying mechanisms. Its formulations are capable of describing the functions of a universe of devices that may all behave the same but that may all be based on totally different internal structures and mechanisms. Thus, mathematics provides a system of representation that is at once so powerful in describing and so limited in reductively explaining that it often provides an irresistible impulse to lead us astray from truth as defined by more valid indicators.

It is not always appreciated how easy it is to extrapolate from mathematical formulas to mechanisms that have no physical reality. The best illustration of this is Fourier frequency analysis. Another is the control system engineer's realization theory, both of which were discussed earlier. The important general point to keep in mind is that the outputs of these analytical tools are mathematical fictions! The engineer's internal model is based on specific assumptions and constraints that need not hold in the system that is being modeled. It is all too easy, however, to forget that both realization and Fourier analysis produce fictional components and, in our forgetfulness, to reify those components as real physical entities.

This is one of the most tantalizing problems with mathematics—its seductive tendency to have its intangible abstractions misinterpreted as tangible physical entities. There is another problem that must also be considered, and that is the inappropriateness of many, if not most, kinds of mathematics to the problem at hand—the study of the mind–brain relationship. With the exception of a very few novel and recent developments, most of our mathematical tools were invented to help understand rather simple and usually linear physical systems. For example, most forms of analysis using calculus or integral and differential equations arose from the study of problems in astronomy and mechanics. As a further example, another great tradition in mathematics is statistics. Descriptive statistical approaches were originally aimed at finding the central tendencies of sets of observations. Inferential statistics sought to explicate the interactions between different variables, many of which were stimulated by problems encountered in agriculture.

Another contemporary approach is to use the computer as a quasi-mathematical tool. The power of the computer to simulate and model is one of the most important developments of our times. However, here, too, there is a proclivity toward misinterpretation of what the results of a computational model may mean. Computer architectures and programming strategies are essentially oriented toward the processing of local properties or features. Programmed algorithms, as a result, produce intellectual forces toward an elementalist emphasis and push us more and more toward an emphasis on local features rather than the global or organizational properties of images.

The reason for this is simple. We have methods for manipulating local regional interactions, but there is a shortage of both computer algorithms and other mathematical methods that allow us to examine or model the broad, molar, organizational attributes of human visual perception and cognition. Yet, when one examines the basic nature of human vision—the classic demonstrations and illusions—one is repeatedly reminded of its basically molar precedence. Even such basic properties as color appearance and apparent lightness seem to depend more on the interactions of widely distributed subregions of a scene than on the wavelength components of the physical luminance of the objects contained in a complex scene.

The successes of analysis, statistics, and computer modeling have been enormous in their respective fields of application. Nothing I have said is intended to diminish this accomplishment. However, even though they succeeded so well there, it is not at all clear that these kinds of mathematics are appropriate for studying the mind–brain problem. The point is that modern mathematical analysis techniques are generally inappropriate methods for the analysis of large-scale neural networks. Our science is in great need of significant breakthroughs in mathematical techniques that will be suitable for studying the broad, molar, interactive aspects of vision that are largely obscured by the local elementalist, feature-oriented mathematics currently in favor.

New approaches to analyzing neurophysiological data that utilize contemporary ideas from chaos theory (e.g., Skarda & Freeman, 1987) also produce representations and measures that quantify the global behavior of a system. Hoffman's (1966) application of Lie groups to visual perception was promising and might have met the need for a bridge between the action of the microscopic components and the macroscopic behavior. However, there has not been general acceptance of any of these ideas in perceptual science, and the need for an appropriate mathematics remains.

THE NEW BEHAVIORISM

Some Comments

What is to be the nature of a new behaviorally oriented perceptual science that would meet the criticisms that I have raised throughout this book? One set of answers to this question was given by Killeen (1984). He cited the following criteria for his modern version of behaviorism, which he refers to as a form of emergent behaviorism.

First, of course, Killeen said that it must be "behavioral." The significant data must be the data of observed behavior, as opposed to inferences about hypothetical constructs, either neural or cognitive. Killeen also believed, as I do, that one must not deny the existence or the causal relevance of some neural substrate for mental events.

Second, Killeen suggested that it must be inductive and, contrary to the classic Skinnerian tradition, allow hypotheses to concern events "at another level." It is not clear to me if Killeen was accepting some kind of neuroreductionism here or if he was merely reasserting the utility and necessity of some form of postulated mental events. If the former, I disagree; if the latter, of course, I agree.

Third, Killeen championed a pragmatic standard for his new behaviorism. He repudiated those theory-generating forces that are based on fad, fiat, doctrine, or imitation—a repudiation that should guide all science, not just a new behaviorism.

Fourth and finally, he astutely noted that his ideal of an emergent behaviorism should be "prudent with its resources but not parsimonious." Again, I agree that this is an entirely appropriate standard for any science.

Killeen set high standards for his emergent behaviorism and, indeed, for any scientific endeavor. There are, however, some additional and somewhat more specific criteria that, in my opinion, should guide and constrain any new behaviorist approach to perceptual as well as more general forms of cognitive research. The following comments are presented to define more precisely the nature of these criteria and the new version of behaviorism with which I am now most comfortable. These admonitions collectively represent the framework for the new behaviorism that I believe is necessary for the continued progress of perceptual and cognitive science.

A New Mathematical Approach Suitable for Describing Molar Behavior Must Be Developed

We must now acknowledge that human perception is primarily and initially molar, as opposed to elementalistically reductionist, in its operation. The Gestalt psychologists understood and correctly taught this principle, but their wisdom was not sustained because the computational and mathematical technology needed to pursue the molar strategy was just as unavailable a half century ago as it is today. We need some new mathematical approach and therefore have an enormous obligation to convince mathematicians to develop techniques better suited to studying arrangement than parts. A major effort is necessary to develop the appropriate mathematics so that some future equivalent of some non-Euclidean mathematics can be utilized by some future psychological Einstein or Bohr to make much-needed breakthroughs in perceptual theory. This step is essential if perceptual science is to enjoy the same kind of growth in understanding that has graced the physical sciences. These breakthroughs may require a softer kind of mathematics able to handle different kinds of relationships other than +, −, ×, and /. It would be very useful to have available a formal symbol manipulation system that could handle such object relations as "a lot alike," "means the same," or even "came from the same place." In other words, we must develop mathematical models that concentrate on quantifying, formalizing, and describing reported perceptual phenomena with symbols and relations that are appropriate for this science and are not borrowed from physics or agriculture. It is mandatory that there be a conscious effort to develop techniques that emphasize the global and organizational attributes of a stimulus form. The glimmering of such "softer" and perhaps more appropriate mathematics can be observed in the novel statistical approaches of fuzzy logic (Zadeh, 1973) and Dempster–Shafer theory (Shafer, 1976).

Realistic Limits on Theory Must Be Elucidated

We must determine what limits apply to the primary goal of theory building. I have dealt in this book with the idea that there are in principle barriers between models and mechanisms. The main idea is that there are serious misinterpretations in what theories and model do and can mean. There is, therefore, a deep need for additional efforts to determine what constraints are operating on perceptual science so that we can avoid a naive and enormous waste of fanciful theory-building energy aimed at impossible goals. That there should be limits is in no sense a condemnation of perceptual psychologists or of perceptual psychology any more than the limits on perpetual motion, time travel, or speed of light are of physics.[2] That we should ignore clear signals that we may have gone astray is not, however, excusable. Perceptual science can be justifiably criticized for not paying sufficient attention to the logical and mathematical fundamentals before imprudently attempting demonstrably untenable neurophysiological or cognitive process reductionism. I am convinced that a few more skeptical combinatorial, automata, or chaos theorists interested in the problems raised by a modern perceptual psychology would do more for the future progress of our science than an army of "true believers" in the ultimate solubility of all our problems with traditional methods.

The Empirical Exploration of Perceptual Science Must Be Continued

The empirical psychophysical approach in which new phenomena are sought, discovered, and described must be the centerpiece of any new development in this science. This empirical effort, however, should be directed to emphasize more fully the global or molar properties of stimuli, rather than the local ones currently in vogue. This is probably the most effective means of diverting the *zeitgeist* from what it is to what it should be until such time as a balance and understanding of the many forces that operate in perception can be achieved.

A major modification of the paradigm of perceptual research is also called for. Too long have we been unidimensional. It is now reasonable to carry out more complex experimental designs that acknowledge the multidimensionality of most experimental scenarios.

---

[2]It has recently been suggested that these limits on time and faster-than-light travel may not be completely rigid constraints. Alcubierre (1994) interpreted the general theory of relativity in a way that may permit such barriers to be penetrated in a way not allowed by the special theory. However, ideas of this kind are considered to be highly controversial and are generally rejected by cosmologists.

Description, Rather Than Neuroreduction, Must Be Emphasized

Reluctantly, given my own scientific background and training in what was called "physiological psychology," I am now convinced that we must ultimately abandon the idea that perceptual processes can be reduced to neurophysiological terms by drawing inferences from psychophysical data. Similarly, I do not believe that it will be possible to conclude from the vast compilations of cellular neurophysiological data anything about mental mechanisms that is relevant to the fundamental problem of mind–brain relationships. This romantic notion, this will-of-the-wisp, this chimera, this dream that we call neuroreductionism, is almost certainly unobtainable in principle as well as in practice if complexity, combinatorial, automata, and chaos theories do turn out to be applicable to perceptual science. What we know about the metabolism and physiological functioning of individual neurons, although a distinguished intellectual and scientific accomplishment in its own right, can probably never be transformed into knowledge of how they operate collectively in the enormous networks of the brain to produce molar behavior.

Of course, the neurosciences are not completely irrelevant. Considerable knowledge has been obtained about the synapse, the final common paths, and localization, among many other highly respected pieces of knowledge. I am calling attention specifically to the unbridgeable gap between the microscopic details of the interactions in the essential neural network and the macroscopic mental processes.

Description, Rather Than Cognitive Reductionism, Must Be Emphasized

Equally reluctantly, I believe that an appreciation must emerge that the major goal of cognitive psychology—to determine the functional processes that are carried out by the nervous system in perception or, for that matter, in any other kind of mental activity—will always be elusive. Not only have the data been inconsistent, but so too have the drawn conclusions. These outcomes reflect the enormous adaptability of the perceiver, on the one hand, and on the other, the fundamental indeterminativeness of any theory of the processes going on within what for any conceivable future is a closed system.

One of the great mysteries of this science is why there has been so little recognition of the fact that the interpretation of data has been so variable. It is almost the norm that a particular set of observations is used as an argument for one hypothesis, and then subsequently as an argument for exactly the opposite theory. My discussion of the phenomena of mental rotation in chapter 4 was a clear example of a case in which the findings were not sufficiently well anchored to the underlying mechanisms to justify the prevailing model of a pictographic representation.

Information, Rather Than Energy, Must Be Emphasized

We will also have to come to appreciate that the study of perception, like all of the other cognitive processes, is an information-processing science, and not an energy- or matter-processing one. The nature of the internal codes and representations of a perceptual experience, therefore, is far less tangible and far more complex a variable than those emerging from the study of simple physical systems. To put it very baldly, psychology is a much more complicated subject matter than are the quantum-mechanical microcosm or the cosmological macrocosm. Indeed, there is even a question arising of whether or not the general concept (which is operative in the simpler energy/matter-dominated fields of science) that universal "laws" exist may be transferred to this much more multivariate domain of perception. Certainly, they are rare beyond the simplest kind of single-variable psychophysics.

The new behaviorism must also take into account the twin aspects of mental processes. That is, they are both empiricist and rationalist in character, with both direct (stimulus attribute driven) and automatic processes, on the one hand, and logical (meaning and context driven) and mediated processes, on the other, playing important roles in the determination of our thoughts. The century-old philosophical debate between the empiricist and rationalist schools can only be resolved by a rapprochement that acknowledges that the reason there has been such a persistent debate is that both were partially correct.

Thus, we must acknowledge that stimuli do not lead solely and inexorably to responses by simple switching circuit-like behavior. Rather, a modern neo-behaviorist perceptual science must accept the fact that there is a rational, meaningful, adaptive, utilitarian, and active construction of percepts and responses by mechanisms that depend more on the meaning of a message than its temporal or spatial geometry. In the perceptual world information can actually be created, unlike matter or energy in the physical world. Many perceptual "illusions" illustrate the truism that we can see that which is only implied as well as we can see real stimuli.

The main point is that "cognitive penetration" plays a very much more important role in perception than is often acknowledged, particularly by those who seek to show the neural correlates of some psychophysical response. The ubiquity of cognitive penetration argues strongly that neuroreductionist strategies attributing perceptual experience to a few peripheral neurons will be hard to justify.

The Reality of Mental Events as Processes
Must Be Accepted

We must accept the reality of mental processes, and the psychobiological premise that these natural processes are nothing more or less than the result of ultracomplex neural mechanisms. This point can be summed up in two axiomatic statements, both of which are fundamental to a new behaviorist perceptual psychology. First, mental states are real. It is, of course, still a matter of dispute whether these mental states directly cause behavior or are merely concomitant to the neurophysiological forces that drive our behavior.

The second principle—psychobiological monism—asserts that there is nothing extraneural, mystical, or even separate at work during mental activity—perception is nothing more nor less than one of the emergent processes of neural activity.

Furthermore, we have to appreciate the danger that is raised by the fact that complexity and numerousness themselves can exert influences that come perilously close to producing exactly the same kind of results that would appear if there were in actual fact such mysterious forces as "free will" at work. As we reaffirm our commitment to psychobiological monism (without which any scientific study of perception or any other aspect of the mind would certainly perish), we must also acknowledge that the gap between the two levels of discourse—neuronal network state and mental phenomenon—may never be crossed. This requires an epistemological or methodological behaviorism in practice and an ontological neuroreductionism in principle. An appreciation of this theory dualism is a necessity for the progress of perceptual science.

Obviously, one of the most salient implications of this admonition for me personally is that perception must regain a place in the new behaviorist strategy I am proposing. Classical behaviorism rejected the study of perception because it represented a type of "mental" response that was supposedly too distant from behavioral measures. A little thought, however, suggests that virtually any topic in psychology faces this same difficulty, and perceptual responses are no different from any of the others. We are capable of appreciating the phenomenology of visual experiences as well as any other mental process. The measurement and description of those phenomena, therefore, can and must be included in the range of topics in any new behaviorist version of perceptual science.

Nevertheless, the intrapersonal privacy of perception (i.e., only we can directly experience our precepts) must also be acknowledged. We can measure perception, but the new behaviorist approach must conclude that the experiences, or measures of them, are equally neutral with regard to the underlying mechanism to both experimenter and observer. Again, there is nothing unique in this statement; mathematics, powerful descriptive tool that it is, is also neutral with regard to the underlying mechanisms.

A most important corollary, therefore, is that we cannot communicate the processes underlying these experiences (or the course of any other cognitive processes) to others. As observers, we can experience the outcome, but not the steps that led to the outcome. This is a generalization of both Moore's theorem and new ideas in other areas of cognitive psychology. Many psychologists (e.g., Nisbett & Wilson, 1977; Nisbett & Ross, 1980) have shown that introspective speculations about one's own mental processes can be terribly misleading.

The neutrality of phenomena is another manifestation of the black box phenomenon. Subjects typically do very poorly in evaluating their own performance in cognitive experiments. The intrapersonal privacy of a percept is as much a barrier to scientific analysis as is the combinatorial limit or the "black box" constraint. The end of this line of logic is that the measurable behavioral or phenomenological response must be considered primary and introspective reports in which subjects are required to interpret what they think they are doing relegated to the same unprivileged level of any other behavior or response. Just as classical behaviorism eschewed introspective reports, so too must this new behaviorism. In their place, response measures must be substituted that are as immune to subjective interpretation or distortion as possible—for example, such experimental designs as Brindley's Class A paradigms. These are key reasons for a new version of the behaviorist approach to perceptual science.

The Primacy of Behaviorally Measured Phenomena Must Be Appreciated

Next, we are going to have to accept the primacy of the phenomena in any controversy between different points of view or theories in perceptual science. That is, the final arbiter of any explanatory disagreement or controversy must be some behavioral measurement of the perceptual experience. Neurophysiology, mathematics, computational convenience, parsimony, and even some kind of simplistic plausibility are all secondary and incomplete criteria for resolving such disputes. This echoes Killeen's plea for prudence, rather than parsimony. But this prudence must be tempered by solid links to the measured response data. The measurable phenomena are the final outcome of a concatenation of processes and are complete in the sense that they reflect all of the relevant previous and intermediate steps. Anything else—idea, introspective report, theory, formal model, neural data, or verbal explanation—that is in conflict with the phenomenon, in principle, requires modification or rejection. This does not mean that the nature of the perceptual experience, as reflected in the measured behavior, can explain or even suggest the underlying processing steps. Rather, in those cases where a conflict between observation and explanation (or any of the other hypothetical estimates of intervening states) does occur, the final result—the phenomenal outcome—must be definitive.

At a qualitative level, however, the perceptual phenomenon is an excellent source of heuristics for theory building simply because it is the stuff of this science: Perceptual psychologists are primarily in business to describe and explain the psychobiological reality we call perceptual experience, not to exercise computers or to speculate about uses for the increasingly large number of anatomically or physiologically specialized neurons that are appearing at the tips of our microelectrodes.

Taxonomic Classification and Organization of the Data and Theories of Our Science Must Be Emphasized

Finally, I repeat my conviction that there is a vast unmet need in perceptual science for efforts to classify and organize our collective knowledge. We urgently require a substantial effort to organize our theories and findings. All too often there has been unnecessary replication or unappreciated analogous experiments that have ignored the identity of two processes. Not only would some rather minor problems of research economics be resolved by an intelligent systemization of our science, but the relationships, similarities, and even the identity of perceptual processes and phenomena, which may seem superficially to be quite different, will become evident.

Some Concluding Advice

In sum, what I am proposing is a mathematically descriptive, nonreductionist, molar, empiricist,[3] rationalist, multidimensional, psychophysical neobehaviorism that is guided more by the relevant phenomena and observations than by the availability and convenience of analytic or methodological tools. This neobehaviorism would be ambitious in seeking solutions to some of the classic problems of perceptual psychology, but modest in avoiding recourse to strategies that are patently beyond the limits of this or any other science. It would place a strong emphasis on the development of more integrated and inclusive descriptive theories. All too much of our effort has been spent on unattainable goals, especially those false but seductively reductionist ones, in the past few decades. I believe such a strategic redirection would be a major step toward a realistic and mature scientific approach to perceptual science.

---

[3]For the philosophers among you who notice the clash between *empiricist* and *rationalist* in this final paragraph, I am specifically suggesting that this false dichotomous debate can be best resolved by accepting that both automatic and interpretive processes take place in perception. The new behaviorism must also be a rapprochement between these two classical antagonistic positions.

6

EMERGING PRINCIPLES

This final chapter is a statement of what I believe are the fundamental guiding principles of perceptual science today. It is a list without further explanation or discussion. This list places heavy emphasis on those issues surrounding neuro- and cognitive reductionism. Other lists expressing my views of more specific principles of perceptual science can be found in my earlier works (Uttal, 1973, 1978a, 1981a, 1988a).

It is important for my readers to appreciate that the significant word in the previous paragraph was *believe*. Many of the principles expressed in this kind of scientific creed cannot be absolutely or rigorously proven any more than can the belief structure of any other scientist. Rather, each of us, after a period of training and experience, comes to a set of expectations and convictions that modulate and guide his or her scientific career. These convictions arise as an integrative interpretation of everything learned or observed. Many of these principles are not the direct consequences of any particular empirical observation, but are the indirect outcome of the global significance of many related findings. Just as we have not been successful in defining a mathematics for global form and arrangement, so too it is difficult to establish the precise pathways by means of which scientists arrive at their own personal points of view.

It is unfortunate that an appreciation of the power of these personal attitudes, belief structures, and theoretical perspectives is not more widely accepted. Many scientists exhibit a reluctant unwillingness to accept the idea that there are often differing points of view based on what might equally be reasonable criteria. Perhaps this is a desirable feature of science. This reluctance can also be considered to be a necessary conservative and stabilizing force that keeps science from wandering off onto fantastic by-ways. Be that as it may be, differing scientific views, premises, beliefs, and creeds do provide the basis for the ferment that characterizes the best science. Universality of opinion is usually a sign of stagnation.

In a field such as perception or more generally, cognitive neuroscience, where the complexities are so great and the empirical and logical difficulties preventing us from achieving rigor so profound, our scientific work is especially heavily influenced by our beliefs. I know that I read and interpret technical reports differently now than a few decades ago when my scientific perspective was different.

In the rush to collect *data*, the integrative role of science is all too often forgotten. American cognitive science is often criticized by many Europeans as being much too empirical and not sufficiently thoughtful. We are criticized as "barefoot empiricists" or experimental "mechanics" unconcerned with the conceptual foundations on which our science is based. All too often, we hear some of the most eminent of our colleagues asserting that a particular issue "is much too philosophical" or "too far from the data" to merit discussion at a scientific conference or inclusion in a journal article. Interpretive speculation (in the best sense of the term) is eschewed as being beyond the pale and a consideration of the fundamental premises of our science is deprecated.

The following list of principles is not likely to completely reverse this trend, but perhaps it can help to stimulate discussion of some of the fundamental issues of our science by making explicit one person's view of where perceptual science stands today.

EMERGING PRINCIPLES OF PERCEPTUAL SCIENCE

The Nature of the Problem

1. The basic metaphysical statement of the nature of psychobiological reality is known as *Material Monism*. This premise asserts that all mental acts are nothing more nor less than one set of the many functions carried out by the nervous system. This is the fundamental principle on which all subsequent ones rest.

2. At the present time, the best estimate of the psychoneural equivalent of mind (the neural equivalent of thought or the essential level of analysis) is the ensemble details of the interactions among vast networks of huge numbers of neurons in the higher reaches of the cerebral cortex. The ensemble or statistical nature of the information patterns embodied in these nets is what emerges as mental activity and cognitively relevant behavior. Individual neurons are relatively unimportant except to the degree they play

a role as constituents in these great neuronal networks. The role of any given neuron may be fleeting without undo instability being introduced in the perceptual experience.

3. The mind is an information processing activity of the brain. The metabolism and chemistry of neurons may set some limits on processing or transmission speeds and are interesting to the degree they define the technology in which mind is instantiated. However, neurochemistry is fundamentally irrelevant to the organizational and informational nature of the process. In principle, any other machine, built on any other technology, but arranged in the same way as the brain (whatever way that might be), would produce the same cognitive and perceptual processes—including conscious awareness.

4. The ideal goal of a science is *Ontological Reductionism* in which the phenomena at one level of discourse are explained in terms of mechanisms and processes at more microscopic levels. However, true ontological reductionism for perception and other cognitive processes, both neurophysiological and cognitive, is elusive, and for a number of reasons, both fundamental and practical, may be unobtainable.

5. Scientific examination of the nature of the relationship between perception, in particular, and mental activity, in general, and neurophysiological activity is so severely constrained and bounded that there exists serious doubt about the possibility of building explanatory bridges from one domain to the other. This suggests that the material monistic ontology expressed in Principle 1 may have to be paired with what is actually a dualistic epistemology.

Fundamental Barriers to Reductionism

6. Obstacles to reductionism can arise from matters of fundamental principle (e.g., the irreversibility of thermodynamic systems) as well as from practical matters (e.g., the vast numbers of neurons involved in a psychologically significant neural network).

7. One of the most fundamental and most ignored principles opposing reduction of mental processes to brain mechanisms is the "Black Box" theorem, well known to engineers and automata theorists. This is identical to Moore's second theorem, which asserts that there are always many more possible internal mechanisms in a closed system than there are experiments that could be used to determine the system's internal structure. Therefore, there is no way to deduce the internal structure from input–output experiments. This holds for all psychophysical and cognitive experiments as well as attempts to infer internal structure of electronic or mechanical hardware.

8. In some cases, the black box may be opened only to discover that it is so complicated that it remains "functionally" closed.

9. In some cases, attempts are made to circumvent the "black box" barrier by applying other constraints such as least energy, elegance, parsimony, or economy. While these criteria may be partially useful in some simple systems, such additional constraints are usually irrelevant in the context of the brain. The huge number of neurons in the brain obviates the need for parsimony or economy. It is impossible to know what "elegance" represents in a system about which we do not even know the basic logical rules being used.

10. Currently two diametrically opposed points of view contend over the possibility of reduction. One side says—"Given enough time anything is possible: We shall reduce mind to brain functions." The other says: "For reasons of fundamental and inescapable principles, the attempt to build a bridge between brain and mind is forever unachievable." I believe that the latter assertion is the correct one. This is not a pessimistic view; it is a realistic one.

Some Caveats for Neuroreductionists

11. Many proposed neuroreductionist "explanations" are based on false analogies or spurious correlations between the neural and cognitive domains. Often this misidentification is based on nothing more than a play on words whose similarity is more poetic than real.

12. In other instances it is based on a similarity of functional form or some superficial isomorphism. Isomorphic representation, however, is not a satisfactory criterion for psychoneural equivalence. Some codes cannot be isomorphic (e.g., greenness). Some isomorphic relationships (e.g., retinotopic mapping) may be only indirectly relevant merely characterizing the nature of the early, low level transmission codes conveying information to the more symbolic representation of perceptual processes at higher levels.

13. There is such an enormous variety of neurophysiological activities resulting from the enormous variety of neural responses involved in even the simplest cognitive process) that it is usually possible to find virtually anything one needs to support almost any reductionist theory of neural coding or representation by injudicious selection of data.

14. Many proposed neuroreductionist "explanations" of perceptual or cognitive functions are based on dramatic, but misinterpreted, findings from the neurophysiological laboratory. The raw observations can usually be replicated, but their meaning may vary with changes in the current theoretical consensus.

15. Correlations between percepts and a neural response in some region of the brain do not necessarily signify that that location is the site of psychoneural equivalence. Some brain location or group of locations must be responsible for perceptual experience, but correlation is not tantamount to equivalence. This principle must be kept in mind particularly when one

applies the criterion of the first (or lowest) level of explicit correlation between a perceptual experience and a neural response as, for example, a
proof of low-level vision.

16. Psychophysical data take precedence over neurophysiological data.
Psychophysical data are the final outcome of the entire perceptual brain–
mind system. Any contradictory neural data must, by definition, be incorrect
or irrelevant in the information processes that lie between stimuli and perceptions.

17. Different questions of perceptual science are often confused. The
attempt to answer the *localization question* may possibly be moving ahead
under the impetus of new devices capable of examining the macroscopic
places in the brain where activity seems to be correlated with some mental
activity. The quite separate *representation question* is one of microscopic
neuronal network interactions: It remains refractory and intractable. Unfortunately, it is this latter issue that lies at the heart of the effort to build
mind–brain bridges. Representation (i.e., psychoneural equivalence) is the
essential question and is the one dealt with in this book.

Some Caveats for Cognitive Reductionists

18. Reduction of mind to the components of an underlying cognitive architecture may also be an impossible quest. The reasons behind this principle are based on the fact that unlikely assumptions have to be made about
the nature of thought for such an enterprise to be achieved. Most of these
unlikely assumptions are based on a functional rigidity of the putative components that is in conflict with our observations of the actual adaptability
of human cognitive processes.

19. Many dichotomous arguments (e.g., serial vs. parallel processing)
that have driven perceptual science throughout its history are extremist
"straw men." In almost all cases, the ultimate resolution is in the form of a
compromise that adopts neither extreme view.

20. Psychophysical, behavioral, or cognitive data, the observations of
molar psychology, are neutral with regard to the underlying neural or cognitive mechanisms to both the perceptual scientist and the perceiver. Neither the external nor the internal observer can have any insight in the logical
processes that lead from a stimulus to a percept. Only the outcomes are
observable or perceivable.

Some Caveats for Modelers

21. Mathematics, the "queen of the sciences," does not provide a means
of avoiding the barriers that lie between mind and neural activity or cognitive
components. Mathematics is exclusively a descriptive endeavor. It is a means
of describing the functional course of a process, but is also absolutely neutral

with regard to the inner workings of the system. The physiological premises of a theory are always distinguishable and separate from the mathematical ones. Mathematics is so powerful that it can introduce irrelevant attributes into our understanding of a system and so fragile that it can ignore critical ones. It shares these limitations with all other forms of modeling.

22. Many forms of mathematics are powerful tools for describing, manipulating, and measuring stimuli and responses. For example, Fourier analysis provides an effective means to manipulate stimuli precisely. However, such methods may also carry with them superfluous meaning that can be misinterpreted as psychobiological reality.

23. Many putatively distinct mathematical theories actually turn out to be duals of each other. That is, the theories are often derivable, one from the other, and may differ only in secondary issues such as their neural premises.

24. A new mathematics is needed for the description of perceptual processes. It must be sensitive to the global organization (i.e., the arrangement of the parts) of the scene as opposed to the local features (i.e., the nature of the parts) in a way that is not achieved by such analytic devices as Fourier or other feature superimposition type methods.

Some General Caveats

25. The indisputable observation of cognitive penetration by meaningful or relational factors in some of the most basic perceptual experiences suggests that "low-level" vision is a misnomer. Cognitive penetration implies high level influences on all visual experience and a high cortical level location for the actual psychoneural equivalent of perception.

26. Many attempts to justify the existence of low-level vision or peripheral neural explanatory models can be understood as either (a) confusions of the representative role of neurons with their transmission role; or (b) the misdirection of research direction to accessible regions and obtainable observations when the true locus is inaccessibly obscured by complexity or numerosity; or (c) the tendency to seek justification for some preexisting theory.

27. The inaccessibility of the higher regions is due to the complexity of the neural networks. These regions are the locus of the essential representative functions of the brain. It is disappointing to have to acknowledge that we do not know anything about the rules or logic by which neural activity becomes the equivalent of mental activity. It seems likely, although it cannot be proven, that the rules of cerebral logic are not well modeled by either conventional mathematics or current neural network computational models.

28. Many of the words used in discussions of mental processes are extremely difficult to define. Efforts to be more precise usually founder on the

shoals of the intrapersonal privacy of our mental experience. Most definitions are limited to a kind of phenomenalistic reductionism (see p. 141) in which the words are simply equated to what is assumed to be common experience.

29. Our perception of perceptual phenomena—the data and phenomenological observations themselves—is conditioned by the theories that have evolved in our science. We more often than not see what we want to see.

30. Many of the findings of perceptual science reflect the design of our experiments rather than the psychobiological realities of the mind–brain system.

31. Many generally accepted and superficially direct methods for examining the brain (such as the PET scan) may not mean what they seem to at the present. Even the "hardest" and most direct data not only may be difficult to replicate, but, even more fundamentally, may prove to be sending different messages at different times in our scientific history. The meaning of a finding is strongly theory dependent.

Future Directions

32. The future of a vigorous perceptual science depends on its return to its behaviorist roots. The siren songs of neuroreductionist and cognitive reductionist theories notwithstanding, there are sufficient arguments to suggest that the ideal goal of an ontological reductionism is unobtainable.

33. The new behaviorism does not reject the existence of the process we call mind or of any of the underlying mechanisms. It does, however, say that most internal processes are not accessible. It does not deal with introspection as anything different from any other form of verbal response with all of the attendant frailties and deficiencies. It does accept all kinds of observable behavior, including verbal behavior, as the data of the science.

34. The new behaviorism will not be the same as the classic version. It has its own premises and principles, some of which have been presented here.

35. The future of this new behaviorist perceptual science does not diminish the value of nor the need for formal modeling, or neurophysiological, biochemical, or cognitive research of other kinds. Each of these fields of study is useful, interesting, and elegant in its own right. What this book does call for is an appreciation of the limits of the reductionist enterprise, the fantastic nature of some bridge building efforts, and a reevaluation of the meaning of our theories.

REFERENCES

Adelson, E. H. (1993). Perceptual organization and the judgment of brightness. *Science, 262*, 2042–2044.

Alcubierre, M. (1994). The warp drive: Hyper-fast travel within general relativity. *Classical and Quantum Gravity, 11*, L73–L77.

Allman, J. (1981). Reconstructing the evolution of the brain in primates through the use of comparative neurophysiological and neuroanatomical data. In E. Armstrong & D. Falk (Eds.), *Primate brain evolution: Methods and concepts* (pp. 13–28). New York: Plenum.

Anderson, J. A. (1968). A memory model utilizing spatial correlation functions. *Kybernetik, 5*, 113–119.

Anderson, J. A. (1972). A simple neural network generating an interactive memory. *Mathematical Biosciences, 14*, 197–220.

Anderson, J. A., Pellionisz, A., & Rosenfeld, E. (Eds.). (1990). *Neurocomputing: Vol. 2. Directions for research*. Cambridge, MA: MIT Press.

Anderson, J. A., & Rosenfeld, R. E. (Eds.). (1988). *Neurocomputing: Foundations of research*. Cambridge, MA: MIT Press.

Anderson, J. R. (1978). Argument concerning representations for mental imagery. *Psychological Review, 85*, 249–277.

Arieli, A., Sterkin, A., Grinvald, A., & Aertsen, A. (1996). Dynamics of ongoing activity: Explanation of large variability in evoked cortical responses. *Science, 273*, 1868–1871.

Armstrong, D. M. (1962). *Bodily sensations*. New York: Routledge & Kegan Paul and Humanities Press.

Atkinson, R. C., & Shiffrin, R. M. (1968). Human memory: A proposed system and it control processes. In S. K. W. & J. T. Spence (Eds.), *The psychology of learning and motivation: Advances in research and theory* (Vol. 2). New York: Academic Press.

Baddeley, A. D. (1992). Working memory. *Science, 255*, 556–559.

Barlow, H. B. (1972). Single units and perception: A neuron doctrine for perceptual psychology. *Perception, 1*, 371–394.

Barlow, H. B. (1978). The efficiency of detecting changes of density in random dot patterns. *Vision Research, 18*, 637–650.

Barlow, H. B. (1995). The neuron doctrine in perception. In M. S. Gazzaniga (Ed.), *The cognitive neurosciences*. Cambridge, MA: MIT Press.

Bennett, B. M., Hoffman, D. D., & Prakash, C. (1989). *Observer mechanics: A formal theory of perception*. San Diego: Academic Press.

Blakemore, C., & Campbell, F. W. (1969). On the existence of neurons in the human visual system selectively sensitive to the orientation and size of retinal images. *Journal of Physiology, 203*, 237–260.

Blakemore, C., & Cooper, G. F. (1970). Development of the brain depends on the visual environment. *Nature, 228*, 477–478.

Blum, H. F. (1951). *Time's arrow and evolution*. Princeton, NJ: Princeton University Press.

Boyd, R. (1980). Materialism without reductionism: What physicalism does not entail. In R. Block (Ed.), *Readings in the philosophy of psychology* (Vol. 1, pp. 67–106). Cambridge, MA: Harvard University Press.

Braje, W. L., Tjan, B. S., & Legge, G. E. (1995). Human efficiency for recognizing and detecting low-pass filtered objects. *Vision Research, 35*, 2955–2966.

Braunstein, M. L., Hoffman, D. D., Shapiro, L. R., Andersen, G. J., & Bennett, B. M. (1987). Minimum points and views for the recovery of three-dimensional structure. *Journal of Experimental Psychology: Human Perception and Performance, 13*, 335–343.

Breitmeyer, B. G. (1984). *Visual masking: An integrative approach*. New York: Oxford University Press.

Breitmeyer, B. G., & Ganz, L. (1976). Implications of sustained and transient channels for theories of visual pattern matching, saccadic suppression, and information processing. *Psychological Review, 83*, 1–36.

Bridgeman, B. (1987). Metacontrast and lateral inhibition. *Psychological Review, 78*, 528–539.

Brindley, G. S. (1960). *Physiology of the retina and the visual pathway*. London: Edward Arnold.

Campbell, F. W., & Robson, J. G. (1968). An application of Fourier analysis to the visibility of gratings. *Journal of Physiology, 197*, 551–566.

Carpenter, G. A., & Grossberg, S. (Eds.). (1991). *Pattern recognition by self organizing neural networks*. Cambridge, MA: MIT Press.

Casti, J. L. (1996, October). Confronting science's logical limits. *Scientific American*, pp. 102–105.

Chalmers, D. J. (1995, December). The puzzle of conscious experience. *Scientific American*, pp. 80–86.

Cheal, M. L., & Lyon, D. R. (1992). *Allocation of attention in texture segregation, visual search, and location-precuing paradigms*. Williams AFB, AZ: Armstrong Laboratory.

Churchland, P. M. (1979). *Scientific realism and the plasticity of mind*. Cambridge, MA: MIT Press.

Churchland, P. M. (1981). Eliminative materialism and the propositional attitudes. *Journal of Philosophy, 78*, 67–90.

Churchland, P. M. (1988). *Matter and consciousness*. Cambridge, MA: MIT Press.

Churchland, P. S. (1986). *Neurophilosophy: Toward a unified science of the mind–brain*. Cambridge, MA: MIT Press.

Churchland, P. S., & Sejnowski, T. J. (1988). Perspectives on cognitive neuroscience. *Science, 242*, 741–745.

Churchland, P. S., & Sejnowski, T. J. (1989). Neural representation and neural computation. In L. Nadel, L. A. Cooper, P. Culicover, & R. M. Harnish (Eds.), *Neural connections, mental computation* (pp. 15–48). Cambridge, MA: MIT Press.

Churchland, P. S., & Sejnowski, T. J. (1992). *The computational brain*. Cambridge, MA: MIT Press.

Cohen, M. A., & Grossberg, S. (1984). Neural dynamics of brightness perception: Features, boundaries, diffusion, and resonance. *Perception and Psychophysics, 36*, 428–456.

Coren, S., & Girgus, J. S. (1978). *Seeing is deceiving: The psychology of visual illusions*. Hillsdale, NJ: Lawrence Erlbaum Associates.

Cosgriff, R. L. (1960). *Identification of shape* (Report No. 820-11). Columbus: Ohio State University Research Foundation.

Cox, D. R., & Smith, W. L. (1954). On the superimposition of renewal processes. *Biometrika, 41,* 91–99.

Crick, F. (1994). *The astonishing hypothesis: The scientific search for the soul.* New York: Scribner's.

Crutchfield, J. P., Farmer, J. D., Packard, N. H., & Shaw, R. S. (1986). Chaos. *Scientific American, 256,* 46–57.

Cummins, R. (1983). *The nature of psychological explanation.* Cambridge, MA: MIT Press.

Cutting, J. E. (1986). *Perception with an eye for motion.* Cambridge, MA: MIT Press.

Cutting, J. E. (1987). Perception and information. *Annual Review of Psychology, 38,* 61–90.

Daubechies, I. (1988). Orthonormal bases of compactly supported wavelets. *Communication on Pure and Applied Mathematics, 41,* 909–996.

Davies, D. R., & Parasuraman, R. (1982). *The psychology of vigilance.* London: Academic Press.

Deadwyler, S. A., & Hampson, R. E. (1995). Ensemble activity and behavior: What's the code? *Science, 270,* 1316–1318.

DeMonasterio, F. M., & Gouras, P. (1975). Functional properties of ganglion cells of the rhesus monkey retina. *Journal of Physiology (London), 251,* 167–195.

Dennett, D. C. (1981). *Brainstorms: Philosophical essays on mind and psychology.* Cambridge, MA: MIT Press.

De Valois, R. L., & De Valois, K. K. (1988). *Spatial vision.* New York: Oxford University Press.

Donders, F. C. (1868, 1969). On the speed of mental processes. W. G. Koster, Trans. *Acta Psychologica, 30,* 412–431.

Dresp, B., & Bonnet, C. (1991). Psychophysical evidence for low level processing of illusory contours. *Vision Research, 10,* 1813–1817.

Dresp, B., & Bonnet, C. (1993). Psychophysical measures of illusory form induction: Further evidence for local mechanisms. *Vision Research, 33,* 759–766.

Dresp, B., & Bonnet, C. (1995). Subthreshold summation with illusory contours. *Vision Research, 35*(8), 1071–1078.

Dreyfus, H. L. (1972). *What computers can't do: The limits of artificial intelligence* (rev. ed.). New York: Harper & Row.

Dreyfus, H. L. (1992). *What computers still can't do.* Cambridge, MA: MIT Press.

Eccles, J. C. (1953). *The neurophysiological basis of mind.* Oxford: Clarendon Press.

Eddington, A. (1928). *The nature of the physical world.* New York: AMS Press.

Edwards, P. E. (1967). *The encyclopedia of philosophy* (Vol. 5). New York: Collier Macmillan.

Ericksen, C. W., & Collins, J. F. (1967). Some temporal characteristics of visual pattern perception. *Journal of Experimental Psychology, 74,* 476–484.

Farley, B. G., & Clark, W. A. (1954). Simulation of a self-organizing system by a digital computer. *Institute of Radio Engineers Transactions of Information Theory, 4,* 76–84.

Feigl, H. (1960). Mind-body not a pseudo problem. In S. Hook (Ed.), *Dimensions of mind* (pp. 33–34). New York: New York University.

Felleman, D. J., & Van Essen, D. C. (1991). Distributed hierarchical processing in primate visual cortex. *Cerebral Cortex, 1,* 1–47.

Ferster, D., & Spruston, N. (1995). Cracking the neural code. *Science, 270,* 756–757.

Finke, R. A., & Schmidt, M. H. (1978). The quantitative measure of pattern representation in images using orientation-specific after effects. *Perception and Psychophysics, 23,* 515.

Fodor, J. A. (1968). *Psychological explanation.* New York: Random House.

Fodor, J. A. (1981). *Representations: Philosophical essays on the foundations of cognitive science.* Cambridge, MA: MIT Press.

Fodor, J., & Pylyshyn, Z. (1988). Connectionism and cognitive architecture. *Cognition, 28,* 3–71.

Fourier, J. (1822). *Theorie analytique de la chaleur.* Paris: F. Didot.

Freeman, W. J. (1995). *Societies of brains: A study in the neuroscience of love and hate.* Hillsdale, NJ: Lawrence Erlbaum Associates.

Gabor, D. (1946). Theory of communication. *Journal of the IEEE, 93,* 429–457.

Gazzaniga, M. S. (Ed.). (1995). *The cognitive neurosciences.* Cambridge, MA: MIT Press.

Gell-Mann, M. (1964). A schematic model of baryons and mesons. *Physics Letters, 8*, 214–215.

Gilchrist, A. L. (1977). Perceived lightness depends upon spatial arrangement. *Science, 195*, 185–187.

Ginsburg, A. P. (1983). Visual form perception based on biological filtering. In L. Spillman & B. R. Wooten (Eds.), *Sensory experience, adaptation and perception: Festschrift for Ivo Kohler.* Hillsdale, NJ: Lawrence Erlbaum Associates.

Gleick, S. (1987). New images of chaos that are stirring a science revolution. *Smithsonian, 18*(9), 122–137.

Graham, N. V. S. (1989). *Visual pattern analyzers.* New York: Oxford University Press.

Granit, R. (1955). *Receptors and sensory perception.* New Haven, CT: Yale University Press.

Grebogi, C., Ott, E., & Yorke, J. A. (1987). Chaos, strange attractors, and fractal basin boundaries in nonlinear dynamics. *Science, 238*, 632–638.

Green, M. (1991). Visual search, visual streams, and visual architectures. *Perception and Psychophysics, 50*(4), 388–403.

Greengard, L. (1988). *The rapid evaluation of potential fields in particle systems.* Cambridge, MA: MIT Press.

Gregory, R. L. (1963). Distortion of visual space as inappropriate constancy scaling. *Nature, 199*, 678–680.

Gregory, R. L., & Gombrich, E. H. (1973). *Illusion in nature and art.* London: Duckworth.

Grosof, D. H., Shapley, R. M., & Hawken, M. J. (1993). Macaque V1 neurons can signal "illusory" contours. *Nature, 365*, 550–552.

Gross, C. G. (1992). Representation of visual stimuli in inferior temporal cortex. *Proceedings of the Royal Society of London (B), 335*, 3–10.

Gross, C. G., Rocha-Miranda, C. E., & Bender, D. B. (1972). Visual properties of neurons in infero-temporal cortex of macaque. *Journal of Neurophysiology, 35*, 96–111.

Grossberg, S. (1968). Some nonlinear networks capable of learning a spatial pattern of arbitrary complexity. *Proceedings of the National Academy of Sciences, 59*, 368–372.

Grossberg, S. (1969). On learning of spatiotemporal patterns by networks with ordered sensory and motor components. *Studies in Applied Mathematics, 49*, 135–166.

Grossberg, S. (1982). *Studies of mind and brain: Neural principles of learning, perception, development, cognition, and motor control.* Boston: Reidel Press.

Grossberg, S. (1988a). Nonlinear neural networks: Principles, mechanisms, and architectures. *Neural Networks, 1*, 17–61.

Grossberg, S. (Ed.). (1988b). *Neural networks and natural intelligence.* Cambridge, MA: MIT Press.

Grossberg, S., & Mingolla, E. (1985a). Neural dynamics of form perception: Boundary completion, illusory figures, and neon color spreading. *Psychological Review, 92*, 173–211.

Grossberg, S., & Mingolla, E. (1985b). Neural dynamics of perceptual grouping: Texture, boundaries, and emergent segmentations. *Perception and Psychophysics, 38*, 141–171.

Harmon, L. D., & Julesz, B. (1972). Masking in visual recognition: Effects of two-dimensional filtered noise. *Science, 180*, 1194–1197.

Harris, J. R., Shaw, M. L., & Altom, M. J. (1985). Serial position curves for reaction times and accuracy in visual search: Tests of a model of overlapping processing. *Perception and Psychophysics, 38*, 178–187.

Harris, J. R., Shaw, M. L., & Bates, M. (1979). Visual search in multicharacter arrays with and without gaps. *Perception and Psychophysics, 26*, 69–84.

Hartline, H. K. (1938). The response of single optic fibers of the vertebrate eye to illumination of the retina. *American Journal of Physiology, 121*, 400–415.

Hartline, H. K., Wagner, H., & Ratliff, F. (1956). Inhibition in the eye of *Limulus. Journal of General Physiology, 39*, 651–673.

Hawkins, R. D., & Kandel, E. R. (1984). Is there a cell-biological alphabet for simple forms of learning? *Psychological Review, 91*, 375–391.

Hecht, S., Shalaer, S., & Pirenne, M. H. (1942). Energy, quanta, and vision. *Journal of General Psychology, 25,* 819–840.

Helmholtz, H. v. (1925). *Excerpts from treaties on physiological optics* (3rd ed.). New York: Wiley.

Hermann, L. (1870). Eine Erscheinung des simultanen Contrastes. *Pflugers Archiv, 3,* 13–15.

Hick, W. E. (1952). On the rate of gain of information. *Quarterly Journal of Experimental Psychology, 4,* 11–26.

Hilgetag, C. C., O'Neill, M. A., & Young, M. P. (1996). Indeterminate organization of the visual system. *Science, 271,* 76–777.

Hoffman, W. C. (1966). The Lie algebra of visual perception. *Journal of Mathematical Psychology, 3,* 349–367.

Hubel, D. H., & Wiesel, T. N. (1959). Receptive fields of single neurons in the cat's striate cortex. *Journal of Physiology, 148,* 574–591.

Hubel, D. H., & Wiesel, T. N. (1962). Receptive fields, binocular interaction, and functional architecture in the cat's visual cortex. *Journal of Physiology, 160,* 106–154.

Hubel, D. H., & Wiesel, T. N. (1965). Binocular interaction in striate cortex of kittens reared with artificial squint. *Journal of Neurophysiology, 28,* 1041–1059.

Hubel, D. H., & Wiesel, T. N. (1968). Receptive fields and functional architecture of monkey striate cortex. *Journal of Physiology, 195,* 215–243.

Hubel, D. H., & Wiesel, T. N. (1974). Uniformity of monkey striate cortex: A parallel relationship between field size, scatter, and magnification factor. *Journal of Comparative Neurology, 158,* 295–306.

Hull, C. L. (1943). *Principles of behavior.* New York: Appleton-Century-Crofts.

Humphrey, G. K., Goodale, M. A., & Gurnsey, R. (1991). Orientation discrimination in a visual form agnostic: Evidence from the McCullough effect. *Psychological Science, 2,* 331–335.

Hurvich, L. M., & Jameson, D. (1955). Some quantitative aspects of an opponent color theory. II. Brightness, saturation, and hue in normal and dichromatic vision. *Journal of the Optical Society of America, 45,* 602–616.

Hurvich, L. M., & Jameson, D. (1957). An opponent-process theory of color vision. *Psychological Review, 64,* 384–404.

Hyman, R. (1953). Stimulus information as a determinant of reaction time. *Journal of Experimental Psychology, 45,* 188–196.

Ishai, A., & Sagi, D. (1995). Common mechanisms of visual imagery and perception. *Science, 268,* 1172–1774.

Jackson, F. (1989). Epiphenomenal qualia. *Philosophical Quarterly, 32,* 127–136.

Jenkins, B., & Ross, J. (1977). McCullough effects depends upon perceived orientation. *Perception, 6,* 399–400.

Johanson, D. C., & Shreeve, J. (1989). *Lucy's child: The discovery of a human ancestor.* New York: Morrow.

Jones, D. D., & Holding, D. H. (1975). Extremely long persistence of the McCullough effect. *Journal of Experimental Psychology: Human Perception and Performance, 1,* 323–327.

Jordan, M. I. (1986). *Serial order: A parallel distributed processing approach.* San Diego, CA: Institute for Cognitive Studies.

Julesz, B. (1981). Textons, the elements of texture perception, and their interactions. *Nature, 290,* 91–97.

Julesz, B. (1983). Textons, the fundamental elements in preattentive vision and perception of texture. *Bell System Technical Journal, 62,* 1619–1645.

Kaas, J. H. (1978). *The organization of visual cortex in primates.* New York: Plenum Press.

Kabrisky, M. (1966). *A proposed model for information processing in the human brain.* Urbana: University of Illinois Press.

Kaniza, G. (1955). Margini quasi-percettivi in campi con stimolaxione omogenea. *Rivista di Psicologia, 49,* 7–30.

Kaniza, G. (1974). Contours without gradients or cognitive contours. *Italian Journal of Psychology, 1,* 93–112.

Kaufman, J. H., May, J. G., & Kunen, S. (1981). Interocular transfer of orientation-contingent color aftereffects with external and internal adaptation. *Perception and Psychophysics, 30*(6), 54–551.

Kellogg, O. D. (1953). *Foundations of potential theory.* New York: Dover.

Killeen, P. R. (1984). Emergent behaviorism. *Behaviorism, 12,* 25–39.

Killeen, P. R. (1988). The reflex reserve. *Journal of Experimental Analysis of Behavior, 50,* 319–331.

Klein, S. A. (1992). The duality of psychophysics. In A. Gorea, Y. Fregnac, & Z. Kapoula (Eds.), *Representations of vision: Trends and tacit assumptions in vision research* (pp. 232–249). Cambridge: Cambridge University Press.

Koffka, K. (1935). *Principles of Gestalt psychology.* New York: Harcourt, Brace, and World.

Konorski, J. (1967). *The integrative activity of the brain.* Chicago: University of Chicago Press.

Kosslyn, S. M. (1980). *Image and mind.* Cambridge, MA: Harvard University Press.

Kosslyn, S. M. (1995). *Image and brain: The resolution of the imagery debate.* Cambridge, MA: MIT Press.

Kosslyn, S. M., Alpert, N. M., Thompson, W., Maljkovic, V., Weiss, S. B., Chabris, C. F., Hamilton, S. E., Ruch, S. L., & Buonanno, F. S. (1993). Visual mental imagery activates topographically organized visual cortex: PET investigations. *Journal of Cognitive Neuroscience, 5,* 263–287.

Kosslyn, S. M., & Ochsner, K. N. (1994). In search of occipital activation during visual mental imagery. *Trends in Neuroscience, 17,* 290–292.

Kulikowski, J. J., & King-Smith, P. E. (1977). Spatial arrangement of line, edge, and grating detectors revealed by subthreshold summation. *Vision Research, 13,* 1455–1478.

Kunen, S., & May, J. G. (1980). Spatial frequency content of visual imagery. *Perception and Psychophysics, 28,* 555–559.

Land, E. H. (1959a). Color vision and the natural image: I. *Proceedings of the National Academy of Sciences, USA, 45,* 115–129.

Land, E. H. (1959b). Color vision and the natural image: II. *Proceedings of the National Academy of Sciences, USA, 45,* 636–644.

Land, E. H. (1977). The Retinex theory of color vision. *Scientific American, 237,* 108–128.

Landy, M. S., & Movshon, J. A. (Eds.). (1991). *Computational models of visual processing.* Cambridge, MA: MIT Press.

Lesher, G. W. (1995). Illusory contours: Toward a neurally based perceptual theory. *Psychonomic Bulletin and Review, 2,* 279–321.

Lettvin, J. Y., Maturana, H. R., McCulloch, W. S., & Pitts, W. H. (1959). What the frog's eye tells the frog's brain. *Proceedings of the Institute of Radio Engineers, 47,* 1940–1951.

Ling, G., & Gerard, R. W. (1949). The normal membrane potential of frog satorius fibers. *Journal of Cellular and Comparative Physiology, 34,* 383–385.

Link, S. W. (1992). *The wave theory of difference and similarity.* Hillsdale, NJ: Lawrence Erlbaum Associates.

Livingstone, M. S., Nori, S., Freeman, D. C., & Hubel, D. H. (1995). Stereopsis and binocularity in the squirrel monkey. *Vision Research, 35,* 345–354.

Loewenstein, W. R. (1961). Excitation and inactivation in a receptor membrane. *Annals of the New York Academy of Science, 94,* 510–534.

Luckiesh, M. (1965). *Visual illusions: Their causes, characteristics and applications.* New York: Dover.

MacCorquodale, K., & Meehl, P. E. (1948). Hypothetical constructs and intervening variables. *Psychological Review, 55,* 95–107.

Mallat, S. (1989). A theory for multiresolution signal decomposition: The wavelet representation. *IEEE Transactions on Pattern Analysis and Machine Intelligence, 11,* 674–693.

Marr, D. (1982). *Vision.* San Francisco: W. H. Freeman.

Massaro, D. W. (1986). The computer as a metaphor for psychological inquiry: Considerations and recommendations. *Behavior Research Methods, Instruments, & Computers, 18*(2), 73–92.

Massaro, D. W. (1988). Some criticisms of connectionist models of human performance. *Journal of Memory and Language, 27,* 213–234.

Maunsell, J. H. R. (1995). The brain's visual world: Representation of visual targets in cerebral cortex. *Science, 270,* 764–769.

McClelland, J. L., Rumelhart, D. E., & the PDP Research Group. (1986). *Parallel distributed processing. Vol. 2: Psychological and biological models.* Cambridge, MA: MIT Press.

McCullough, C. (1965). Color adaptation of the edge-detectors in the human visual system. *Science, 149,* 1115–1116.

McDonough, R. (1991). Wittgenstein's critique of mechanistic atomism. *Philosophical Investigations, 14,* 231–251.

McGinn, C. (1989). Can we solve the mind-body problem? *Mind, 98,* 349–366.

Meyer, G. E., & Phillips, D. (1980). Faces, vases, subjective contours, and the McCullough effect. *Perception, 9,* 603–606.

Miller, G. S., Galanter, E., & Pribram, K. (1960). *Plans and the structure of behavior.* New York: Holt, Rinehart & Winston.

Miyashita, Y. (1995). How the brain creates imagery: Projection to the primary visual cortex. *Science, 268,* 1719–1720.

Moore, E. F. (1956). Gedanken-experiments on sequential machines. In C. E. Shannon & J. McCarthy (Eds.), *Automata studies* (pp. 129–153). Princeton, NJ: Princeton University Press.

Moscovitch, M., Behrman, M., & Winocur, G. (1994). Do PETS have long or short ears? Mental imagery and neuroimaging. *Trends in Neuroscience, 17,* 292–294.

Nagel, T. (1986). *The view from nowhere.* New York: Oxford University Press.

Nakayama, K. (1990). The iconic bottleneck and the tenuous link between early visual processing and perception. In C. Blakemore (Ed.), *Vision: Coding and efficiency* (pp. 411–422). Cambridge: Cambridge University Press.

Necker, L. A. (1832). On an apparent change of position in a drawing of an engraved figure of a crystal. *Philosophical Magazine, 1,* 329–337.

Neisser, U. (1967). *Cognitive psychology.* New York: Appleton-Century-Crofts.

Newell, A. (1990). *Unified theories of cognition.* Cambridge, MA: Harvard University Press.

Niall, K. K. (1997). "Mental rotation," pictured rotation, and tandem rotation in depth. *Acta Psychologica, 95,* 31–83.

Nisbett, R. E., & Ross, L. (1980). *Human inference: Strategies and shortcomings of social judgment.* Englewood Cliffs, NJ: Prentice-Hall.

Nisbett, R. E., & Wilson, T. D. (1977). Telling more than we can know: Verbal reports on mental processes. *Psychological Review, 84,* 231–259.

Olson, P. L., Cleveland, D. E., Fancher, P. S., Kostyniuk, L. P., & Schneider, L. W. (1984). *Parameters affecting stopping sight distance* (Report No. 270). Washington, DC: National Cooperative Highway Research Program.

Pachella, R. G. (1974). The interpretation of reaction time in information processing research. In B. H. Kantowitz (Ed.), *Human information processing: Tutorials in performance and cognition* (pp. 41–82). Hillsdale, NJ: Lawrence Erlbaum Associates.

Papathomas, T. V., Chubb, C., Gorea, A., & Kowler, E. (Eds.). (1995). *Early vision and beyond.* Cambridge, MA: MIT Press.

Parasuraman, R. (1986). Vigilance, monitoring, and search. In K. R. Boff, L. Kaufman, & J. P. Thomas (Eds.), *Handbook of perception and human performance* (pp. 43-1 to 43-39). New York: Wiley.

Peichl, B., & Wassle, H. (1979). Size, scatter, and coverage of receptive field centers in the cat retina. *Journal of Physiology (London), 291,* 117–141.

Penfield, W. (1958). *The excitable cortex in conscious man.* Springfield, IL: Charles C. Thomas.

Pentland, A. P. (1984). Local shading analysis. *IEEE Transactions on Pattern Analysis and Machine Intelligence, 6,* 170–187.

Perrett, D. I., Heitanen, J. K., Oram, M. W., & Benson, P. J. (1992). Organizations and functions of cells responsive to faces in the temporal cortex. *Philosophical Transactions of the Royal Society of London (B), 335*, 31–38.

Pfeifer, R., & Verschure, P. (1992). Beyond rationalism: Symbols, patterns, and behavior. *Connection Science, 4*, 313–325.

Pinker, S., & Prince, A. (1988). On language and connectionism: Analysis of a parallel distributed processing model of language acquisition. *Cognition, 28*, 73–123.

Poggio, T., & Girosi, F. (1990). Networks for approximation and learning. *Proceedings of the IEEE, 78*, 1481–1497.

Pollack, I. (1972). Visual discrimination of "unseen" objects: Forced choice testing of Mayzner–Tressalt sequential blanking effects. *Perception and Psychophysics, 11*, 121–128.

Polyak, S. L. (1941). *The retina*. Chicago: University of Chicago Press.

Polyak, S. L. (1957). *The vertebrate visual system*. Chicago: University of Chicago Press.

Popper, K. R. (1959). *The logic of scientific discovery*. New York: Basic Books.

Posner, M. I. (1978). *Chronometric explorations of mind*. Hillsdale, NJ: Lawrence Erlbaum Associates.

Prigogine, I. (1980). *From being to becoming*. San Francisco: W. H. Freeman.

Proctor, R. W., & Rao, K. V. (1981). On the "misguided" use of reaction time differences: A discussion of Ratcliff and Hacker (1981). *Perception and Psychophysics, 31*, 601–602.

Pylyshyn, Z. W. (1979). Validating computational models: A critique of Anderson's indeterminacy of representation claim. *Psychological Review, 86*, 383–394.

Rachlin, H. (1994). *Behavior and mind: The roots of modern psychology*. New York: Oxford University Press.

Rakover, S. S. (1986). Breaking the myth that behaviorism is a trivial science. *New Ideas in Psychology, 4*, 305–310.

Rakover, S. S. (1990). *Metapsychology: Missing links in behavior*. New York: Paragon/Solomon.

Rakover, S. S. (1992). Outflanking the mind–body problem: Scientific progress in the history of psychology. *Journal for the Theory of Social Behavior, 22*, 145–173.

Ramachandran, V. S. (1988). Perception of shape from shading. *Science, 331*, 163–166.

Ratcliff, R. (1981). A theory of order relations in perceptual matching. *Psychological Review, 88*, 552–572.

Ratcliff, R., & Hacker, M. J. (1982). On the misguided use of reaction time differences. A reply to Proctor and Rao. *Perception and Psychophysics, 31*, 603–604.

Ratliff, F. (1965). *Mach bands: Quantitative studies on neural networks in the retina*. San Francisco: Holden-Day.

Ratliff, F., & Hartline, H. K. (1959). The response of *Limulus* optic nerve fibers to patterns of illumination on the receptor mosaic. *Journal of General Physiology, 42*, 1241–1255.

Redies, C., Crook, J. M., & Creutzfeldt, O. D. (1986). Neuronal responses to borders with and without luminance gradients in cats visual cortex and dorsal lateral geniculate nucleus. *Experimental Brain Research, 61*, 469–481.

Robinson, D. N. (1995). The logic of reductionistic models. *New Ideas in Psychology, 13*(1), 1–8.

Robinson, J. O. (1972). *The psychology of visual illusion*. London: Hutchinson University Library.

Roland, P. E., & Guly'as, B. (1994). Visual imagery and visual representation. *Trends in Neuroscience, 17*, 281–287.

Rosenblatt, F. (1962). *The principles of neurodynamics*. Washington, DC: Spartan Books.

Rumelhart, D. E., & McClelland, J. L. (1987). Learning the past tenses of English verbs: Implicit rules or parallel distributed processing? In B. MacWhinney (Ed.), *Mechanisms of language acquisition*. Hillsdale, NJ: Lawrence Erlbaum Associates.

Rumelhart, D. E., McClelland, J. L., & the PDP Research Group. (1986a). *Parallel distributed processing. Vol. 1: Foundations*. Cambridge, MA: MIT Press.

Rumelhart, D. E., & McClelland, J. L. (1986b). On learning the past tenses of English verbs. In J. L. McClelland & D. E. Rumelhart (Eds.), *Parallel distributed processing: Explorations in the microstructures of cognition, Vol. 2: Psychological and biological models* (pp. 216–271). Cambridge, MA: MIT Press.

Saarinen, J., & Levi, D. M. (1995). Perceptual learning in Vernier acuity: What is learned? *Vision Research, 35,* 519–528.

Safranek, R. J., Gottshlich, S., & Kak, A. C. (1990). Evidence accumulation using binary frames of discernment for verification vision. *IEEE Transactions on robotics and automation, 6*(4), 405–417.

Sahoo, P. K., Soltani, S., Wong, A. K. C., & Chen, Y. C. (1988). A survey of thresholding techniques. *Computer Vision, Graphics, and Image Processing, 41,* 233–260.

Sakai, K., & Miyashita, Y. (1994). Visual imagery: An interaction between memory retrieval and focal attention. *Trends in Neuroscience, 17,* 287–289.

Sakitt, B. (1972). Counting every quantum. *Journal of Physiology, 223,* 131–150.

Savoy, R. L., & Gabrielli, J. D. E. (1991). Normal McCullough effect in Alzheimer's disease and global amnesia. *Perception and Psychophysics, 49,* 448–455.

Schneider, W., & Shiffrin, R. M. (1977). Controlled and automatic human information processing. I. Detection, search, and attention. *Psychological Review, 84,* 1–66.

Scragg, G. W. (1975). Answering questions about processes. In D. Norman & D. Rumelhart (Eds.), *Explorations in cognition* (pp. 349–375). San Francisco: W. H. Freeman.

Sejnowski, T. J., Koch, C., & Churchland, P. S. (1988). Computational neuroscience. *Science, 241,* 1299–1306.

Selfridge, O. G. (1958, November). *Pandemonium: A paradigm for learning.* Paper presented at the Mechanization of Thought Processes, London. London: Her Majesty's Stationary Office. pp. 513–526

Sereno, M. I., Dale, A. M., Reppas, J. B., Kwong, K. K., Belliveau, J. W., Brady, T. J., Rosen, B. R., & Tootell, R. B. H. (1995). Borders of multiple visual areas in humans revealed by functioning magnetic resonance imaging. *Science, 268,* 889–893.

Shafer, G. (1976). *A mathematical theory of evidence.* Princeton, NJ: Princeton University Press.

Shaw, M. L. (1978). A capacity allocation model for reaction time. *Journal of Experimental Psychology: Human Perception and Performance, 4,* 586–598.

Shepard, R. N., & Cooper, L. A. (1982). *Mental images and their transformations.* Cambridge, MA: MIT Press.

Shepard, R. N., & Metzler, J. (1971). Mental rotation of three-dimensional objects. *Science, 171,* 701–703.

Sherrington, C. S. (1940). *Selected writings of Sir Charles Sherrington.* New York: Hoeber.

Shiffrin, R. M., & Atkinson, R. C. (1969). Storage and retrieval processes in long term memory. *Psychological Review, 56,* 179–193.

Shiffrin, R. M., & Schneider, W. (1977). Controlled and automatic human information processing. II. Perceptual learning, automatic attending, and a general theory. *Psychological Review, 84,* 127–190.

Skarda, C. A., & Freeman, W. J. (1987). How brains make chaos in order to make sense of the world. *Behavioral and Brain Sciences, 10,* 161–195.

Skinner, B. F. (1938). *The behavior of organisms: An experimental analysis.* New York: Appleton-Century-Crofts.

Skinner, B. F. (1953). *Science and human behavior.* New York: Free Press.

Skinner, B. F. (1963). Behaviorism at fifty. *Science, 140,* 951–958.

Smith, L. D. (1992). On prediction and control: B. F. Skinner and the technological ideal of science. *American Psychologist, 47,* 216–223.

Sperling, G. (1960). The information available in brief visual presentations. *Psychological Monographs: General and Applied, 74,* 1–29.

Spillman, L., Ransom-Hogg, A., & Oehler, R. (1987). A comparison of perceptive and receptive fields in man and monkey. *Human Neurobiology, 6,* 51–62.

Spinelli, D. N., Hirsch, H. V. B., Phelps, R. W., & Metzler, J. (1972). Visual experience as a determinant of the response characteristics of cortical receptive fields in cats. *Experimental Brain Research, 15*, 289–304.

Staddon, J. (1993). *Behaviorism: Mind, mechanism, and society*. London: Duckworth.

Sternberg, S. (1966). High speed scanning in human memory. *Science, 153*, 652–654.

Sternberg, S. (1967). Two operations in character recognition. Some evidence from reaction time experiments. *Perception and Psychophysics, 2*, 45–53.

Sternberg, S. (1969a). The discovery of processing stages: Extension of Donders' method. *Acta Psychologica, 30*, 276–315.

Sternberg, S. (1969b). Memory scanning: Mental processes revealed by reaction time experiments. *American Scientist, 57*, 421–457.

Sternberg, S. (1975). Memory scanning: New findings and current controversies. *Quarterly Journal of Experimental Psychology, 27*, 1–32.

Stewart, A. L., & Pinkham, R. S. (1991). A space-variant operator for visual sensitivity. *Biological Cybernetics, 64*, 373–379.

Stewart, A. L., & Pinkham, R. S. (1994). Space-variant models of visual acuity using self-adjoint integral operators. *Biological Cybernetics, 71*, 161–167.

Stewart, A. L., & Pinkham, R. S. (1997). Representing contrast sensitivity as an eigenvalue problem. *Personal Communication*.

Stockmeyer, L. J., & Chandra, A. K. (1979). Intrinsically difficult problems. *Scientific American, 240*, 140–159.

Stoner, G. R., & Albright, T. D. (1993). Image segmentation cues in motion processing: Implications for modularity in vision. *Journal of Cognitive Neuroscience, 5*, 129–149.

Stryker, M. P., & Sherk, H. (1975). Modification of cortical orientation selectivity in the cat by restricted visual experience. *Science, 190*, 904–906.

Swets, J. A. (1977). Signal detection theory applied to vigilance. In R. R. Mackie (Ed.), *Vigilance: Theory, operational performance, and physiological correlates* (pp. 705–718). New York: Plenum.

Tanaka, K. (1993). Neuronal mechanisms of object recognition. *Science, 262*, 685–688.

Taylor, D. A. (1976). Stage analysis of reaction time. *Psychological Bulletin, 83*, 161–191.

Teller, D. Y. (1980). Locus questions in visual science. In C. S. Harris (Ed.), *Visual coding and adaptability* (pp. 151–176). Hillsdale, NJ: Lawrence Erlbaum Associates.

Teller, D. Y. (1984). Linking propositions. *Vision Research, 24*, 1233–1246.

Tjan, B. S., Braje, W. L., Legge, G. E., & Kersten, D. (1995). Human efficiency for recognizing 3-D objects in luminance noise. *Vision Research, 35*, 3053–3069.

Tolansky, S. (1964). *Optical illusions*. Oxford, England: Pergamon.

Tomita, T. (1965). Electrophysiological study of the mechanisms subserving color coding in the fish retina. *Cold Spring Harbor Symposia on Quantitative Biology, 30*, 559–566.

Townsend, J. T. (1969). Mock parallel and serial models and experimental detection of these. *Proceedings of The Purdue Symposium on Information Processing, 2*, 617–628.

Townsend, J. T. (1971). A note on the identifiability of parallel and serial processes. *Perception and Psychophysics, 10*, 161–163.

Townsend, J. T. (1972). Some results concerning the identifiability of parallel and serial processes. *British Journal of Mathematical and Statistical Psychology, 25*, 168–199.

Townsend, J. T. (1974). Issues and models concerning the processing of a finite number of inputs. In B. H. Kantowitz (Ed.), *Human information processing: Tutorials in performance and cognition*. New York: Wiley.

Townsend, J. T. (1990). Chaos theory: A brief tutorial and discussion. In A. F. Healy, S. M. Kosslyn, & R. M. Shiffrin (Eds.), *From learning processes to cognitive process: Essays in honor of W. K. Estes* (Vol. 1, pp. 65–96). Hillsdale, NJ: Lawrence Erlbaum Associates.

Townsend, J. T., & Ashby, F. G. (1983). *The stochastic modeling of elementary psychological processes*. Cambridge, England: Cambridge University Press.

Townsend, J. T., & Thomas, R. D. (1994). Stochastic dependencies in parallel and serial models: Effects on systems factorial interactions. *Journal of Mathematical Psychology, 38*(1), 1–34.

Triesman, A., & Patterson, R. (1984). Emergent features, attention, object perception. *Journal of Experimental Psychology: Human Perception and Performance, 10,* 12–31.

Ungerleider, G. (1995). Functional brain imaging studies of cortical mechanisms for memory. *Science, 270,* 769–775.

Uttal, W. R. (1965). Do compound evoked potentials reflect psychological codes? *Psychological Bulletin, 64,* 377–392.

Uttal, W. R. (1967). Evoked brain potentials: Signs or codes. *Perspectives in Biology and Medicine, 10,* 627–639.

Uttal, W. R. (1969). Emerging principles of sensory coding. *Perspectives in Biology and Medicine, 12,* 344–368.

Uttal, W. R. (1971a). The psychobiological silly season, or what happens when neurophysiological data becomes psychological theories. *Journal of General Psychology, 84,* 151–166.

Uttal, W. R. (1971b). The effect of interval and number on masking with dot bursts. *Perception and Psychophysics, 9,* 469–473.

Uttal, W. R. (1973). *The psychobiology of sensory coding.* New York: Harper & Row.

Uttal, W. R. (1975). *An autocorrelation theory of form detection.* Hillsdale, NJ: Lawrence Erlbaum Associates.

Uttal, W. R. (1978a). *The psychobiology of mind.* Hillsdale, NJ: Lawrence Erlbaum Associates.

Uttal, W. R. (1978b). Codes, sensations and the mind–body problem. *Behavioral and Brain Sciences, 1,* 368.

Uttal, W. R. (1981a). *A taxonomy of visual processes.* Hillsdale, NJ: Lawrence Erlbaum Associates.

Uttal, W. R. (1981b). On the limits of sensory reductionism. In *Relating physiology to psychophysics: Current problems and approaches. Proceedings of the 12th Symposium.* Rochester, NY: Center for Visual Science.

Uttal, W. R. (1982). Neuroreductionistic dogma: A heretical counterview. In D. G. Albrecht (Ed.), *Lecture notes in biomathematics: Recognition of pattern and form* (pp. 193–225). Berlin: Springer-Verlag.

Uttal, W. R. (1988). *On seeing forms.* Hillsdale, NJ: Lawrence Erlbaum Associates.

Uttal, W. R. (1990). On some two way barriers between theories and mechanisms. *Perception and Psychophysics, 48,* 188–203.

Uttal, W. R. (1993). Toward a new behaviorism. In S. C. Masin (Ed.), *Foundations of perceptual theory* (pp. 3–42). Amsterdam: North-Holland.

Uttal, W. R., Baruch, T., & Allen, L. (1995a). The effect of combinations of image degradations in a discrimination task. *Perception and Psychophysics, 57,* 668–681.

Uttal, W. R., Baruch, T., & Allen, L. (1995b). Combining image degradations in a recognition task. *Perception and Psychophysics, 57,* 681–691.

Uttal, W. R., Baruch, T., & Allen, L. (1997). A parametric study of face recognition when image degradations are combined. *Spatial Vision.*

Uttal, W. R., Bradshaw, G., Dayanand, S., Lovell, R., Shepherd, T., Kakarala, R., Skifsted, K., & Tupper, K. (1992). *The swimmer: An integrated computational model of a perceptual-motor system.* Hillsdale, NJ: Lawrence Erlbaum Associates.

Uttal, W. R., Davis, N. S., Welke, C., & Kakarala, R. (1988). The reconstruction of static visual forms from sparse dotted samples. *Perception and Psychophysics, 43,* 223–240.

Uttal, W. R., Kakarala, R., Dayanand, S., Shepherd, T., Kalki, J., Lunskis, C. F., & Liu, N. (1998). *A vision system.*

Uttal, W. R., & Smith, P. M. (1967). On the psychophysical discriminability of somatosensory nerve action potentials with irregular intervals. *Perception and Psychophysics, 2,* 341–348.

Valenstein, E. (1986). *Great and desperate cures: The rise and decline of psychosurgery and other radical treatments for mental illness.* New York: Basic Books.

Van Essen, D. C. (1985). Functional organization of the primate visual cortex. *Cerebral cortex 3* (pp. 259–329).

Van Orden, G. C., & Papp, K. R. (in press). Functional neuroimages fail to discover pieces of the mind in parts of the brain. *Philosophy of Science.*

von der Heydt, R., & Peterhans, E. (1989). Mechanisms of contour perception in the monkey visual cortex. I. Lines of pattern discontinuity. *The Journal of Neuroscience, 9*(5), 1731–1748.

Wald, G. (1945). Human vision and the spectrum. *Science, 132*, 316–317.

Warren, R. M., & Warren, R. P. (1968). *Helmholtz on perception: Its physiology and development.* New York: Wiley.

Watanabe, T. (1995). Orientation and color processing for partially occluded objects. *Vision Research, 35*(5), 647–656.

Watson, A. B. (1982). Summation of grating patches indicates many types of receptors at one retinal location. *Vision Research, 22*, 17–26.

Watson, A. B. (1987a). The cortex transform: Rapid computation of simulated neural images. *Computer Vision Graphics and Image Processing, 39*, 311–327.

Watson, A. B. (1987b). Efficiency of a model human image code. *Journal of the Optical Society of America, A-4*, 2401–2417.

Watson, A. B. (Ed.). (1993). *Digital images and human vision.* Cambridge, MA: MIT Press.

Watson, J. B. (1919). *Psychology from the standpoint of a behaviorist.* Philadelphia: Lippincott.

Watson, J. B. (1925). *Behaviorism.* New York: Norton.

Weisstein, N. (1972). Metacontrast. In D. Jameson & L. M. Hurvich (Eds.), *Handbook of sensory physiology: Visual psychophysics* (Vol. VII/4, pp. 233–272). New York: Springer-Verlag.

Weisstein, N., Ozog, G., & Szoc, R. (1975). A comparison and elaboration of two models of metacontrast. *Psychological Review, 82*, 325–343.

Westheimer, G. (1965). Spatial interactions in the human retina during scotopic vision. *Journal of Physiology (London), 181*, 881–894.

Westheimer, G. (1967). Spatial interactions in human cone vision. *Journal Physiology (London), 190*, 139–154.

White, M. J. (1985). On the status of cognitive psychology. *American Psychologist, 40*, 117–119.

Widrow, B. (1962). *Generalization and information storage in networks of Adaline neurons.* Washington, DC: Spartan.

Wilson, H. R., & Bergen, J. R. (1979). A four mechanism model for threshold spatial vision. *Vision Research, 19*, 19–32.

Woodworth, R. S. (1938). *Experimental psychology.* New York: Holt.

Zadeh, L. A. (1973). Outline of a new approach to the analysis of complex systems and decision processes. *IEEE Transactions on Systems, Man, and Cybernetics, SMC-3*(1), 28–44.

Zeki, S. (1993). *A vision of the brain.* Oxford, England: Blackwell.

Zuriff, G. E. (1985). *Behaviorism: A conceptual reconstruction.* New York: Columbia University Press.

Author Index

SUBJECT INDEX

A

"A" reaction, 176
"B" reaction, 176
"C" reaction, 176
Acuity, 97
Additive factor theoreticians, 181
Additive factors method, 106, 178-181
Additivity, 186
Algorithmic transformations, 122
Amplifier, 1
Analog computers, 60
Analogies, 60, 103
Analogy, 109, 135
Analytic function models, 66
Anthropomorphized, 90
Antireductionist views, 33
Aplysia, 57
Apparently random, 47-48, 58
Applied epistemology, 7
Architecture, 173
Artificial intelligence (AI), 54, 63, 194
Attention allocation, 155
Attention, 45, 148-149, 184
Attentive-preattentive dichotomy, 119
Attractors, 48
Automatic processing, 169
Aware, 149
Awareness, 140, 144

B

Barefoot empiricism, 203, 218

Barriers to theory, 68
Behavior, 23-24, 70, 142, 146, 155
Behavioral macrocosm, 59
Behavior-brain issue, 44
Behaviorism, 6, 23, 138, 190, 192
Behaviorist epistemology, 46
Binding problem, 201
Biochemistry, 2, 56
Biopsychological bridge building, 25
Bipolar neurons, 88
Black box barrier, 47
Black box problem, 44, 46-47, 62, 77, 137, 182, 186, 205, 219, 220
Block diagram, 146, 157, 159,160
Bottom-up, 77, 120
Boundaries, 16
Brain centers, 192
Brain functions, 220
Brain imaging studies, 76
Brain scan methods, 21
Brain state, 150-151
Brain, 6
Brain-mind complex, 137
Brain-mind relations, 207
Bridging theories, 69, 104, 109

C

Candidate code, 115
Cardinal cell, 17
Cellular action, 124
Cellular neurophysiology, 15
Centrifugal activation, 92
Cerebellum, 57
Cerebral cortex, 72, 89